28 DAY BOOK

DATE			
9/12 P.O. 4/09 ①			©1993

UNDERSTANDING
JOSÉ DONOSO

UNDERSTANDING MODERN EUROPEAN and LATIN AMERICAN LITERATURE

James Hardin, *Series Editor*

Understanding

JOSÉ
DONOSO

SHARON MAGNARELLI

UNIVERSITY OF SOUTH CAROLINA PRESS

Published in Columbia, South Carolina, by the
University of South Carolina Press

Manufactured in the United States of America

Library of Congress Cataloging-in-Publication Data

Magnarelli, Sharon, 1946–
      Understanding José Donoso / Sharon Magnarelli.
          p.   cm. — (Understanding modern European and Latin American
      literature)
      Includes bibliographical references and index.
      ISBN 0-87249-844-1 (hc : alk. paper)
      1. Donoso, José, 1924– —Criticism and interpretation.
   I. Title.   II. Series.
   PQ8097.D617Z74   1992   92–19103
   863—dc20

CONTENTS

EDITOR'S PREFACE

Understanding Modern European and Latin American Literature has been planned as a series of guides for undergraduate and graduate students and nonacademic readers. Like its companion series, *Understanding Contemporary American Literature,* these books provide introductions to the lives and writings of prominent modern authors and explicate their most important works.

Modern literature makes special demands, and this is particularly true of foreign literature, in which the reader must contend not only with unfamiliar, often arcane artistic conventions and philosophical concepts, but also with the handicap of reading the literature in translation. It is a truism that the nuances of one language can be rendered in another only imperfectly (and this problem is especially acute in fiction), but the fact that the works of European and Latin American writers are situated in a historical and cultural setting quite different from our own can be as great a hindrance to the understanding of these works as the linguistic barrier. For this reason, the UMELL series emphasizes the sociological and historical backgrounds of the writers treated. The peculiar philosophical and cultural traditions of a given culture may be particularly important for an understanding of certain authors, and these are taken up in the introductory chapter and also in the discussion of those works to which this information is relevant. Beyond this, the books treat the specifically literary aspects of the author under discussion and attempt to explain the complexities of contemporary literature lucidly. The books are conceived as introductions to the authors covered, not as comprehensive analyses. They do not provide detailed summaries of plot because they are meant to be used in conjunction with the books they treat, not as a substitute for the study of the original works. The purpose of the books is to provide information and judicious literary assessment of the major works in the most compact, readable form. It is our hope that the UMELL series will help to increase our knowledge and understanding of the European and Latin American cultures and will serve to make the literature of those cultures more accessible.

J. H.

EDITIONS CITED

Quotations from the books treated in this text are taken from the editions listed below unless otherwise noted. Page numbers are given in parentheses following quotations, first for the English edition and then for the Spanish. Books are listed in the order in which they are treated.

Charleston and Other Stories. Trans. Andrée Conrad. Boston: Godine, 1977.

Cuentos. Barcelona: Seix Barral, 1981.

Coronation. Trans. Jocasta Goodwin. New York: Knopf, 1965.

Coronación. Barcelona: Seix Barral, 1968.

This Sunday. Trans. Lorraine O'Grady Freeman. New York: Knopf, 1967.

Este domingo. Mexico: Joaquín Mortiz, 1968.

Hell Has No Limits. Trans. Suzanne Jill Levine and Hallie Taylor. In *Triple Cross,* by Carlos Fuentes, José Donoso, and Severo Sarduy. New York: Dutton, 1972.

El lugar sin límites. Mexico: Joaquín Mortiz, 1971.

The Obscene Bird of Night. Trans. Hardie St. Martin and Leonard Mades. Boston: Knopf, 1973.

El obsceno pájaro de la noche. Barcelona: Seix Barral, 1970.

Sacred Families. Trans. Andrée Conrad. New York: Knopf, 1977.

Tres novelitas burguesas. Barcelona: Seix Barral, 1973.

A House in the Country. Trans. David Pritchard with Suzanne Jill Levine. New York: Random House, 1984.

Casa de campo. Barcelona: Seix Barral, 1978.

Curfew. Trans. Alfred MacAdam. New York: Weidenfeld and Nicolson, 1988.

La desesperanza. Barcelona: Seix Barral, 1987.

CHRONOLOGY

1924   Born in Santiago, Chile, October 5

1932   Begins attending an English school, The Grange

1943   Drops out of school

1945   Leaves Santiago destined for Chilean pampas

1946   Hitchhikes from Patagonia to Buenos Aires; parents come to get him in Buenos Aires because he is ill

1947   Finishes *bachillerato* (high school degree) and enters university

1949   Receives Doherty Foundation scholarship to Princeton

1950   Publishes "The Blue Woman" in English in *MSS* at Princeton

1951   Publishes "Poisoned Pastries" in English in *MSS*

1952   Returns to Chile after hitchhiking through the United States, Mexico, and Central America; begins teaching English at the Kent School and the Catholic University

1954   Writes " 'China' " for literary contest

1955   Publishes *Veraneo y otros cuentos* (Summer Vacation and Other Stories)

1956   Publishes *Dos cuentos* (Two Stories) ("Ana Maria" and "El hombrecito")

1957   Goes to Isla Negra to complete *Coronación (Coronation)*, which is published in December of the same year

1958   Sets off on tour through South America with introductory letter from Pablo Neruda; gets only as far as Buenos Aires, where he meets future wife

1959   Publishes "The Closed Door" and "The Walk"

1960   Publishes *El charlestón* (The Charleston), returns to Chile, and gets job at weekly news magazine *Ercilla*

1961   Marries María del Pilar Serrano

1962   Attends Writers' Congress at University of Concepción and becomes friends with Carlos Fuentes; publishes "Santelices" in *El Mercurio*

1963   Knopf agrees to publish translation of *Coronación,* and Donoso begins to work on a "little tale" that will eventually become *El obsceno pájaro de la noche (The Obscene Bird of Night)*

1964   Goes to Mexico with wife for Writers' Congress and does not return to Chile for seventeen years

1965   Writes *El lugar sin límites (Hell Has No Limits)* at home of Carlos Fuentes in Mexico and finishes *Este domingo (This Sunday);* goes to Iowa City, where he will teach creative writing at the Writers' Workshop for two years

1966   *This Sunday* and *Hell Has No Limits* are published

1967   Moves to Madrid, and then on to Mallorca

1969   Goes to Fort Collins, Colorado, to teach; has emergency ulcer operation after two weeks; returns to Mallorca and moves to Barcelona; finishes *The Obscene Bird of Night*

1970   *The Obscene Bird of Night* is published in Spain and encounters problems of censorship

1971   Moves with his wife to Calaceite, Teruel, Spain

1972   Publishes *Historia personal del "boom" (The Boom in Spanish American Literature: A Personal History)*

1973   Publishes *Tres novelitas burguesas (Sacred Families)*

1976   Moves to Sitges, Barcelona, Spain

1978   Publishes *Casa de campo (A House in the Country)*

1980   Publishes *La misteriosa desaparición de la Marquesita de Loria* (The Mysterious Disappearance of the Little Marquise of Loria)

1981   Publishes *El jardín de al lado* (The Garden Next Door) and returns to Chile

1982   Publishes *Cuatro para Delfina* (Four for Delfina)

1986   Publishes *La desesperanza (Curfew)*

1990   Publishes *Taratuta/Naturaleza muerta con cachimba* (Taratuta/ Still Life with a Pipe)

UNDERSTANDING
JOSÉ DONOSO

LIFE AND WORKS

José Donoso was born on October 5, 1924, into a family of doctors and lawyers in Santiago, Chile. He studied at an English day school, "The Grange," and later majored in English language and literature at the University of Chile. A 1949 Doherty Fellowship brought him to the United States to Princeton University, where he studied with some of the leading literary figures of that time and published (in English) his first two short stories: "The Poisoned Pastries" and "The Blue Woman." He returned to Chile in 1952 and, after a long, difficult readjustment, taught English at the Kent School and later at the Catholic University. Although Donoso claims that he always knew he wanted to be and in fact would be a writer, it was not until 1954 that he finally wrote his first short story in Spanish, " 'China'," and submitted it to a literary contest. That story formed part of an anthology of young writers who eventually achieved some renown, and a year later his first collection of short stories, *Veraneo y otros cuentos* (Summer Vacation and Other Stories), was published.

After the 1957 release of his first novel, *Coronación (Coronation)*, which won him the William Faulkner Foundation Prize for Latin American Literature in 1962, and another volume of stories, *El charlestón* (The Charleston), in 1960, Donoso and his wife, María del Pilar Serrano, left Chile to attend a writers' conference in Mexico in 1964. It was not until seventeen years later that they finally returned to their homeland. In the meantime, Donoso wrote *El lugar sin límites (Hell Has No Limits)* in 1965 while staying at the home of Mexican writer Carlos Fuentes and his wife. From 1965 to 1967 he taught creative writing at the University of Iowa's Writers' Workshop and worked on *El obsceno pájaro de la noche (The Obscene Bird of Night)*. In 1966 both *Este domingo (This Sunday)* and *Hell Has No Limits* were published. After his stay in the United States, he moved to Madrid and later to Mallorca, but in 1969 he left his family in

1

Mallorca to return to the United States and teach in Fort Collins, Colorado. There he underwent an emergency operation for the stomach ulcers that have plagued him most of his life. He assures his critics that this operation and his experiences under morphine led him to finish *The Obscene Bird of Night* later that same year in Barcelona; he had worked on the novel, surely his greatest work to date, for some seven or eight years.

In 1971 Donoso and his family moved to a small town in Spain, where he wrote *Casa de campo (A House in the Country)* (1978). He wrote three other works in various parts of Spain: *Tres novelitas burguesas (Sacred Families)* (1973), *La misteriosa desaparición de la Marquesita de Loria* (The Mysterious Disappearance of the Little Marquise of Loria) (1980), and *El jardín de al lado* (The Garden Next Door) (1981), which at that time he classified as his most realistic novel. He did not return to Chile until 1981, eight years after Augusto Pinochet's September 11, 1973, military coup d'état, which overthrew duly elected Marxist president Salvador Allende. Since his return to his native land, he has written *Cuatro para Delfina* (Four for Delfina) (1982), *La desesperanza (Curfew)* (1986), and most recently, *Taratuta/Naturaleza muerta con cachimba* (Taratuta/ Still Life with a Pipe) (1990). He has also published a collection of poetry, *Poemas de un novelista* (Poems of a Novelist) (1981) and has written the stage play of "Sueños de mala muerte" (Dreams of a Bad Death or Bad Luck, produced in 1983) and, with Carlos Cerda, a stage version of *This Sunday* (produced in 1990).

Although Donoso's prose is highly original, he claims to be influenced, directly or indirectly, by his vast reading of authors of international acclaim such as Henry James, Isak Dinesen, Charles Dickens, Laurence Sterne, Virginia Woolf, Jean-Paul Sartre, Marcel Proust, Franz Kafka, William Faulkner, Carlos Fuentes, and Ernesto Sábato, among others. He acknowledges that his childhood was bookish but maintains that it was his family and their servants who exercised the greatest influence on him.

Though Donoso might not agree, he is one of the leading figures in the Latin American literary phenomenon known as the "Boom," the period during the 1960s and 1970s that witnessed the publication of some of the most important works of Jorge Luis Borges, Gabriel García Márquez, Carlos Fuentes, Mario Vargas Llosa, Alejo Carpentier, and Julio Cortázar, among others. This same phenomenon, simultaneously literary and commercial, led to a significant increase of interest in Latin American literature around the world and placed that literature at the front of the world avant-garde in terms of literary technique.

CHAPTER ONE

How to Read José Donoso

Critics disagree, often vehemently, about how to read the works of José Donoso. Many, particularly his early critics, have insisted on perceiving his works in a traditional, realistic, or naturalistic mode, specifically as social realism whose goal is to critique the Chilean bourgeois society. Donoso maintains, and it would be hard for the careful reader to disagree, that on some level his work always encompasses a fissure with realism or social reality and that the social message is only one aspect of his work. For Donoso, reality is little more than a word, and not a very reliable one at that. Unlike the static, tangible, objective entity implied by the term as it is generally used, reality is for Donoso always fluid, always provisional, always subjective—that is, subject to the individual's perception, which is frequently metamorphosed, if not created, by language. Thus when his character Santelices looks out of his office window, he perceives not a dark, mundane, empty, quiet patio in its nighttime tranquillity (as another might view it) but a jungle teeming with ferocious beasts and fraught with danger. Although the two perceptions are contradictory, one interpretation of the physical surroundings is no more valid than the other. As presented by the author, neither vision is completely accurate nor completely erroneous. Both evoke, if indeed on different planes or within different focal points, our complex world, which includes the psychological as well as the physical and, as Donoso recognizes, is a world that can never be grasped in its totality at any given moment or by any given perceiver. It is for this reason that Donoso's fiction invites, indeed exacts, such disparate and multivocal readings.

Thus Donoso's prose can never be read simplistically on one level alone. On the contrary, it demands multiple readings and interpretations (as does any good piece of literature). Although his fiction creates a cosmos that may parallel the realities of quotidian experience, those literary worlds are unequivocally different and subject to their own rules. Donoso's narrative universe is not simply a reflection of some external referent (generally labeled reality) but rather an artistic invention in which he employs metaphors and other literary tropes and figures in order to embody multifarious meanings and thereby highlight the plurality of that world.

For that reason, Donoso specifically deplores readers' attempts to reduce and simplify his prose by "boiling down the complexities of a metaphor to the false lucidity of one word."[1] As a result, he refuses to deal with symbols that have an exact correlative in reality. Furthermore, he wants his readers to see not just the "what" and the "why" but also the "how" of his prose. For him style and technique are as important as his thematic concerns. *How* we perceive is as much an issue in his prose as *what* we perceive. That is why the questions of art (literature), artistic (literary) techniques, and artistic materials (language, discourse) are so frequently the subject as well as the material of his work.

Masks and Changing Faces

The "how" in Donoso, his technique, is often an endless superimposition of layers or levels—hence the mask or the disguise that figures in so much of his work and that ultimately is less a mask than simply another version or perception. The result of this technique is often a multilayered product in which the layers have become either inseparable or indiscernible, and thus the hierarchy implicit in the layering or masking (first layer, second layer, one *above* the other) is rendered null and void. At the same time, the mask consistently functions in a paradoxical fashion. It not only distorts the purportedly hidden, covered "face" but also inevitably allows that veiled layer to peek through. In this respect, both his thematic and his stylistic masks emphasize the gesture of disguising while they blur the ostensibly distinct and separate layers, as they produce new perceptions that combine the previous ones. This technique is perhaps best metaphorized in the image of the package in *The Obscene Bird of Night*. In that novel numerous packages are wrapped again and again, becoming ever more bulky and unwieldy, not with the goal of hiding or protecting anything but rather just for the sake of wrapping, as one stratum is superimposed on another. Similarly, for the Chilean author, human personality or selfhood (ontological being in the world) is a series of masks or disguises, ever changing and ever (inter)changeable, with no ultimate coherence or integrity.

4

Thematically the question of mask is treated in two principal ways in the works of Donoso. At times the characters are shown to be so rigidly restricted by social structures that their "authentic" selves cannot show through; nor, perhaps, are they even conscious of having an "authentic" self apart from the social role. Again one of Donoso's points is that the mask is or becomes the self. Humberto of *The Obscene Bird of Night* wants nothing more than to don the mask of Don Jerónimo and to be him. The brothers of "Paseo" ("The Walk"), like those of *This Sunday,* never disclose their emotions but feign a self-sufficiency they surely do not feel. In other words the motif of the mask reveals itself in a form of transvestism. Sometimes it is a transvestism in the traditional sense of wearing the clothing of the opposite sex, as in *Hell Has No Limits,* but at other times it is an interchangeability of characters when one character places himself in the clothes and thus the social position of another, such as Mauricio and his double in "Gaspard de la Nuit." A similar commutation of characters is apparent in the relationship between Peta Ponce and Inés as well as that of Humberto and Don Jerónimo in *The Obscene Bird of Night,* while the device reaches its apogee in "Chatanooga Choo-choo," in which not only are the characters replaceable one with another, but even their individual body parts are detachable and reusable on other characters.

On the level of technique this layering or mask manifests itself in a number of ways. One is the framing technique by means of which Donoso embeds one narrative within another. An example of this can be found in *This Sunday,* in which the grandparents' stories are embedded within the grandson's. Similarly, in *The Obscene Bird of Night* the story of the landowner's daughter and the nanny/witch is inscribed within the larger narrative of Inés's attempts to have her ancestor canonized, a narrative which in turn is embedded within the still larger frame narrative that tells the tale of the Casa de los Ejercicios Espirituales, the asylum for old servants and other discarded possessions. Within this frame narrative the story of the Rinconada is embedded, much as its narrator, Humberto/Mudito, is enclosed within the Casa and its tale. By enclosing this series of tales one within the other, Donoso produces a Chinese box effect while at the same time he highlights both the metaphoric and the metonymic relations among the stories. The stories relate to each other metaphorically in that they exhibit significant similarities and metonymically because they exist in physical proximity. Yet the metaphoric similarities tend to blur the differences among the stories and lead us to an erroneous assumption of identity between the frame story and the embedded one. In turn, it is the metonymic relation, the embedding or layering, that underlines the error of this assumption and reminds us that the individual situations are only similar in appearance (surface, mask) and not in essence.

Another stylistic layering technique is found in Donoso's frequent utilization of the simile *X* is like *Y*. More than the metaphor (*X* is *Y*), the simile evokes similarity while underlining difference. By saying "*X* is like *Y*," one concurrently implies that *X* is not *Y*. Thus, to say *X* is like *Y* is to allow us to perceive both *X* and *Y*, their points of contact *and* their divergence, as so many Donoso masks do. Although the two entities blend, to some degree, neither totally loses its unique qualities while we are led to a new perception.

Although the mask is one of the most important techniques and motifs in Donoso's works, my reading of his fiction will necessarily center on seven additional topics. Like the question of mask, each of these seven topics must be analyzed as both content and technique, for the issues he raises are always treated in both dimensions.

The Bourgeoisie in Chile

It would be impossible to comprehend Donoso's works without some understanding of the Chilean bourgeoisie to which his family belonged and from which the majority of his characters proceed. Like many Latin American countries, Chile is defined by a rigid class structure and the institution of the extended family with its numerous servants. In this extended family system, unmarried female relatives and less affluent relatives reside with the more prosperous members of the family in a home governed, nominally at least, by a male patriarchal figure. Like most upper-middle-class children in Santiago, Donoso spent much of his childhood in a large home surrounded not only by his immediate family (parents and brothers) but also by relatives, predominantly female (two of them elderly), as well as numerous servants, also predominantly female. Because the female servants are frequently charged with the care and early education of the children, they inevitably exert considerable influence over those children, as his prose demonstrates. Yet this system of household servants should not to be confused with the slavery system of the Southern United States during the eighteenth and nineteenth centuries. Servants in Chilean society, in spite of their lack of education and the fact that they belong to a different socioeconomic class, consider themselves members of the family they serve and on some level are considered by the family as members, though honorary ones. The esteem granted those servants is surely evidenced by the fact that Donoso dedicated his first book to Teresa Vergara, the servant who effectively raised him. It is noteworthy too that traditionally, even in their old age, after they have outlived their function and usefulness within the household, the servants are provided for by the family. This structure is reflected in his works: in *The Obscene Bird of Night* one finds an asylum for aged servants, while in *This Sunday* the elderly Violeta is comfortably established in a house provided by the family she had long served.

Such a family structure, marked as it is by the presence of numerous female relatives and servants, combines with the frequent absence of the father figure (because of responsibilities away from the home or simply his greater freedom and mobility) to imbue the Chilean bourgeois society with a distinctly matriarchal flavor. Children grow up surrounded by figures of immediate if not ultimate authority who are female. It is for this reason that the old servants in *The Obscene Bird of Night* are characterized as witchlike with a combination of natural powers (probably those actually wielded by the female servants over the children) and supernatural powers (perhaps those the child feared the female servant might exert).

Throughout Donoso's work the complex status of the servants is underscored. Subordinate to their "masters," they nonetheless enjoy a position of tacit, though not always recognized, power to the extent that the life of the household and the family could not continue as it is without them. At the same time, they assume much of the responsibility of caring for the young children and enjoy a dimension of influence in this respect. In fact, in *A House in the Country,* they tyrannize the children, especially after curfew, when their jurisdiction is total. More important, as Donoso himself has noted on several occasions, the subculture of the servant class not only provides an inverted mirror of the dominant culture but also exposes the children of that dominant culture to set a of "unorthodox," alternative cultural myths, value systems, and hierarchies. By means of their interrelationships as well as the stories they tell the children, the servants provide and represent the "other," alternative society that exists contingent to but separate from the dominant one, both metaphorically and metonymically. The servants bridge the two worlds, belonging to both, yet are never completely subject to the rules, rituals, and social decorum of the dominant class. It is presumed the servants can do things and feel emotions denied to their more rigidly masked masters. This is perhaps the germinal experience from which Donoso has developed his perception of the world as a series of tangential layers.

For those members of Chilean society not privy to an extended upper-middle-class family with servants, a different, if indeed parallel, social structure is available: the pension, which simulates the extended family in many ways. It is generally governed by a matriarchal figure who either presides over the servants or performs the labors of cooking and cleaning herself. This same woman frequently controls, to a greater or lesser degree, the activities as well as the moral conduct of her lodgers. Because of their close living conditions, the boarders at the pension mirror the family in that each is likely to know the intimate details of the others' lives while, like siblings, they alternately support and rival one another.

Nevertheless, in Donoso's prose fiction, the pension often marks the inveterate isolation and impotence felt by protagonists such as Santelices. Although there is probably no moment in Donoso's work when the social, familial structure is presented in a positive light—it is always either a sham (as in *A House in the Country*) or on the brink of destruction (as in "The Walk" and *This Sunday*)—the institution of the pension is perceived as little more than an unfortunate imitation of the family structure.

Nannies and Witches:
Female Power and the Supernatural

The matriarchal bent that characterizes the social institutions of the home and the pension results in a society of females who maintain, or at least are perceived to maintain, quite a different position from that of women in the United States. Although it is doubtful that women wield or have wielded control in any significant measure on the national level in Chile (at least not overtly), they apparently wield significant control on the familial level, and that produces an awe, if not fear, of those women, particularly in the male child. Thus in Donoso one finds the repeated themes of the nanny and the witch. Throughout Donoso's works it is women who are the powerful ones, often in an evil fashion, while men are frequently portrayed as weak, ineffectual, and pathetic. When, on rare occasion, the text depicts an ostensibly strong, powerful man, that power is undercut by females. For example, Don Jerónimo's power in *The Obscene Bird of Night* is effectively nullified by the nanny/witch Peta Ponce, and masculine "strength" proves to be a sham that masks latent homosexuality in *Hell Has No Limits*. At other moments those males are openly controlled or emasculated by powerful mother figures, like Santelices or Andrés *(Coronation)*.

Children, Games, and Rituals

Children frequently assume leading roles in Donoso's fiction. *A House in the Country* and a number of his short stories provide examples of this thematic concern. At times the events of the plot are even told from a child's point of view, as in *This Sunday* and "The Walk." There are several reasons for this procedure. First, the child's perspective provides a means of manipulating point of view; the child can share the adult reader's values, tell events as she or he sees them, and yet be incapable of comprehending their significance. Obviously, the narrator who cannot grasp the meaning of an experience is incapable of selecting those events and details that merit narration. As a result, readers are left, as they often are in life, with a mixture of relevant and irrelevant information from which to draw conclusions. Through the child's eyes, then, not only can readers understand their own limited comprehension of what surrounds them but at the same time, paradoxically, they can come to a new understanding. Clearly, such is both the theme and technique of *This Sunday,* in which the story of the last years of the narrator's grandparents—their personal demise and the end of a social era—is embedded within his adult speculations about those moments of his childhood. The result is a multilayered and multivocal tale that dramatizes not a moment or even a process of comprehension but an ongoing state of ignorance. As in "The Walk," the narrator understands little more at the end of the process (the narration from his adult perspective, the contemplation of things past) than he did at the beginning or as a child.

Another professed motivation of Donoso's for focusing on children and their antithesis, the elderly, is that both groups live in a form of anarchy. Like the servants, children and the elderly exist on the fringes of society and are not subject to all the rules, role playing, and hierarchies to which adults are subject. Their actions and language tend to be freer, less self-conscious, less manipulated and manipulative. At the same time, however, the children imitate the adult world and reproduce it on a microcosmic level. As a result, the reader is proffered a new perspective that underlines the absurdities of adult (the reader's) society.

His concern with children also leads Donoso to employ the motif of the child's game. Again, however, he proffers a thinly veiled allegory of adult life, for he posits that children's games reflect, in structure and content, the more formalized ritualistic behavior (social decorum) that shapes adult lives. Thus the games are simultaneously similar to and different from adult rituals, but it would be difficult to decide which exerts more influence over the other. Think, for example, of *La Marquise Est Sortie á Cinq Heures* (The Marquise Left at Five o' Clock), the theatrical game of *A House in the Country,* or the games in *This Sunday.* Donoso's suggestion is that each makes the other problematic: adult rituals are absurd because of the traces they retain from childhood games; the latter are perverse because they resemble, perhaps even consciously imitate, adult rituals.

The Inexplicable:
The Call of the Wild

Throughout Donoso's works, one encounters an element of the inexplicable, often depicted (or at least interpreted) as an element of supernatural power. None of our empirical experience seems to provide explanations for the strange allure of Maya in *This Sunday,* the interchangeability of physical parts in "Chatanooga Choo-choo," Mauricio's strange whistling in "Gaspard de la Nuit," Matilde's fascination for the dog in "The Walk," or the protagonist's obsession with pictures of wild animals in "Santelices." What leads Andrés to opt consciously for insanity in *Coronation?* What does the father hide behind his poncho in *The Obscene Bird?*

Questions such as these necessarily punctuate any reading of Donoso's fiction. One of his points is surely that one can never "know" anything unequivocally. In many cases this inexplicable something, this call to another level of nature or reality, is resolved both stylistically and thematically by eradication or disappearance. The texts often end without resolution, or the characters simply disappear while their world disintegrates. *This Sunday* and *Coronation* both conclude with the death of the characters and the disintegration of the world as they knew it. *The Obscene Bird of Night* concludes with the burning of all the packages and papers that presumably were the text the reader has just finished; Marta and Roberto disappear into the night in "Atomo verde número cinco" ("Green Atom Number Five"), as does Matilde in "The Walk."

The unusual conclusions, or even nonconclusions, of so many of Donoso's works pose a curious contradiction. On one level his works seem to open up, letting in the unexpected and the unnatural or supernatural. Yet all his works close up around that possibility and somehow cover or negate it. Indeed, in many of the works in which the main character disappears, a new closure is effectuated in two ways. First, on the level of plot, the society or family depicted turns its back on the disappearance or erasure and carries on with life as if nothing had happened. Thus the brothers return to their ritualistic existence in "The Walk" after Matilde disappears and never make any direct reference to her disappearance. After the highly unusual happenings in *A House in the Country,* the parents return and life ostensibly goes on as usual—for a while, at least, until nature (the thistledown) "swallows" one group and perhaps the other. This erasure functions on the stylistic level too, for the reference to the disappearance or inexplicable event is frequently followed by a number of paragraphs about mundane events and written in the most apparently naturalistic, prosaic, and transparent of languages. In this way, the discourse of the text also denies that anything unusual has happened and lures the reader back into a false sense of complacency even after having shattered that complacency.

Space

The ostensibly circular structure that dominates much of Donoso's work is reflected in his use of space. The majority of his works take place either within the city or inside a carefully delimited and defined space—most often the home or a building that evokes a homelike structure. Generally the outside, be it a natural setting, the city, or the rest of society, is viewed as threatening and dangerous. Still, on the few occasions when the action takes place out of doors, even that exterior space tends to be markedly limited and confined. For example, the vineyards of *Hell Has No Limits* are bounded even as they surround the town. The Venturas' fence defines the "safe" spaces and separates them from the threatening outside, nature. Significantly, once outside the physical confines, characters tend to disappear, to be swallowed by the external world.

Surely the enclosed physical spaces evoke closed psychological spaces. Characters in the Donoso texts can function only within a rigidly ordered society and universe. The outside or exterior always threatens to destroy that social, psychological order and control. Nonetheless, Donoso's works are also characterized by the number of windows and doors (or even fences) that allow the characters to glimpse the "external" world and feel its allure from a safe distance. At the same time, physical space tends to close in upon itself, as in *The Obscene Bird of Night,* in which Mudito's

11

physical enclosure becomes ever smaller as the book draws to a conclusion. Obviously the delimitation of physical space mirrors the space limitations of the literary work, also closed, structured, and excluding the threatening outside while it paradoxically proffers a relatively unthreatening glimpse of that threatening other, the world outside the confines and rigid structure of the book or society. Space in Donoso's works is necessarily a projection of the mind, as is dramatically demonstrated in Santelices's projection of the jungle onto the patio of his office building (an enclosure within an already severely delimited world).

Art and Language:
The Blending of Content and Form

This depiction of space and the projection of mental rigidity reflect Donoso's preoccupation with art and literature or language. In much of Donoso's work the world is depicted as already a reproduction of some earlier works of art or literature. Western aesthetics, particularly since the nineteenth century, has generally viewed art as a reproduction or mimesis of reality, but Donoso continually demonstrates the degree to which the opposite is also true: reality (or what we perceive as and then insist is reality) is frequently a reproduction or mimesis of artistic works. For this reason, in many of his works the principal action is presented as fiction, as fantasy even within the work. For example, the principal action of *This Sunday,* the relationship of the grandparents to each other and that of the grandmother to Maya, is presented as the recollections, not necessarily reliable, of an adult who reviews his childhood. Within that principal action the narrator includes the grandfather's memories of his youth. The continual embedding of one story within the other, combined with a repeated undermining of the reliability of the narrators, marks the fictitiousness of those tales and their distance from what might be labeled reality. It marks them as already reproduction. In this way Donoso suggests that art is not merely a mirror of some external reality; art and reality mutually influence, shape, and mold each other.

At the same time, language and the embedding technique, like the fences, doors, and windows, frequently provide limiting structures, for, consciously and intentionally or not, Donoso continually proposes that we perceive what we have words for and tend not to perceive what we cannot name. Like art and literature, language shapes and limits perception. When confronted with a situation for which we have no word, we perceive nothing. Thus an inability to name leads logically to the erasure or disappearance that so often marks the conclusion of his works.

As we examine the trajectory of Donoso's prose over the course of forty years, we shall find that some combination of these eight characteristics is present in every work.

Note

1. Ronald Christ, "An Interview with José Donoso," *Partisan Review* 49, 1 (1982): 30.

CHAPTER TWO

The Short Stories

Donoso's short stories mark his earliest incursions into the literary realm. His first story in Spanish, "'China,'" was published in 1954 by Zig-Zag in Enrique Lafourcade's *Antología del nuevo cuento chileno* (Anthology of the New Chilean Short Story). His first volume of stories, *Veraneo y otros cuentos* (Summer Vacation and Other Stories), appeared in 1955 and included "Veraneo" ("Summertime"), "Tocayos" (Namesakes), "El güero" ("The 'Güero'"), "Una señora" ("A Lady"), "Fiesta en grande" (A Grand Party), "Dos cartas" (Two Letters), and "Dinamarquero" ("The Dane's Place"). This book won him the Premio Municipal in 1956. His second volume, *El charlestón* (The Charleston), included "El charlestón" ("Charleston"), "La puerta cerrada" ("The Closed Door"), "Ana María" ("Ana Maria"), "Paseo" ("The Walk"), and "El hombrecito" (The Handyman), most of which had been published previously in literary magazines. These two volumes of stories plus "Santelices" and his earlier "'China'" were collected in 1965 and published as *Los mejores cuentos de Donoso* (Donoso's Best Short Stories). That collection was reprinted in 1971 and 1985 and entitled simply *Cuentos* (Stories). An English translation, *Charleston and Other Stories*, includes nine narratives from that group.

In general the stories share a number of characteristics. First, they portray a society that is rigidly structured and leaves little margin for deviance from predetermined behavior patterns. Second, the stories evince a strong sense of inside and outside, both in the spatial sense (inside the house as opposed to outside) and in a sociopsychological sense (inclusion in or exclusion from a group or social class). In turn, this rigidity of structure and space provides the framework for the inevitable rebellion, successful or not. While some characters defy parental authority, others overtly turn their backs on social mores; refuse to play the game, as it were; and disappear. Thus in one form or another almost all Donoso's protagonists rebel against the status quo. In addition, the stories demonstrate a preoccupation with vision and perspective. Stylistically this leads to a technique that centers on point of view and subtly questions the reliability of the narrative voice.[1] Thematically it manifests itself as a concentration on the sense of sight and the eyes and leads to the notion that one perceives what one wishes, what society has deemed appropriate, or what one has words for and can articulate. What one cannot name, one cannot or will not "see."

In spite of the fact that Donoso's short stories have not been frequently analyzed by critics and scholars, they certainly are valuable works in and of themselves and foreshadow the author's later works. Unfortunately, space limitations do not allow a fuller discussion of them here. As perhaps the best known and most representative, "The Walk" and "Santelices" are the focus of this chapter.

"The Walk"

"The Walk" is one of Donoso's most superbly crafted stories and probably the one most frequently acclaimed by critics. Here the author employs the techniques of the first-person narration and the embedded narrative as he juxtaposes the perspective of a young boy with that of an adult narrator. Reduced to its core, "The Walk" is the story of an adult as he remembers and tries to comprehend the circumstances that surrounded the turning point of his childhood: the disappearance of his Aunt Matilde. Before that momentous event but after the death of the boy's mother, his Aunt Matilde and two bachelor uncles had come to live with him and his father so that there would be a woman to care for him. Their home life was characterized by physical comforts and reassuring routines, epitomized in the ritualistic billiard game each evening.[2] Although the family acknowledged the existence of the world outside the confines of their "perfect" home, a world evoked by distant foghorns and lights but always perceived through the filter of a window, that "other" world never infringed upon theirs, where the fortuitous and the unexpected had no place. In fact, heaven is imaged as an exact replica of their house (78/212). In the family's carefully delimited world, screened from the outside by windows, walls, and fences (both physical and psychological), misfortunes such as hunger, cold, discomfort, poverty, or weakness were perceived only as "mere errors in a world that ought to be—no, *had* to be—perfect" (76/210; the emphasis is Donoso's). The self-correcting gesture is significant. More important, their "perfect" house is imaged in relation to a book: "narrow and vertical as a book slipped in between the thick shapes of the new buildings" (75/208).[3] However, it was a closed book—"that deep house which, like a book, revealed only its narrow spine to the street" (76/209); it never opened itself up to the threat of the exterior, and it hid as much as it revealed, not unlike "the thick [library] door [that] screened the meaning of the words, allowing [him] to hear only the deep, deliberate counterpoint of their voices" (73/205).

The perfection of this prelapsarian structure was apparently broken by the appearance of a small white dog. To the boy, the dog heralded the beginning of disintegration and chaos: first Matilde stopped playing billiards with the brothers, then she forgot the shooting order, later she laughed (perhaps for the first time), and finally she walked the dog each evening. Those "walks," excursions beyond the confines of their neat, ordered, bookish house into the outside world, eventually led to the final, title "walk" and Matilde's "disappearance."

Although her disappearance is incomprehensible to the narrator, he does define it as the end of the secure, neatly ordered, ritualistic life he had known up to that point: "I went to bed terrified that this would be the end. And I wasn't wrong" (94/230). He was terrified because, as he noted in the preceding sentence, he had realized that his aunt had her whole life before her and was capable of anything. Surely that included turning her back on the established order, opting not to continue caring for the males (narrator, father, and uncles), and leaving them to perpetuate their own structure and order. While there can be no question that they do reinstitute that order, they accomplish it in part by imposing a self-serving blindness and refusing to "see" anything that might threaten it. This blindness and the narrative correcting factor that signals it are apparent throughout the story. For example, although the narrator posits his aunt's disappearance as a major threat to, indeed as the termination of, the status quo, he subsequently negates that concept and assures the reader (or himself), "Life went on in our house as if Aunt Matilde were still living with us" (94/230). His confidence quickly falters, however, and in the next statement he corrects himself by noting that the brothers began to meet regularly behind the closed doors of the library. One of the recurrent elements of the text is this self-correcting tendency that leaves the reader dangling over a void of ignorance paralleling that of the narrator. In fact, the story might be read as the dramatization of order reestablished by means of the act of narration.

Nonetheless, Matilde's disappearance is never labeled as such, for it can be encompassed by none of the terms with which the narrator is familiar. In the story's title it is euphemistically designated by the unthreatening term "walk," and within the text he simply concedes that she "never came back" (94/230). By not naming the event, the narrator silences it (and blinds himself to it) much as the brothers do, in both cases in order to avoid "the useless terror of having to accept that the streets of a city can swallow a human being, annul it, leave it without life or death, suspended in a dimension more threatening than any dimension with a name" (73–74/206)—threatening precisely because it does not have a name.

In this respect it is not so much the streets of the city that "annul" Matilde and leave her suspended in a dimension without a name as it is the narrator himself, for it is he (perhaps along with the brothers) who does not or will not know and cannot or will not name—either as the child who lived the experience or as the adult who has become a mirror image of the brothers and who narrates in an attempt to understand events that have no place in his neatly organized world. When he makes an ineffectual attempt to label the event in the first word of the text, he employs *"Esto,"* "This," an indefinite, neuter, demonstrative pronoun, marked by uncertainty and nonreferentiality. In this way he calls attention to the fact that the event lies outside his frame of reference and cannot be named.[4] Certainly, throughout the story he accentuates his lack of comprehension. At the same time his inability to understand is always linked to the bipolar, antithetical nature of all his perceptions: now/then, before/after, inside/outside the house, inside/outside his aunt's circle of recognition, they/he. Surely his aunt's disappearance falls somewhere between his antitheses. Similarly, throughout the text the narrator highlights his own position as neither inside nor outside (or conversely as both inside and outside): he is part of the family but outside the more intimate circle formed by the siblings; he understands and took part in some of the events but not in all (his role was peripheral, more that of witness). Only in the text he narrates does he overcome his marginality by placing himself at the center. At last he has a role in the family unit: he narrates.

It is significant too that his narration is peppered with desire, with how he wanted things to be (which, like the simile discussed in chapter one, simultaneously evokes how they were not): "I'd rather think" (73/205), "I *wanted* them to be talking" (73/205; emphasis added), "I desperately *wanted* this contained affection to overflow" (76/209; emphasis added), he *wanted* her to turn down his bed (77/210–11), he *prayed* one of the brothers would break the rigid order (79/213), he *wants* her to beckon him with a look (89/224), he *wants* to fall ill so she will pay attention to him (90/226). As a result, one should perhaps conclude that the narrative itself, with its emphasis on the dog's culpability, also represents things as he would have liked them to be. While on the one hand he acknowledges that the changes slowly took place in Matilde even before she started walking the dog, on the other hand he must still blame the dog for dragging her away, in spite of the fact that he portrays her as an active participant, carrying the dog in her arms when she returns at night (93–94/229–30). Does he blame the dog because he "never liked dogs" (80/215) or because he cannot name or does not wish to acknowledge the possibility that Matilde might be subject to such circumstances as love and adventure, "fortuitous" events in which he and the brothers were not central?[5] Significantly, with the exception of the indirect allusion (in his premonition) that she was capable of anything, the narrator rarely credits Matilde with any will or dynamic force of her own. For him she was more often a passive being, swallowed by the city street or dragged by the dog. Indeed he would prefer to believe her dead than to "torture" himself with questions and the possibility that she had a will and an existence in which they formed no part.

Chronologically the story ends with a renewed attempt to establish order and centrality and thereby mitigate that threatening external, unnameable element. Although the narrator never designates that element, he encloses it within the circularity of the text. For that reason, his final statement must echo his earlier one even as it repeats the brothers' gesture of shutting a door on the event: "The door of the library was too thick, too heavy, and I never knew if Aunt Matilde, dragged along by the white dog, had got lost in the city, or in death, or in a region more mysterious than either" (94/230). The reader will never know either; the limitations of the vision and discursive mastery of the narrator provide as much a barrier as the library door; both contain and retain literary worlds. At the same time, his egocentric need to place himself at the center of the world he portrays blinds him and the reader.

"Santelices"

Santelices's approach to the void or the uncertainties differs from that of the narrator of "The Walk" in that Santelices tries to fill the void in his life with art—drawings and photographs of ferocious wild beasts that fascinate him. Like any number of Donoso's other characters, he apparently fails to fill that void and plunges into it, literally and figuratively, in part because he fails to differentiate between art and life, fantasy and reality, inside and outside. Contemporary philosophers and theorists have posited that a perception of difference is essential to both our interaction with our world and our sense of order and stability within that world. That is, one must continually be able to differentiate between X and not X, between self and other, and to recognize the dividing line between the two. To a greater or lesser degree Santelices's demise is the result of an erasure of difference.

Santelices is a middle-aged archivist entrenched in the tedium and inflexible routine of his office and the pension where he boards, the latter run by the also middle-aged, unmarried Bertita and her elderly father, Don Eusebio. Presumably Santelices's office life is filled with the repetitious facts and figures of papers and files while his life at the pension is marked by the nightly canasta games (like the billiard games of "The Walk," games with ritualistic rigidity) and punctuated by weekend excursions to the movies (a projected world of fiction). In sum, Santelices is quiet, neat, punctual, polite, organized, and punctilious—totally "normal" but exceedingly dull.

Nonetheless, normality is only the mask Santelices presents to the world, for he has another, less visible side. The text opens as he has been caught in a flagrant display of this other side, his "perversion": his collection of illustrations and photographs of wild animals. His vice is made public when he decides "to do it" (155/260)—to take the illustrations from the bottom drawer where he has been keeping (hiding) them and hang them on the wall (make them visible to all). From his perspective, this act of assertion or defiance transforms his pension room into a jungle: "New odors, powerful and animal, overcame the tired everyday ones. . . . Animal effusions sullied the air" (158/263–64). Santelices's dual nature and the latent eroticism suggested by the animal pictures are foregrounded in the text's description of his encounter with Bertita the next morning. In a scene marked by grotesque eroticism (she is obese but clad only in a semi-transparent nightgown), Bertita reflects Santelices's perhaps unconscious assumption of a mask, for she wraps her eroticism in the guise of maternalism and then projects that eroticism onto him as she calls him a pig who takes advantage of her and accuses him of being a "wolf in sheep's clothing" (164/270).[6] This use of a metaphor based on animals, combined with the implication of a disguise or mask, is neither irrelevant nor totally erroneous, as shall become apparent. Nonetheless, this encounter, followed by his certainty that Bertita has destroyed his pictures, leads him to flee the pension and take refuge in his office and other public locales for several days. He finally returns to the pension and his "old" way of life just long enough to prevaricate by announcing his plans to move in with a widow, thus metaphorically destroying both Bertita and her dream as she had literally destroyed his drawings.

In the meantime, while hiding out in his office, he has been watching the activities of a blonde girl in the patio below his window. His progressively more detailed, sensorial, and dramatic perceptions of what is happening there reflect his increasing alienation from tangible reality and his immersion in a world of sensorial imagination (perhaps also symbolic of latent eroticism) that contrast dramatically with and are punctuated by returns to the prosaic reality of the pension. The evolution and expansion of his perceptions of the girl mirror his earlier "immersion" in the world of his illustrations: his "anxiety . . . grew like a *blinding,* paralyzing vine which left no room for anything but itself" (160/265; emphasis added).

Let us examine the growth of that metaphoric vine. At first, Santelices simply perceives a blonde girl playing in the patio (165/270). In the next paragraph the girl is playing with a cat. A page later the text alludes to the distance that separates them and to the difficulty of perception by noting that she is five stories down. Santelices's fantasy continues to grow, and on the next page, as the girl sews, he begins to imagine how her face (which he cannot see) would look when she plays with her female cat, which he "knows" is female because he has "seen" the litter. By now there are five or six animals around the girl. Curiously, it is his fascination with the birth of those kittens that makes him forget his fears and return to the pension, Bertita, and his former life, for a while at least. In the next reference to the girl (170/277), he sees her through the binoculars he has borrowed and decides she is about seventeen and does not seem to "belong to anybody or anything" (170/278). Now there are eight or nine cats, and the mother cat is enormous. On the next page even more cats have come into the patio, and the reader is told it is a well known fact that they become treacherous at night. Two pages later the patio is lit by the brilliance of animal eyes that greedily watch the unwary girl (172–3/280). At this point Santelices returns once more to the pension and "destroys" Bertita: "this was what he had wanted to *see with his own eyes* for a long time: Bertita destroyed" (174/281; emphasis added). Note, however, that the destruction he "sees" is but metaphoric; she is unhappy but not "destroyed" in the literal sense of the word, a fact that encourages the reader to question all Santelices "sees."

The motif of the eyes is particularly significant here. In his final image of the patio, Santelices perceives the cats, not in their corporeal totality, but only as multicolored eyes; later one of the cats will steal his binoculars. And of course the tale itself brings into doubt one's capacity to see anything that one does not invent or project. What Santelices "sees" does not exist for others. Indeed, the text notes that, like the earlier vine, "the jungle was growing inside him now, with its roars and heat, with its effusions of death and life" (174/281), reinforcing the notion that what he sees is a projection of his own mind. Still, the projection expands to include other sensory perceptions—sounds, temperature. Metaphoric or not, it is becoming all-consuming. Finally the patio teems with beasts that watch him while the jungle grows before his eyes: the trees, which at first do not quite reach his window, moments later are above his vantage point and smother him. What was outside is now inside. He searches for the girl with his eyes. When he locates her down below (note the symbolism: he is above, she below, in the animal, inferior kingdom or hell), where the animals are destroying each other, she is begging him to save her. Since he acknowledges that he cannot hear her, she must be begging him with her eyes, thus suggesting that the projected gaze, his projected vision, has been so well projected that it is perceived as external and returns to him: she and the animals look at him. He is now the viewer *and* the viewed, a status that affords the importance and sense of superiority he had lost when his illustrations were destroyed ("all he needed was this intimate contemplation [of his collection] to feel superior, solid, and proud" [159/264]). His projection and identification are now complete and echo his earlier identification with both the victims and the aggressors of his illustrations. Deprived of them, he feels an imperative and makes "his richest and most ambitious decision" (175/283): he jumps from his window to save her, five stories down, immersing himself in a world of bestiality (and by inference, eroticism) of victim and aggressor. Earlier he had felt "an enervating incitement to . . . risk himself by *becoming . . . victim and aggressor*" (161/266; emphasis added) in "the torturing invitation that for years he himself had prolonged . . . never really taking part except in distant, harmless echoes" (168/275). Now he will forever be a part of the void his illustrations could not fill.

The void (and its danger), first intuited by Eusebio when he discovers the pictures, is dramatically evoked by the tack holes made when Santelices hung the pictures and on which Eusebio focuses in order to avoid the larger blank space, the question mark, the "why." As the text opens, normal order and ritual have already been broken twice: first by the inconsistencies in the card game the night before and then by the hanging of the pictures. The first segment of the story depicts the characters' attempts to reestablish that order through language. Indeed, the first pages are marked by the question of language and the nonconcordance of the two men's language and perspectives. "I'm sure you'll understand," says Eusebio. "It was incomprehensible," responds Santelices mentally, in reference to a different topic. Eusebio calls them nails and insists there are twenty-five; Santelices labels them tacks and corrects the number to twenty-three. The former responds, "It's all the same . . . what's the difference?" His point seems to be that difference is not desirable. Santelices should be like all the other tenants, although admittedly he is not—he is superior. He should put himself in Eusebio's shoes, even though he certainly does not want to "put himself in" his false teeth. Santelices's pictures should be of scantily clad women, like everyone else's, even though that is perverse also. No wonder Santelices is confused; he is receiving contradictory messages here just as he does from Bertita (maternal concern combined with erotic desire). Incapable of distinguishing and deciding between the often undifferentiated antitheses, he slips into the void, the gap of nothingness, the unnameable that lies between the two extremes when his artistic imagination blurs the dividing line between self and other, same and different. Thus he leaps *down* into the primordial void: the metaphoric other, subconsciousness, death, sexuality, animalism, artistic imagination (perhaps the original sin)—all, paradoxically, in order to elude the void, the question mark that, as *Coronation* will suggest, is inevitable and lies within. Difference is erased, and Santelices becomes a part of the question mark, as do so many Donoso characters who follow him.

Notes

1. A number of critics have noted or analyzed Donoso's use of narrators with limited vision in the style of Henry James.

2. The game of billiards is noted for its strict order and rigid rules. It is a game that allows nothing unexpected or gratuitous.

3. The adjectives "narrow" and "vertical" are also intended to evoke the limitation and narrow-mindedness of the family as well as their lofty position.

4. The opening word, *Esto,* is validly rendered "It" in the English translation, but the indefiniteness of the word is more evident in Spanish, in which the neuter demonstrative pronoun indicates that the narrator does not know the name (or gender) of what he describes.

5. Matilde's disappearance is also fraught with erotic overtones. Only after the dog enters their lives does she demonstrate characteristics of femininity: she eats bonbons "that came in boxes tied with frivolous bows" (90/225) and chatters with the dog. At the same time, the boy is inexplicably annoyed that the dog's tail is "curled up like a plume, *leaving its hindquarters shamelessly exposed*" (86/221–22; emphasis added), and Matilde comes home, one time with her hair disheveled, another time with a tear in her skirt. Perhaps we are to understand that her escapades are of an erotic nature that the young boy can intuit but not articulate.

6. Although the Spanish original states, "pasarle gato por liebre," which means to swindle or con someone (literally, pass a cat off for a hare), the figure still depends upon animals and suggests deceit, masquerade.

Even earlier the reader is encouraged to view Santelices's reaction to his illustrations in relation to a latent eroticism. His reaction to the sensational photos is described: "he felt the nape of his neck grow cold with emotion . . . until his hands were damp and his eyelids flickered" (159/265).

23

CHAPTER THREE

Coronation

In the years between the publications of Donoso's two collections of short stories, *Veraneo* and *Charleston,* his first novel, *Coronation* (1957), appeared. In spite of the success of his earlier *Veraneo,* finding a publisher for this novel was not easy. It was finally published by Nascimiento after Donoso agreed to accept seven hundred copies (to be sold privately) in lieu of royalties. In 1962 it won the William Faulkner Foundation Prize for the best Chilean novel since World War II. As might be expected, given its chronological location in Donoso's literary production, *Coronation* exhibits a number of similarities to Donoso's short stories and prefigures many of the themes and techniques that dominate his later works.

Chronicling the final spasms of life and sanity in the last two vestiges of the Abalos family, the nonagenarian Misiá Elisa and her grandson Andrés, who is about fifty-three years old, the novel takes place during the few months before she slips into death and he into a state perhaps worse than death—voluntary insanity.[1] Already bedridden for many years when the novel opens, Misiá Elisa is the widow of a prominent lawyer, Don Ramón Abalos. She is afflicted with a smoldering hatred or diabolical force that drives her to spit vicious, obscene insults at anyone nearby. The problem first manifested itself more than thirty-five years earlier when, still gracious, beautiful, and clever, she began reviling her husband and servants, accusing them all of lewd and sinful behavior and the latter of thievery in addition. The obscenity and explicitness of her language, which defiles everything it touches, contrast sharply with her religiousness, purity, and ostensible ignorance of anything related to the body. In fact, she often insists on how pure and self-sacrificing she is, worthy of wearing a saint's crown. Her self-righteousness is accompanied by the conviction that she has descended from royalty and is thus entitled to wear a royal crown as well. Although according to her husband such a belief is unfounded, no one ever challenges her confusion between coronation and canonization. Furthermore, as Andrés recalls, his grandmother's obscenities destroyed the peace and tranquillity (the paradise lost) that had reigned in their home, in which she still lives at the start of the narrative and which is described, like her, as moribund. Like her too, the house is in a state of deterioration but still envinces half-hidden signs of its former life and glory. Earlier, as her alienation worsened, her husband apparently took a mistress and spent as little time as possible in the house until he was driven to his own form of alienation, becoming gloomy, irritable, and indifferent to both his profession and his appearance.[2] He died when Misiá Elisa was almost seventy, more than twenty years before the events chronicled in the novel.[3]

Meanwhile, the couple raised their grandson, Andrés, whose mother had died when he was born and his father a year later, some say from grief. A product of upper-middle-class education and values, Andrés has paradoxically accepted and rejected both models incarnated by his grandparents. He disdains the ideology of his grandmother and the priests who taught him, but he is still haunted by the terrors of hell, sex, and death they inculcated in him. Similarly, he has followed his grandfather's footsteps and become a lawyer, but he does not practice that profession. His comfortable financial situation affords him the luxury of not working. As a result, at the start of the novel he is firmly ensconced in a bachelor life marked by physical comforts but also by rigid routine, tedium, inertia, and irresolution. He is first portrayed in the decrepitated garden, half asleep, half awake, unable to motivate himself enough to open the newspaper. Content with the life of regimented moderation he has chosen, he allows himself pleasures but no excesses and devotes his hours to collecting antique walking sticks (but never more than ten) and to reading French history (but mostly those texts, such as that of Saint-Simon, that memorialize irrelevant and often erroneous detail).[4] He has learned to avoid all unpleasantness in life simply by averting his eyes and not seeing, although his grandmother's easy familiarity with death still occasionally forces him to face that horrifying eventuality. The turning point, which comes early in the novel, is his recognition of the absurdity of his life, precipitated by his grandmother's recriminations that he is a "pathetic, useless old bachelor" (56/52) who has frittered his life away and who is wicked in addition. His grandmother's depiction of him is confirmed by his friend Carlos's allegations that he is a hypocrite who has never lived (82/72) and does not know what life is. Much of the novel centers on Andrés's efforts to convert his "living death" into life: first by considering a trip to Europe, then by breaking with tradition and buying an eleventh walking stick, and finally by deciding that he must have Estela. When the last endeavor fails, he opts for insanity and reverts to childhood games and irresponsibility.

The story of this bourgeois family is juxtaposed with that of an indigent family composed of René, Dora, and the former's younger half brother, Mario, who has lived with them since the death of his parents. Mario's relationship to Dora and René parallels that of Andrés to his grandparents in that he too simultaneously accepts and rejects their model. Similarly, the poor family's search for a better, more meaningful life echoes Andrés's, even if the specifics of their ironic quests are different. To that end, René is continually involved in dubious schemes to acquire money since he believes their lives would be different if only they had it. Unquestionably, one of the novel's main themes is the irony of this conviction; Andrés has economic security, and his life may appear more enviable than that of the poor family, but it is as hollow and lacking as theirs, though in different ways.

Although scholars have frequently hailed *Coronation* as a critique of the Chilean class system, and although Donoso does depict two social extremes, he does not criticize, analyze, or even acknowledge the ideological structures that support the social divisions, for that is not his intention. Neither class is presented in a particularly favorable light or at the mercy of the other. Certainly both classes have their prejudices and predetermined expectations in regard to the other, but then so do all the groups depicted here (young and old, males and females). For example, René's attempt to impose his model on Mario differs little from Misiá Elisa's indoctrinating Andrés in her values, in spite of the years and social distinctions that separate the two heads of family. Similarly, Mario's stereotypic definition of a "real man" varies little in essence from Misiá Elisa's conviction that all men are "pigs" who only want to use women for their pleasures or Estela's "knowledge" that all rich men take advantage of poor girls (a credence that links the questions of age, class, *and* gender). Donoso demonstrates that all groups have problems—different perhaps, but problems all the same—and that although each group believes its situation would improve with the acquisition of X (which varies from group to group), in fact, even if it were feasible, that acquisition would just lead to other problems and other conflicts. Perhaps Andrés's metaphysical problems are less undesirable (and certainly they are sillier) than

René's material problems of survival, but life is ineluctably imperfect in either case. It is merely a question of focus, for the ideal state sought by all is mythic and inaccessible because it is linguistic in construct. Ultimately, none can escape that which threatens them most: their own mortality, continually imaged in this novel as a void or abyss. Indeed, the parallels among the characters' final destinies attest to this assertion, for Misiá Elisa floats off into the nothingness of death; Andrés surrounds himself with the vacuity (and irresponsibility) of madness; and René, Mario, and Estela disappear into the vastness of the night.

These two social classes and their quests are bridged, in all senses of the word, by the Abalos family's servants, Rosario, Lourdes, and the latter's niece, Estela, who comes from the country to care for Misiá Elisa. Rosario's fondness for Mario and Estela's love for him gain him entrance into the Abalos house. There he and René plot to use Estela to steal the silver, the bounty that will buy their utopia. She is to distract Andrés, who desires her and sees her as the solution to his problems. The brothers' plan fails at the last moment when Estela refuses to be used by any of the males and forewarns Andrés about the robbery. As the novel ends, Mario and Estela escape into the night to an unspecified future (but one that probably mirrors the wretched present of Dora and René), and Andrés retreats into voluntary insanity. Upstairs, in a grotesque, carnivallike ceremony, the servants crown Misiá Elisa, and she dies shortly thereafter, costumed as the saint and queen she has always *said* she was. *Coronation* is consistent with other Donoso works in that one of its principal themes is the capacity of discourse to superimpose itself, like a mask, onto reality and alter perceptions of empirical experience. Nevertheless, in this novel Donoso suggests that the only reality is that of the mask, and the only personality is the role one has assumed, often in response to the words (articulated perceptions) of another.

Plot and Structure

An examination of the structure of *Coronation*, the ordering and interrelation of its plot elements, reveals many of its thematic concerns. The text is composed of three sections, reminiscent of an Aristotelian tragedy with its clearly defined beginning, middle, and end: "The Gift," "Absences," and "The Coronation." The first and last sections are dominated by a ritualistic break in the tedium of everyday life. In the first, the daily routine is interrupted by Estela's arrival and its apparently positive influence on Misiá Elisa. In addition, the preparations for and celebration of the elderly woman's birthday break the routine while concurrently marking the cyclical nature of life. On a more subtle yet parallel note, the routine of years is also broken in this section when Andrés belatedly comprehends the meaninglessness of his life and its rigid structure.[5] Later "The Coronation" echoes "The Gift" in its ceremonial break with daily routine in celebration of Misiá Elisa's saint's day.[6] This time, however, the repetitive, cyclical nature of the ritualistic ceremony is transgressed, for no one comes to the party, and the maids substitute their own bizarre party and coronation.

At the same time, the first section, "The Gift," is characterized by ambiguity and the last, "The Coronation," by irony. The first section encompasses not one gift, as its title suggests, but rather at least four: Estela's mother has "given" her to Lourdes; Mario gives Rosario a fabric rabbit made by Dora; Andrés gives his grandmother a pink shawl for her birthday, which she in turn forces on Estela, labeling it a shawl fit for a whore like Estela, not for a saint like herself; and, finally, Lourdes "gives" Estela the key to the Abalos house, a gift that will subsequently lead the young woman to "give" herself to Mario.[7] In turn, the last section is dominated by the irony and paradox of a series of events that are not what they seem. First Andrés "crowns" his lifetime of inactivity and avoidance of commitment with his final alienation into madness. Paradoxically, his one decisive "act" is a decision not to act (not to do anything) except to act (to play a role, that of a madman and child). Simultaneous to this conscious decision to live a theatrical role is the burlesque and theatrical coronation of Misiá Elisa as queen and saint. Similarly, Estela seems to give herself to Andrés but ultimately does not, and the brothers attempt to rob the house but in fact do not. The structure of the text is circular in that it opens with a theatrical scene and closes with a series of theatrical scenes, suggesting that the theatrical roles may have changed during the course of the novel, but the fact of the role playing has not.

In spite of all the pomp and circumstance that punctuate the first and last sections, the middle section, theoretically the core of the novel, is labeled and characterized by absences, by the nothingness and lack that mark the lives of all the characters. Although by concentrating on the style and structure of the novels he reads Andrés may be able to elide the bothersome questions and voids those novels pose (69/62), readers of *Coronation* cannot, for its style and structure lead to those issues as, metaphorically, the reader too confronts the abyss of Andrés's dreams. Yet ironically it is in this section of absences where the only three consummated "love" scenes take place (Dora and René, Mario and Estela, Carlos and Adriana) and where Andrés decides he loves (or desires) Estela. The fact that Donoso has chosen to include these in a section entitled "Absences" suggests that love (or perhaps better expressed, eroticism, for all these scenes center on the sex act itself) is not the solution to anything and, like a novel, is only a temporary distraction from life's voids. In effect, erotic desire is instead a manifestation of the problem—that eternally unfulfilled desire that will always crave what is other and what cannot be possessed. Sexual desire is imaged here as simply one among many of the forms of endless desire for what one does not and cannot possess, for what is inherently other.

Yet the relationship between love and erotic desire parallels the structuring paradigm of the text, for the erotic is a concrete manifestation of desire, while love seems to be the word, mask, or poetic rendition of that desire. Andrés twice interrupts the erotic scene (in the most theatrical sense of the word *scene*) he is playing with Estela, when she pretends to *give* herself to him, by asking if she loves him. Similarly, Estela twice asks the same question of Mario before she agrees to help with the robbery. Both seek ephemeral words rather than tangible demonstrations. They want the poetry that Andrés repeatedly and openly admits he needs. The word *love* would provide that poetry, that linguistic mask which would facilitate the self-delusion. But Mario's curt affirmatives apparently fail to convince Estela for long, and she rebels against his violations of her dignity and the *gift* of her body and subsequently reveals the robbery plans. Similarly, her silence the first time Andrés asks the question leaves him without his poetry and "with nothing but animal lust" (249/209).[8] He flings himself on her and tries to force her—that is, steal what can only be given. Denied the illusion (mask) of the word, both must seek their "poetry" in another form of self-delusion: he in insanity and she in the "proud knowledge of her victory" (252/211) that she experiences as Mario beats her, insults her, and pushes her along in front of him while the reader is left to wonder what victory there is in being mistreated.

The question of illusion is highlighted in the parallels between the opening and closing scenes. It is significant that the novel opens not with any of the main characters, but with a peripheral character, Rosario, and a seemingly irrelevant action, the delivery of groceries to the Abalos kitchen. The scene serves to highlight the physical comfort and immaculate order that reign in the house while it hints at the interdependence of the various social classes: none could survive without the others. In addition, it provides the motive for what will be the meeting of these two classes: Rosario holds the door open for Angel and through him befriends Mario, signaling her instrumentality in Mario and René's access to the house and thus indirectly implicating her in the thwarted robbery. But even more important, the scene focuses on the principal thematic concerns of the novel: theater, mask, and the word that is not always to be trusted. Angel tells Rosario that he has lost his job and that it is Mario's fault. Indeed, he theatrically performs for her, assuming different gestures, staring glumly, and looking as if he might cry, all to lead her to ask him what is wrong and to convince her of the truth of his words. Yet he is lying. His words here do not accurately reflect a situation; they invent one. Nevertheless, because Rosario accepts his words as consistent with the facts, she intercedes for him and in turn uses her words to modify the state of affairs: he has lost his job; she speaks with his boss and gets his job back (employment replaces unemployment).

In this novel the question of robbery is one of the principal motifs. It punctuates much of the action and is closely related to the question of truth or lie, reality or illusion. Indeed, stealing is repeatedly contrasted with giving. In the opening scene the designation "thief," in all its complexity, first surfaces. Angel calls Mario a thief, and Rosario, who believes him, also labels him a thief. Paradoxically, Rosario should be the character least disposed to accept the term at face value since she has been a victim of its erroneous imputation in the past (when Misiá Elisa had accused her and Lourdes of stealing her feathers) and fears she will be again in the future (as Andrés becomes more like his grandmother, the servants worry that he will follow her model and accuse them of stealing [236/ 198]). Nevertheless, all those who are accused of thievery do eventually steal or at least attempt to do so. Mario and René (whose reputation as a thief is without factual basis) do try to rob the Abalos household; Estela, who is called a thief by Misiá Elisa, does steal her money; and some thirty-seven years after Misiá Elisa's initial accusations, Lourdes and Rosario do "steal" her feathers, her feather boa, in preparation for the "coronation." Thus the word *thief* simultaneously does and does not reflect fact; it is merely a question of time. In this manner, Donoso dramatizes the paradoxical power of words to create the situation they would portray while at the same time he demonstrates how the word can reflect what simultaneously is and is not. The thwarted robbery (a robbery that is and is not one) echoes Andrés's escape into madness and regression to childhood (madness and childhood that are and are not) as he opts to withdraw into a more simplistic period, the prelapsarian world before mutually exclusive absolutes began to break down, when things either were or were not stolen or given.

Similarly, the power of words to alter perceptions of the reality they seem to name is also a major theme. For example, his grandmother's accusation that he desires Estela leads Andrés to accept her words as fact. Yet again her words create the situation rather than describing it. Before she names it, Andrés does not know what he feels around Estela; he has simply experienced undefined physical discomfort. It is Misiá Elisa's words coupled with his conversation with Carlos that occasion his desire for the young woman. That desire heightens when he observes her and Mario in a lovers' colloquium. And, just as Misiá Elisa's earlier revilements of her husband and servants are attributed to her imagination, imagination plays a major role in Andrés's desire: his "*imagination* had only to *stretch* up to pluck the answer—he wanted [in Spanish, "desired"] Estela" (134/115; emphasis added).

Yet the elaboration of Andrés's desire is not the only time when Misiá Elisa's words generate the phenomena they presume to represent. Both Estela and Andrés accept the old woman's version of events.[9] One of the major issues of the text is the degree to which the other characters accept her rendition of reality, the degree to which their perception of empirical events is formulated by prior discourse, specifically hers. For example, after being called a whore and a thief, Estela corroborates the words by "giving" herself to Mario and stealing from Misiá Elisa, that is, by assuming both prophesied roles. Thus, metaphorically Misiá Elisa functions much like an omniscient narrator, the oligarchy she represents, or the generic "they say," in that her words shape others' perceptions of their empirical experiences in a manner that favors her and her ideological group while maintaining that group in its central, controlling position.

Misiá Elisa's rendition of "truth" is directly related to the question of sight and vision. In fact, the text contrasts metaphoric sight and blindness on numerous occasions. Although both Estela and Andrés regard Misiá Elisa as the one who "sees" and therefore knows, her eyes are described as "normally cloudy and lusterless" (41/41).[10] Earlier the text had noted, "It was as if Misiá Elisa's field of vision had been obscured by a cloud of filth which prevented things from growing straight . . . and poisoning everything natural and simple at the roots" (18/22–23). Her nearsightedness (a myopia with which she infects others by means of her words) is particularly evident in the final scene and echoes Rosario's limited vision in the first. In the final paragraphs the nonagenarian can barely differentiate wakefulness from sleep (reality from dream or illusion) and has lost the capacity to distinguish between far and near. As a result she "sees" herself surrounded by stars and concludes that she is dead and ascending into heaven. But again she is wrong; she does not die until moments later. Like her verbal recriminations, her vision has predated rather than postdated the phenomenon. Through these scenes Donoso proposes that even "seeing" can be the illusory product of what one expects to see, or it can be created by someone else's cloudy perceptions. Where then lies the reality and where the theater or mask is the question of the novel. "Reality" seems to be what one sees, but one "sees" only the surface, the theater, the mask.

At the same time, the characters consistently fail to comprehend the figurative or metaphoric quality of language; they take the metaphor literally, often to its absurd conclusion. Misiá Elisa is crowned saint because her servants fail to recognize the metaphor as such (she is *like* a saint). When the simile is converted into a metaphor, only the similarity is perceptible, not the difference. Then, because the word is taken literally rather than metaphorically, it becomes more authoritative and weighty than empirical experience. Similarly, the characters maintain a paradoxical and bidirectional relation with discourse. All escape the tedium of their lives in some form of literature or discourse—Andrés in French history, Misiá Elisa in the discourse of religion and sin, the maids in the radio soap operas, Mario in magazines (28/30–31) and the movies—but that discourse in turn shapes their perceptions of their lives and influences how they perceive and react to future events. Each is the product of the other.

Style and Techniques

As the structure of *Coronation* evokes and leads to many of its primary thematic concerns, so do its style and narrative technique. The novel is narrated by means of selective, limited omniscience; that is, the narrator enters the minds and thoughts of the characters but refuses to tell or clarify everything. The message is that everything depends on perspective and that one person's illusion is another's reality. It is up to the reader to decide. By employing a number of techniques to compel the reader to reach conclusions (perhaps erroneous ones), the text demonstrates that the reader's vision is as "selective" as the characters'. To this end, the narrator sometimes proffers alternate or contradictory explanations, expressing no preference for one over the other. For example, early in the text the cactus plant of the garden is "withered *or* rotted *or* . . . eaten by worms" (6/13; emphasis added). Andrés, the consciousness through which the reader perceives here, does not know, and the narrator leaves it that way. Later the welder who has just donned his mask is either a "demi-god or demon" (44/43). At other moments sentences end with ellipses or question marks that encourage readers to terminate the thought or to answer the question. Both forms of punctuation produce a situation that parallels that of Andrés in his recurrent dream of the bridge suspended over the void. Like the bridge, the punctuation marks invite readers to risk themselves and try to reach the metaphoric other side, but just as Andrés repeatedly falls into the void, the reader is left to confront the blank space that such punctuation evokes both visually and thematically.

Much of the novel's "action" is embedded within the characters' memories. This embedding technique serves two related purposes. First, since much of the action passes through the filter of the characters' recollections and is therefore doubly distanced by means of subjectivity *and* time, the legitimacy of those perceptions is placed in question. Second, the embedding produces a temporal layering and a synchronic perception of past and present that does not totally obscure their sequential nature. Although the past influences the present, it predates the present; the paradise lost (imaginary though it may be) has definitively been "lost," but like the robbery that is and is not, that past exists (in the minds of the characters) but does not exist (in actuality). Indeed, the question of time and the characters' desire (often unconscious) to arrest temporal progress or return to a past utopia, coupled with their inexorable inability to accomplish the same, is the catalyst for much of the action as well as one of the primary themes.

In terms of style, *Coronation* begins in what appears to be (and what critics have often labeled) the mimetic tradition of the social realist novel of the end of the nineteenth century, when the relation between language or perception and reality was deemed unproblematic. In that tradition, as well as in early parts of the Donoso novel, descriptions of physical characteristics and surroundings are detailed because they are presumed to reflect and be extensions of the characters themselves. These descriptions may be symbolic, of course, but the words used to name are not disputed. For example, early in *Coronation* the Abalos house and garden are described in some detail. The decay of the physical facilities mirrors the decline of the individuals and their society. Similarly, the first part of the novel includes dream sequences that portray the character's personality. Donoso's purpose is not to challenge the validity of those dreams or even to emphasize their fictional quality but to dramatize how events from the past have haunted the protagonist and shaped his personality.

By the end of the novel, however, this confidence in language and perception, as well as the rigidity implied in the mimetic tradition, have disintegrated, as has the society depicted, and by his own admission Donoso has moved into a different realm. He credits this change in medias res to his reading of Alejo Carpentier's novel *Los pasos perdidos* (*The Lost Steps*). The Cuban novel, published in 1953, describes the journey of a man who leaves all behind to search for origins, physical and psychological. In his journey the past becomes the present while illusion and reality coexist. In the Donoso novel those "origins" are embodied in the ever-present void and question mark, in death and insanity. Misiá Elisa returns to her origins (imaginary though they might be) when she dons the crown of her royal ancestors and subsequently dies ("ashes to ashes"); Andrés reverts to childhood and is last seen cutting out paper birds as he did "when he was very, very young" (261/218). By the end of *Coronation*, "reality" (like that of *The Lost Steps*) encompasses the subjectivity of the mind as well as the external and objective.

Nonetheless, in spite of appearances to the contrary and Donoso's own observations, I would propose that the technique of the later part of the novel differs less from that of the earlier technique than may have been assumed. The mimetic tradition and ostensibly unproblematic relation between the word and its referent in the first part of the novel might even be read as a mask that parallels that of the society portrayed (note again the close interrelationship between content and form). Surely Andrés must be viewed as a metaphor for the late-nineteenth-century social realism prevalent in Chilean literature at the time Donoso wrote *Coronation*—stylized and ossified. Just as Andrés's cool exterior and rational guise hide the terror and insecurity that lie just under that surface, the novel's ostensible traditionalism masks the early signs of the devitalization of that technique, and the technique itself may well mask its perpetuators' unacknowledged suspicions of an incoherent, chaotic world. Just as Andrés averts his eyes to avoid evidence of the chaos he does not wish to confront (the same chaos his life is structured to negate), readers and critics too have averted their eyes and have failed to recognize the discursive mask here. Just beneath the smooth surface of the Donoso text lurks the threat of chaos and the destruction of the established order, on both the level of the society portrayed and the level of literature itself, its accepted forms and procedures. Even in the first scene of the novel, the mask of mimetic traditionalism and the ostensibly unproblematic relation between the word and its referent is already subtly undermined as the word functions not to reproduce or mirror verifiable phenomena but rather to create an illusion that masks the ideological structures that inform that mask. The reader perceives only what Andrés perceives (to the extent the omniscient narrator shares those perceptions) and like the former tends not to question the validity of that perception or to search beyond it.

Donoso's unusual pairing of dream and memory further underlines his departure from social realism and the mimetic tradition. In the second chapter Andrés's recollection of his religious and erotic education (an admixture which proves significant) is presented as a combination of memory and dream, two narrative modes with quite different relations to objective reality: the former is presumed to reflect that reality and have a transparent relation to it, while the latter is also presumed to reflect it but by means of a metaphoric relation. First Andrés remembers and then he dreams, but the line between the two is diffuse, and the reader (like Andrés himself) cannot discern where one ends and the other begins. In addition, both narrative modes include the reproduction of even earlier dreams. Thus, by means of a compendium of techniques, the text undermines the traditional mimetic mode of these earlier segments and encourages the reader to understand that the traditionalism is only pseudo, a mask to divert one's eyes from the dubious premises upon which the notion of literary omniscience is built. Donoso recognizes traditional techniques as mask and artifice and would have readers do the same.

Finally, an examination of the style and technique of *Coronation* would not be complete without some discussion of the recurrent leitmotifs that, like musical motifs, structure and inform meaning in the novelistic symphony. The motif of giving as opposed to stealing has already been discussed, but two other motifs reappear with significant regularity: the color pink and the newspaper.

The color pink is a hue produced by the combination of red (traditional symbol of erotic passion) and white (traditional symbol of purity). Symbolically, therefore, the color evokes a blend of antithetical elements. That the Abalos house is painted these two colors ("white below and red at the tips" [6/13]) is a subtle allusion then to the contraposition of Misiá Elisa's virulent obscenities and her avowed purity. In the color pink, however, the antitheses red and white are no longer discernible (just as they are not when the simile becomes a metaphor); one does not mask the other but rather merges with it to produce a new hue, just as one's role or mask eventually intermingles with one's less visible qualities to produce a new personality.

In *Coronation* the color pink is highlighted each time Andrés sees Estela's hands. It is generally associated in his subconscious with a form of nudity; their pinkness makes the palms *seem* more naked than the rest of her. Note, however, that from the beginning this nakedness is presented as a question of individual perception and projection, and the qualifying expression "as if" is repeatedly used: "as if they were more naked" (11/17). Surely nudity is in the eyes of the beholder as changing fashion modes will attest, but because of his background, Andrés associates nudity with eroticism. Indeed, Donoso's depiction of Andrés's sexual education and "enlightenment" dramatizes the influence of prior discourse on future experience. Andrés's psychological association of pink with eroticism is exacerbated by his grandmother's accusation that he really meant to give Estela the pink shawl in which to wrap herself in bed and then later by Tenchita's coquettish appearance before him, straight from bed, wrapped in a similar pink shawl while she repeats his grandmother's earlier words. The similarities between the two moments (the shawl coupled with the repetition of words) lead Andrés to project Estela's face onto Tenchita. But Andrés's psychological associations go back much further—to his childhood and his education in religion, sexuality, and language, all of which are superimposed one on the others and all of which are revealingly presented in chapter six as it mingles dream and memory.

In that chapter Donoso proposes that one's perception of sin is a product of language and, in Andrés's case, linked to violence (the boys beat him).[11] At the same time sin is associated with eroticism, death, and confession (yet another mode of discourse). In the process of learning what words mean, the child asks Lourdes if she is a whore. Later, when he seems to understand what a whore is, he has erotic dreams about the pink chair, which he names Lourdes because of its shape. It is significant that the chair is located in his grandmother's sewing room, in which she discusses death and hell with him while silencing any discussion of sexuality, and probably the same room in which Estela later sleeps. Surely, just as he metaphorically associates the chair with Lourdes, based on similarity of shape, he later associates pink with eroticism, based on similarity of color, although obviously both associations are arbitrary. Religion and society's juxtaposition of hell, death, and eroticism lead him to fear them all equally and, in turn, to image them as the black hole of Father Damián's gaping mouth, an association that again links death, eroticism, and hell with the word or language, whose source is the mouth. In fact, he reacts to his grandmother's familiarity with death (38/38–39) exactly as he does to the "sensuality" of Estela's hands (40/40): by averting his eyes to avoid having to face those "potential horrors" of what is "lying in wait for him." He has repeatedly been taught to close his senses: in school the drawings of his anatomy books omitted certain parts of the body; his grandmother proclaimed not to know anything about, nor the words for, bodily functions.

This linguistic and imagistic censorship is subtly mirrored in the motif of the newspaper, which first appears in the opening chapter with the description of Andrés in the garden. Among other things the paper functions as an indicator of his lethargy, irresolution, and avoidance of contact with the world outside the confines of the neat, ordered, limited microcosm in which he has barricaded himself. On some level Andrés is already metaphorically averting his eyes here. Although the outside world is embodied only by words, those of the newspaper, Andrés still cannot shake his inactivity sufficiently to open that paper and "see" that other world. In the next chapter there is a fleeting reference to a newspaper as Rosario confronts Angel and Mario and learns that the former had been lying to her. Although it is only a passing reference, the newspaper's appearance is revealing in this scene that raises the question of stealing, counterbalances truth and lie, and depicts the power of the word. Specifically, the newspaper holds some grapes that the boys are eating and thus also subtly evokes the economic contrast between their lives of materialistic concerns (the grapes are their lunch and they are worried about money) and Andrés's life. In the earlier scene Andrés has already eaten to his satiety; he can sit, doing nothing, with the paper on his knees precisely because he has no economic concerns.

The next time the reader encounters a newspaper, it is again connected to economic issues, for it is used to paper the walls and keep the cold out of the rooms where Dora, René, and Mario live. Here too, however, it is linked to the theme of the power of the word, for in the same scene Mario questions Dora about the validity of René's reputation as a thief, and she reminisces about the "good old days." The motif of the newspaper reappears in the final chapters. At the conclusion of the chapter in which Carlos "confirms" Andrés's insanity, the latter is cutting the newspaper and folding the pieces into paper birds as he did when he was a child. For Andrés, to open the paper at the beginning would have meant to face the external; at the end, to open it is to avoid the external. Yet the image leads the reader to the external, for two paragraphs later a sheet of newspaper is seen (the reader does not know by whom) in the city's slums, blown around by the wind, "flying" as Andrés's paper birds might. At this point the paper mirrors the narrative technique: like the novel's words (perceptions and descriptions), the paper flies around, unattached and ungrounded. Thus the newspaper is portrayed as a tool, but one that is not always used as intended (to be read, as a vehicle of information). As a signifier, it has moved further and further from its intended usage and referent and now merely floats in the wind.

Constants

As should be apparent by now, *Coronation* incorporates the constants of Donoso's works, outlined in the first chapter of this study. The Chilean bourgeoisie, with its rigid structure and social role playing, contrasts with the classes of servants and the unemployed. The former is portrayed as enveloped in inertia and tedium, consciously choosing to avoid the unknown. The result, however, is an artificial and superficial order so precarious that, like traditional social realism, it crumbles as soon as it is seriously questioned or closely examined. Although neither of the less privileged groups has achieved the degree of power that both will wield in the future Donoso texts, the interdependence of the various classes and the structural similarity of their problems are already evident.

As in many of Donoso's texts, the manipulation of space in this novel and the establishment of firmly demarcated boundaries embody attempts (though they are inadequate) to conquer the unknown or the potential chaos that underlies sociopolitical structures (and that the latter, like social realism, are designed to disguise). Life within the Abalos house and garden is more controlled than that outside and thus theoretically less menacing. At the same time, the unknown threat and the threat of the unknown are imaged as exterior spaces: the chasm under the bridge in Andrés's dream, the labyrinthine streets of Valparaiso that threaten to engulf Mario, the vast night into which Mario and Estela disappear. The final scene, however, questions the effectiveness of this careful demarcation and imagery, for inside and outside merge: the stars enter Misiá Elisa's room, and antitheses blend as life yields to death, night to day, sanity to insanity.

In this text the constant of women and women's power is clearly related to the question of space and the notion of inside and outside as women are alternately adored or reviled, not for themselves or anything within them but rather for what the males project onto them. Andrés blames first his grandmother and then Estela for the erotic and metaphysical fears that exist only within himself. He at times "loves" Estela and at others wants to kill her (217/183). Similarly, he alternately desires his grandmother's death and prays it will never occur. In a mirror reflection of Andrés, Mario wavers between desiring Estela and wanting to strangle her (245/206). In fact, he hates not himself but her for the words of insecurity he utters when they make love and fears she will lock him into a life resembling that of Dora and René. Thus both males fear the female, Estela, but seek their salvation in her while failing to recognize that their perception of her is a mirror of themselves. Like Santelices, they project outward what is inside and then perceive it as external and beyond their control. Neither male recognizes that his future (like his present), for better or worse, will be primarily of his own making and masking. Yet it is no wonder each assumes this attitude, given his earlier education and the imposed psychological associations between women and sex, hell, and death (arbitrary overlappings carefully dramatized and developed by Donoso). And each male projects his perception of an individual woman onto another (Andrés projects Estela's face onto Tenchita, and Mario projects her face onto the pregnant woman on the streetcar) to produce a personal myth of generic Woman. At the same time it would appear that acceptance or rejection by a woman is an essential catalyst for the inverse rites of initiation that mark the conclusion of the novel—when Mario leaves adolescence to become a "man" and Andrés leaves adulthood to become a child again. In the Donoso novel the generic male can become neither a man nor a boy without her.

Also ever present in *Coronation* is the question of the ritual and game playing. Note has already been made of the ritualistic aspect of the tedious bourgeois life, of the two celebrations that structure the text, and of the fact that the beginning and end of the text are marked by the mask and theatrical role playing. The motifs of the game and theater are further emphasized in the two philosophical conversations between Andrés and his friend Carlos. In the first Carlos labels Andrés's metaphysical terrors an imaginary tragedy he has dreamed up for himself (155/131).[12] Later Andrés counters with the accusation that his friend and people like him make a game of death: they play at dying, for they are promised a longer, better life in the hereafter (185/156–57); that is to say, like the robbery that is not a robbery, death is not really death but rather rebirth in the Christian tradition. All these dramas and games converge in the penultimate chapter as Andrés opts to play out his drama in the guise of a child and reverts to infantile games in his own theatrical rebirth.

The convergence of these two motifs leads to the last major theme to be discussed here: the question of time. As noted earlier, all the principal characters are obsessed with the problem of time and their desire to halt its flow by returning to origins and the paradise lost. Although surely most of that past utopia is verbal creation, the human capacity for living in the past and continually evoking it in language is dramatically emphasized in the scene with Andrés's fellow club members, whose conversation centers around "Do you remember?" (122/105). Similarly, the maids continually reminisce about the old days, when the house was full of life and Misiá Elisa young and vibrant; they hope to recapture those days with the celebration of her birthday and saint's day. Dora too yearns for the wonderful years when she was young, pretty, and had all her teeth. She is convinced that the acquisition of false teeth would reproduce that earlier world and René would love her again. Andrés believes that if he could just have Estela he could live the adolescence he never lived, and even in his dreams he reverts to that childhood. Dora believes money will correct what time has destroyed (as do René and Mario), while Andrés believes love and poetry will. But temporality cannot be denied, erased, or reversed, and all the characters inevitably rush headlong toward the abyss of death, for the watch that Mario prizes so dearly keeps on ticking, whether in his possession or not.

Andrés's final act, when he consciously chooses madness, is surely an endeavor to halt or reverse time, for madness is an atemporal state in which temporal sequence is violated, just as it was for Misiá Elisa: the things she said had happened (in the past) did eventually happen (in the future). Still Andrés's insistence on freezing time by reverting to childhood fails on two levels. First, that childhood is mere sham, theater. Second, time does go on at any rate, and shortly after his "heroic" gesture, Misiá Elisa dies (just as he will one day, regardless of his mask of childhood). Paradoxically, all fail to recognize that even if they could return to origins, those origins (birth) are just another variation of that void of nothingness that terrifies them so.

Notes

1. *Misiá* translates roughly as Miss and is used before a woman's given name. It is loosely comparable to the Spanish terms *don* and *doña* in the male and female forms respectively,

also used with first names to indicate respect and class difference. *Misiá*, however, connotes more familiarity on the part of the speaker than *doña*.

Andrés's age is one of the inexactitudes of the text. First he is said to be fifty-odd years old (7/14), then fifty-three (38/39), then fifty-four (138/117).

2. Although this is the account embraced by Andrés's recollections in the first chapter of the novel, later memories indicate the possibility that his grandfather's frequenting his club predated his grandmother's vituperative behavior. In the dream sequence in chapter six, Andrés recalls the days when he was in school and about to make his first communion; he notes that even at that time his grandfather spent every night at the club while his grandmother stayed in her room and cried (65/59), suggesting that he may have already had a mistress. Since Andrés was only nine at the time, perhaps he was unable to comprehend the significance of the situation.

3. Although the English translation indicates that she was almost sixty years old (20) when the grandfather died, the Seix Barral edition in Spanish indicates that she was almost seventy (*setenta*, 24), and simple mathematics confirm this number. At the start of the novel Andrés is fifty-three or fifty-four. His grandmother's problem first manifested itself when he was seventeen, that is, thirty-seven years ago, when she was fifty-three (she is ninety at the start of the novel). The problem worsened for ten years (until she was sixty-three), but he did not die until some time after that (when she was almost seventy).

4. Louis de Rouvroy, duc de Saint-Simon (1675–1755), was a French writer who tried to write a more lively version of history than had been published at that time. It is generally accepted that his portraits were vivid but not necessarily historically accurate and that he freely mixed anecdotal gossip with minute details and his own opinions about a situation.

5. Andrés perceives his grandmother's birthday as the moment that marks a metaphoric birthday for him, the birth of a new anguished self: "He felt as if he were being painfully severed from the old Andrés Abalos of before his grandmother's birthday, that quiet man who had succeeded in *burying* all his problems" (131/112; emphasis added).

6. Most Spanish Americans are named after Catholic saints and celebrate that saint's day instead of or in addition to their birthdays, although at times the two coincide.

7. Although the English translation states that Estela "was to be left in her care" (10), the original Spanish employs the word *regalar*, "to give as a gift" (16).

8. In the Spanish it is not called animal lust but rather brutality.

9. Estela certainly knows she is not a thief, and Andrés recognizes his grandmother's prevarications on more than one occasion. He never believed that the servants stole from her, and at one point he even contradicts the story she tells Estela about her former admirer (probably imagined), George Lang (40/40).

10. Andrés credits his grandmother's madness with a form of seeing "deep into the truth of things" (133/113), and when Misiá Elisa guesses Estela's loss of virginity, the latter believes that the former knows the truth (178/151).

11. It is significant too that first he hears the words *sin* and *whore* and only later (as a result of an unpleasant experience) learns what they mean.

It should be noted that as the other boys "teach" Andrés about sexuality (in the men's room, which is also significant), he learns that his parents had had sexual relations, the results of which were his birth and his mother's death.

12. Ricardo Gutiérrez Mouat studies the games of the novel more completely in *José Donoso: Impostura e impostación* (Gaithersburg, Md.: Hispamérica, 1983). He has imaged the novel as a series of dramas, written by others, in which each character plays the assigned role (page 52) and notes that in the novel truth becomes one more fiction among many (page 53).

CHAPTER FOUR

This Sunday: I Possess, Therefore I Am

In 1966 Donoso published two novels: *Hell Has No Limits*, which will be considered in the next chapter, and *This Sunday*, which continues many of the themes and preoccupations already evident in *Coronation* and the short stories. In *This Sunday* Donoso is again concerned with overt bourgeois social structures and masks as well as with point of view as both theme and technique.

This Sunday is composed of three interrelated narratives: that of retired lawyer and law professor Alvaro Vives in part one; that of his wife Chepa in part two; and that of their unnamed grandson, the narrator of the opening, closing, and middle sections (all italicized), who, now an adult, recalls his weekly childhood visits to his grandparents' house. The focus of parts one and two is one day of the grandson's childhood, "this Sunday," the turning point that marks the loss of the paradise of his grandparents' house.[1] Although the frame action is limited to one day, the principal characters' streams of consciousness provide access to events (or their perceptions of events) prior to that day. Similarly, the veritable action of the italicized segments is limited to the short span of time during which the now grown grandson remembers, recounts, and thus reproduces the paradise lost. Specifically, he comments, *"Perhaps now, seated at my desk, I make this act of contrition realizing that when my grandfather began to exist in my memory he was the same age I am as I write this, and yet my remembrance of him is still colored by the fact that he was old and absurd"* (11/21).[2] Thus, if we accept his word at face value, his narration is motivated by his grandfather, about whose life, he acknowledges, *"I know nothing"* (11/21). Nonetheless, although he knows even less about his grandmother's life, his portrayal of her is far more sympathetic and suggests that his "act of contrition" is tacitly motivated by his abandonment of her in her old age and infirmity, a paradox to be considered below. In either case, the grandson "knows" of the grandparent's life only how it touches and overlaps his own, only how it frames and is framed by his own childhood (and therefore limited) experiences. In this respect the narrative structure of the text (in which the italicized segments frame the stories of the grandparents) is echoed within both part one and part two since each character's recollections of earlier events are framed by the "present," limited action (in large degree simply that of remembering or inventing). Surely one of the principal themes of the novel is the myopia experienced by each of the characters, a short-sightedness produced by two tangential factors: first, by the characters' egocentrism (already evoked by the grandson in the opening pages), which blinds them to any event or person to which they, the perceivers, are not central; second, by their imprisonment (echoed in Maya's physical imprisonment as well as in the physical framing of the narratives) within social myths and masks, role playing (the fishbowl), perpetuated by discourse, the ubiquitous "they say."

I shall first consider the two more deeply embedded narratives, those of Alvaro and Chepa in parts one and two, and then proceed outward to the framing, italicized sections to consider how they affect any reading of the embedded tales while they simultaneously highlight the ahistoricity of the text. It is the ahistoricity of the text that signals first the universality and repetitiveness of the situations depicted and second, the act of narration as a manifestation of that myopic egocentrism. Not unlike the adult-child narrator of "The Walk," the grandfather and grandson here both "speak" or narrate to focus attention on themselves and situate themselves at the center of a world they fear is indifferent to them. As shall be demonstrated below, one of the structuring motifs of both the "lives" dramatized and the narrative gesture itself is the need to exist in the eyes of others and to confirm one's existence by making oneself central, by accumulating and surrounding oneself with possessions (and in that sense "possessing" the other). Apparently, when the character feels he has been unsuccessful at this, his alternative is to narrate and thus invent a text, a world he can possess and that can encircle him.

The embedded or framed sections of the novel center on four adult characters: the grandfather, fifty-five-year-old Alvaro Vives; a woman who was at one time the family servant, fifty-eight-year-old Violeta, by whom Alvaro earlier fathered a child; the grandmother, fifty-four-year-old Chepa (Josefina Rosas de Vives); and Maya, the convict Chepa helped to free from prison. These central sections include both omniscient narration and streams of consciousness as Alvaro and Chepa are presented through the pronouns *I, you,* and *she* or *he,* a technique that underlines the theme of changing perspectives as well as the ever precarious and shifting center.

Part One

Part one proffers a series of fragmented incidents, recollections from the life of the grandfather, Alvaro. In spite of the ostensible omniscience of the third-person narration, this rendition of events proves to be as partial (in both senses of the word) as the perspective of the grandson of the italicized segments, the child who understood and the adult who still understands very little. The section opens as Alvaro faces the beginning of the end and the terrors of death, for in spite of the irony of his name (*Vives,* "you live") he has discovered what will prove to be a fatal cancerous mole near his left nipple.[3] The motifs of the mole and the nipple are reiterated throughout the text. Maya, the convict, is recognized by a mole near his lip that "signifies" him, and Alvaro repeatedly characterizes Chepa pejoratively as a female dog nursing pups (22, 25, 28, 68/33, 36, 39, 87).[4] This portrayal of Chepa signals a general tendency in the text and one that underlines the structuring issues of (often erroneous) point of view, for although it reflects how Alvaro "sees" Chepa, and although she internalizes it, in fact it is the perception of a myopic and therefore unreliable character. Early in the text Alvaro himself calls into question his capacity to "see" by acknowledging that his eyes are the weakest part of his face (22/32). Later Chepa finds him unattractive when she views him full-face rather than from his profile because his eyes are too close together (108/130). In addition, he is hard of hearing and thus apparently hears and sees only what he wishes or what flatters his self-image.[5] Perhaps even more telling is the grandson's assertion in the first italicized segment that it *"was as though he didn't focus his eyes"* (10/20). Nonetheless, the narrator later learned that this was because Alvaro was not looking at the grandchildren; *"he was scrutinizing his own reflection in the glass doors of the bookcases"* (10/20). This depiction of Alvaro is confirmed in part one as "he scrutinizes himself in the glass of the largest of his bookcases" (21/31). In his myopia, Alvaro perceives little but himself and his own reflection. Throughout he pays little attention to Chepa and consistently fails to "focus" on her, the grandchildren, or anything outside of himself as he attempts to silence them all. Near the conclusion of part one, when he accuses Chepa of being frigid, she retorts, "How do you know *what* I am?" (70/88), and even he recognizes she is right. In this respect the grandson proves to be a mirror reflection.

Still, Alvaro's metaphorical description of Chepa takes what is often a positive characterization of a female—that of self-sacrificing, "giving" mother, source of nourishment and physical well-being—and converts it into a pejorative one by employing the image of the littered bitch. The quality evoked is the same; the connotations have changed. At issue is perspective, for like the adult-child narrator of "The Walk," Alvaro finds himself outside of, not the center or focus of, that maternal care. From his perspective, Chepa is more interested in caring for *her* poor people and grandchildren than for him (note the question of possession, which will be discussed below). Her "maternal instincts" are perceived pejoratively because they are focused elsewhere and do not center on him. On the other hand, in the italicized segments the grandson highlights the same quality in Chepa but images her (and the house that for him is an extension of her) positively as an *"inexhaustible cornucopia"* (13/24) because, from his perspective, he is the center of her world (at least on Saturdays and Sundays).[6] Since those "maternal instincts" are centered on him (he believes) and thus *his* (*"this part of the world that was mine"* [4–5/13]), they are figured in a positive fashion.

Yet just as the grandson is never able to recognize that Chepa's "world" extends far beyond both the house and him and indeed centers on him much less than he would like to imagine, Alvaro is unable to fathom that the isolation he experiences and Chepa's indifference to him are of his own making to a large degree. That isolation and indifference are the products of his need for centrality and possession to compensate for or fend off his own sense of nonexistence. They are also a mirror reflection of his own indifference to her, which is produced by his insistence on placing himself at the center of the world, surrounding himself with reflections of himself, and scrutinizing them. Readers, however, are able to comprehend his isolation (and the fact that it reflects and prefigures the grandson's) because they have access to his memories, his stream of consciousness embedded within part one, because they are outside the fishbowl rather than inside it—or at least believe they are.[7] Indeed, readers are encouraged to perceive the ironies and inconsistencies in Alvaro's character and to understand or "see" more than he himself grasps, just as they are encouraged to perceive the grandson in a similarly ironic light.

After examining his mole a number of times (Alvaro looking at Alvaro), deciding to consult with his son-in-law about it this very Sunday (make himself the center of conversation), and determining that he will not tell Chepa about it for fear she will "steal" his death from him (again he fears loss of centrality), Alvaro drives to Violeta's house to pick up the traditional Sunday *empanadas,* or meat turnovers. In the car, en route to and from Violeta's, he recalls some of the events of his youth (again, Alvaro scrutinizing Alvaro), including his first sexual experience with that former family servant. At that time, as a punishment for not doing well in school, the adolescent Alvaro had been left behind in the city in Violeta's care while his family vacationed in the country. The memory of his first erotic experience with Violeta is stimulated by the festive odor of *empanadas* that fills his car this Sunday morning just as it filled his room that Sunday morning when he first made love to her, when her skin was golden like the *empanadas* and her aroma that of white dough turning gold (46–52/60–68). Thus the Sunday *empanada* became the symbol of the ritual, always the same yet always different.

During the remainder of the remembered summer of "punishment," their relationship was marked by games and role playing. They played erotic games and pretended to be grown up: they dressed up in the parents' clothes, and Violeta served him dinner at his father's place at the head of the table. Each Friday as his father left the city to join the rest of the family in the country for the weekend, Alvaro playacted, pretending he really wanted to go with him. The reader is encouraged to wonder if these games, coupled with what Alvaro labels his solitary games (masturbation [46/61]), are not to be understood as the counterpart to the grandson's "Legitimate Games" of the second italicized segment. Nonetheless, the legitimate games, like much else in the novel, are one among many misnomers that highlight the question of perspective as they impose a version of reality favorable to the narrating self.

But the games of Alvaro and Violeta were fraught with yet more role playing. One of the ironies of the novel, often overlooked by its readers, is that, despite the couple's youth and the seemingly affective bent to the relationship between them, their relationship was unequivocally one of master and servant, predicated on her subservience to him as she focused on him, made him central, and allowed his egocentricity to reign unchallenged. Alvaro underlined this inequality and its relation to his sexuality by recalling as they were about to make love for the first time that his cousins said "servant girls are for that, they expect it" (48/63). The indefinite *that* and *it* here refer to the sexual advances of the patron or patron's sons. Thus, from the beginning, in the "innocence" of childhood and adolescence, Alvaro's perception of gender and social roles was formed by the authoritative "they say" that validates the superiority he apparently must feel in order to function sexually. The "they say" also recalls the children's games of "idealizations," in which one must convert into whatever "they say."

Still the master/servant roles that first surfaced in the "they say" and informed the generic social structure that causes both Maya and Mirella so much chagrin became even more apparent as the relationship between Alvaro and Violeta progressed. During the weekends of the rest of that summer, Violeta served him sumptuous dinners (which she prepared and paid for out of her own savings) in the dining room, while she ate in the kitchen (as both Maya and Mirella do at different moments) and washed the dishes. She invited him to movies, after which she washed and ironed his shirts while he watched (as usual, he did nothing). And in Spanish, she generally used the respectful *don* and *usted* with him and rarely employed the familiar *tú* with which he consistently addressed her.[8] Thus, although he had sexual intercourse with her, in his mind her role never ceased to be that of servant, and he never engaged in any form of egalitarian social intercourse with her. Paradoxically, quite the opposite was the case with the "proper" young women of his social class. Although he was able to engage in social intercourse with them, he could not relate to them sexually, apparently in part because of his sense of inadequacy or inferiority. Thus Donoso posits eroticism as another "game" requiring the assumption of "proper" roles of inferiority and superiority.

Alvaro's egocentrism (metaphoric nearsightedness) is so complete that he never viewed his relationship with Violeta as exploitation on his part. He saw it simply as part of the inherent and thus unquestionable order of things: "the ideal, the norm . . . the place in the universe where doubt can never assail" (60/77). This perception (and prescription) of the ideal or the norm (the prescriptive myth imposed by the word) and, in turn, the role is also one of the major issues in the text. Alvaro justified his attitude by convincing himself (and many of the novel's readers) that Violeta was using him as much as he was using her. Six years after that summer, when his relationship to her was limited to sexual encounters each time he returned from escorting "proper" young ladies of his social class, he rationalized his "use" of her by projecting it onto her (again, Alvaro saw only himself). When she cried one night and he first fathomed the possibility that she might become pregnant, he told himself that if she were crying because of him he would never touch her again (57/74). Still he did nothing: he neither attempted to correct the problem nor stopped having relations with her; he merely turned off the light so he would not have to see.[9]

Yet, as the omniscient narrator notes, because "Violeta sensed the terror in the tense body next to hers" (58/75), she assured him she was not pregnant although apparently she was, as evidenced by the birth of Mirella. She then comforted him further, assuming an acceptable role and declaring that she was really in love with someone else. He believed her story because it was convenient, but its position in the narrative as it immediately follows two other lies on Violeta's part should lead the reader to recognize it as a prevarication and the discourse Alvaro wanted to hear.[10] Furthermore, Violeta's story about the boyfriend prompted more rationalization on Alvaro's part: "What she meant, then, was that there wasn't any other tie between them but this compromise of skin on skin" (59/76). Again, his perception of Violeta was a convenient projection (role playing, game), perhaps exactly the same convenient projection he would later impose on Chepa in blaming her first for trying to possess and control him (steal his death and his masculinity) and then for making him marginal to her life.

Thus one need not enter Chepa's stream of consciousness in part two to understand why her relationship with Alvaro is one of distance and alienation; that information is already given in "Alvaro's" part one. Furthermore, part one provides more than one rendition of their psychological and affective "divorce." One version appears to be the official one, the one they told others and the one that perhaps he would like to believe: they have separate bedrooms because of the children and the grandchildren (24–25/35–36). Another version is that she needed independence (64/82), while still another suggests that the alienation resulted from her discovery of his series of affairs with other women and his assertion to her that he never desired her, even at the beginning (65–66/84). Similarly, he recalls, he married her not because he was in love with her but because she "has everything he needs to love her" (61, 62/79) and "she represents the best, the pinnacle of his world" (62/79). Yet the text is explicit about his self-delusion here: he recalls that he was almost impotent on their wedding night, not because of lack of desire on his part but rather because he was "terrified in the face of so much perfection . . . [and] afraid of mutilating so much perfection" (68/87). He was finally able to make love to her only by imagining she was Violeta (from his perspective, a woman who was inferior and not threatening). Later he repeated this substitutive act and had a series of indiscreet affairs with other women (one of whom committed suicide). Again, role playing and the projection of otherness are essential to Alvaro's erotic fulfillment.

His various affairs point to a series of subplots to which the reader has no access, presumably because his affair with Violeta provides a paradigm of the others. At the same time, those affairs highlight the interchangeability of characters—one of the primary themes of this and later Donoso works. Alvaro makes love to a number of young women (including Chepa) in the body of Violeta, while later he makes love to Violeta in the body of Chepa. Similarly, Chepa substitutes "her" poor people for Alvaro, the children, and the grandchildren, who do not need her sufficiently, while Maya's goal is to "replace" Alvaro by assuming his social position and perceived relationship with Chepa—by "possessing" his property. Indeed Maya is frequently portrayed as a copy of Alvaro: he is as vain about his clothes as Alvaro is and as worried about losing his identity to Chepa. He makes love to Chepa in the bodies of both Violeta and his girlfriend, Marujita. Finally, he metaphorically slays Chepa in the body of Violeta. Similarly, Violeta and Chepa are both characterized by their cleanliness: Alvaro viewed Violeta as clean, unlike the prostitutes his friends visited, while Chepa admits that the only thing she knows and can share with the poor is a sense of cleanliness (96/117).

As in *Coronation,* the question of cleanliness is directly linked with that of eroticism here. Alvaro first has sexual relations with Violeta as he steps out of the bath and later is potent and able to perform sexually with her because she is clean, not dirty and sexually demanding, not devouring. Donoso raises here a question that surfaced in *Coronation* and becomes a constant in his work: the issue of sexuality and sexual education and how the latter perverts, distorts, and metaphorically "soils" any "naturality" that might be inherent in the former. Surely one of the predominant issues in part one, and one that is also linked to the questions of perspective and the outward projection of what lies within one, is that of erotic desire.

Alvaro is obsessed with the erotic throughout the present of the narration ("this Sunday" when all will change). In fact, in part two Chepa accuses him of not being able to think of anything else (113/137). He finds both Chepa's dressing routine and the position of their two cars in the garage obscene. Yet the unique figures and metaphors Alvaro employs in reference to the cars emphasize the projection of his own psychological state: "A little obscene, this coquettish intimacy of the female auto curled up beside the male in the same bed" (28/35). Someone less obsessed with the erotic and the obscene would be unlikely to perceive cars in quite such a way; obscenity/legitimacy ("legitimate games") is in the eye of the beholder. In addition, his memories focus on his earlier erotic relationship with Violeta, and the segment concludes as he accuses Chepa of some sort of illicit or "dirty" relationship with Maya (again in reflection of his own reaction to similar situations).

Curiously, however, in the present of the narration, Alvaro finds the sight of both Violeta's and Chepa's bodies disgusting (32–33, 64–65/56, 82), perhaps because of the inevitable passage of time to which they have been subjected, but also because of his own projection. His own body is decaying, being consumed from within by the cancer he has recently discovered, and he projects that outward onto other bodies just as he earlier projected the body of one lover onto another. Again Alvaro's world centers on himself, and his myopic perceptions of all else are colored by that egocentricity.

At the same time, the action of this Sunday morning is structured on Alvaro's desire to narrate, to tell. Although he is determined not to tell Chepa of what he perceives (correctly, as it turns out) as his impending death, all his gestures and actions are designed to do just that. He leaves the door open between their bedrooms, not so he can hear Chepa talk, but so she might be able to hear him call out should he become too frightened. In a gesture that is repeatedly echoed in other characters (including the narrator), his decision to remain silent provokes discourse about matters that, from his perspective, are irrelevant: he tells the maid where he is going (she knows); later, rather than telling Chepa that he is dying, he tells her he has seen Maya. In a similar gesture of saying other than what one deems most important, Chepa recalls in part two what she would have liked to say to Maya while he tells her what she wants to hear (98/119). Since Violeta repeats this gesture with both Chepa and Alvaro (telling them only what they want to hear), the reader must wonder if the narrator of the italicized sections might not be doing the same. Nonetheless, Alvaro delays in telling Chepa what is most important to him, and then he chooses precisely the wrong moment to tell. He narrates in the wrong order (perhaps like the grandson), and she will neither believe him nor concern herself about his "truth."

There can be little doubt that the "telling" or narrating is designed and motivated by the desire to exist and centralize the self, to assure oneself and others of one's existence: I narrate, therefore I exist—a literary and philosophical stance that prefigures the dominant one of *The Obscene Bird of Night*. The irony, of course, is that when Alvaro does finally assume the role of speaking subject, he articulates only his death: "I am dying," and "I saw Maya," statements that will alienate him even further from Chepa and metaphorically kill whatever remains of their relationship. Just as the children egotistically believe that nothing happens unless they invent it (express it, say it, metaphorically "write" it), Donoso suggests that Alvaro's death can become a "reality" only once he vocalizes it. The word makes it so, just as in part two Violeta's articulation of the possibility of a competition between herself and Chepa (152/182) "frees" Chepa and allows her to compete—that is, search for Maya—while earlier Alvaro's use of the word *love* in reference to her and Maya "cuts all her ties" (148/177).

Part Two

Part two differs from part one in that events are viewed more from Chepa's position, although there is still a section from Alvaro's perspective that again highlights his myopia and inertia: the segment in which he fails or refuses to see Violeta's economic problems and refers her to Chepa rather than taking action himself (116–18/140–42). His myopia and inertia eventually lead to Violeta's murder. Her financial problems, which according to Alvaro are merely her miserliness (note that she is miserly, he is thrifty), lead her, at Chepa's urging, to rent part of her house (left to her by Alvaro's mother in exchange for "services rendered") and become involved with Maya. Thus Alvaro's inactivity is as deadly as Maya's overt violence.

The frame action of part two starts where part one ends, as Chepa takes leave of Alvaro and goes to look for Maya, having stated at the end of part one that even if Alvaro were dying this Sunday (as it turns out he is), she would still search for Maya. In a mirror reflection of part one, this part begins with an oblique economic concern that foreshadows Violeta's and also indirectly evokes the question of possession. Part one opens as Alvaro tries to economize by not turning on the heat in the whole house; part two opens as Chepa tries to economize by buying Christmas gifts at the penitentiary, where they are less expensive. Both images contrast sharply with the grandson's portrayal of their life and home as a cornucopia of prosperity, a contrast that suggests just how little he really comprehended while it foregrounds the socioeconomic issues evoked by the final conversion of the grandparents' home into an unofficial refuge for the poor. Also implicit here, however, is an underlying question of the greed of the self who can never possess enough, for it is unclear whether Alvaro's and Chepa's miserliness (which is projected onto Violeta by Alvaro) is due to a lack of economic resources or simply greed—desire to have more and more and keep it for oneself. The motif of greed surfaces when Chepa and Fanny go to buy pocketbooks from Maya; he has only one, but they want eight. Similarly highlighting the motif, the grandson notes how little his parents received from the sale of the grandparents' house (they wanted more) and how that small sum was exchanged for other goods (174/207).

Just as part one presents the history of the ritual Sundays, and the italicized sections present the children's ritualistic games, part two presents the history of Chepa's ritual Wednesday visits to see Maya in prison; these visits eventually lead her to secure his release and underwrite his business in the outside world. While the motivation for Chepa's interest in Maya is never explicit, it seems to be based on her desire to be needed, to give of herself, a desire directly linked to the question of maternity (thus Alvaro's figure of the littered bitch). At a number of points, her relationship to Maya is overtly imaged, either on her part or his, as that of a mother and son: she wants to take care of him (108/131); it is as though he were her baby (111/134); he needs her (112/135); he needs someone to take care of him and love him like a son (118/143); she felt like kissing him like a child (122/147); he insists he is not a baby (139/167). In addition, her relationship to him is delineated in maternal terms to the extent that his release from prison is viewed as a rebirth (116, 125/140, 150); she educates him in the ways of the world as she helps the "blind" man to see (125/150; note again the motif of vision); and she repeatedly focuses on his tiny hands, those of a child, not those of a murderer or a lover (98, 115/119, 139). Yet when Alvaro accuses her, at the end of part one, of being in love with the ex-convict, she does not deny it but does wonder what to do with the absurd word *love* (148/177). Chepa's problem, it would seem, is one of social games, myths, and role playing gone awry.

The various segments of *This Sunday* portray Chepa as a woman who needs to give and who needs others to be dependent on her, although, as noted above, the positive or negative value afforded this quality varies according to the perspective of the speaker. Apparently, much as Alvaro must assume the socially acceptable role of potent macho (and all the self-doubts that accompany that role), Chepa must assume the only roles allotted her in the society in which she lives: those of mother and wife. These roles are predicated on giving, providing the other with food and other signs of physical well-being. Although Chepa admits she finds these roles unfulfilling (because they do not "fill" the self but rather "empty" it), they are the only roles for which she has been prepared.[11] In a mirror reflection of her childhood education and games when she took care of her dolls (games to which the reader is not privy but which one can imagine, given the context of the italicized sections and her protests over organized games for the grandchildren), Chepa as an adult must take care of people. Hers is a social problem, common to women and the maternal role they assume. Although (ideal) motherhood, as it is emblematized and mythified by society, consists of constant self-sacrifice and unselfish giving, Donoso obliquely proposes that human beings (even mothers) cannot be quite so altruistic and must receive something in return for what they give (if not, they are metaphorically "emptied").[12] What Chepa needs is what the various male characters (including the grandson narrator) get, or would like to get, from her: centrality and possession. But within the portrayed society her only recourse to those "gifts" is the maternal role, hence the "perversion" or distortion of that role in society's mythification of it. Thus the male and female characters' need for centrality is the same. What differs is society's prescription ("they say") of the (pseudo) acceptable means of fulfilling that need.

In this novel Donoso intuits the prescriptive nature of myth and social mask/role playing. Not only is one imprisoned in the limitations of the chosen role/myth, but, more important, one is destined to a sense of inadequacy since one can never quite live up to what one perceives as the description/prescription. As a result, one's sense of self is diminished. Because one does not question or challenge the myth itself (as I believe Donoso is doing here), one sees oneself, not the prescriptive role, as inadequate and must continually struggle not only to assume the mask but also to surround oneself with mirrors and reflections of that mask while attempting to barricade and distance oneself from anything that might undercut that self-perception (mask). Alvaro surrounds himself with mirrors, books, glass bookcases, and Chepa surrounds herself with the needy and the hungry. Donoso suggests that one attempts to possess and make a part or a reflection of oneself all that surrounds the self; one centralizes the self by surrounding it with reflections of the assumed mask. Shortly after the text observes, "Violeta *belonged* to Alvaro, as Maya *belonged* to her" (119/143; emphasis added), the servant is viewed as "the infinite succession of the mirror-image in the mirror, because really . . . Violeta was not important. . . . she lacked any life beyond that conferred on her by others" (124/150). In the society portrayed, Alvaro can "possess" women (or delude himself to that effect) by means of sexual intercourse, and, by means of his psychological substitutions, he can "possess" others (or delude himself to that effect) in the body of Violeta. As he notes, "I possess all of those impossible girls in your [Violeta's] warm, plump flesh" (57/74).[13] At the same time Violeta offers no threat to Alvaro's egocentrism or his sense of self, centrality, masculinity because she "can't expect anything from [him] in the way that they expect" (56/73). They frighten him; she does not, for she reflects back the mask of superiority and self-confidence he would assume. On a similar note, by needing her and her help, others make Chepa central to their lives in a way that Alvaro has not, just as she (from their perspective) would make them central to her life.

Nonetheless, when given outlet in the form of idealized maternity, that need to give, to help, can go too far and become oppressive; it can metaphorically engulf or swallow the other. Although each of the adult male characters wants to be central to Chepa, each also fears the other side of that centrality: enclosure, imprisonment, oppression. Throughout Donoso's works all human qualities and situations are overtly portrayed as one side of a two-sided coin: Maya's inactivity is the other side of his violent nature, just as Alvaro's inactivity produces Violeta's violent demise; the children's attic games are the other side of the poor children's violence (as shall be demonstrated) as well as the other side of the less conscious adult masks; Chepa's need to give is the other side of Alvaro's need to take; adult games (chess and literature) are the other side of passion. Yet, as this novel portrays, it is not only the recipient of the "gift" who is in danger of annihilation; conversely, the giver is also in danger of being devoured by all the hungry mouths that take (again leading back to the concept of an "empty" self). At the end of part two the earlier image of Chepa as a littered bitch is repeated, but now Chepa envisions herself as a being with multiple teats from which thousands of people feed and eventually devour her (161–62/192–93). Nonetheless, in a paradoxical contrast, Maya sees her (and Violeta) as wanting to devour him (143/172), while Alvaro images his fear of her first as one of "stealing" from him what is his (his death) (22/33) and later as one of binding, tying him to her (69/87). It would seem that one is always both inside and outside the fishbowl.

The final scene of part two, in which Chepa sinks into the heap of refuse while the children play around her, is a valid if indeed nightmarish metaphor of the paradoxes of her life as both the devourer (albeit unintentional) and the devoured. At the same time her metaphoric "journey" into the "other" world evokes the labyrinth (a term repeatedly used from pages 153 to 165/183 to 197) of the "they say" that produces social role playing and myths, "that cancer that grows" (153/183), as one travels in circles (154/184) or spirals (162/193) while millions of eyes watch (155/ 185) from the darkness (162/193). In this labyrinth of language and masks, one is surrounded by those who want to take, to devour pieces of the self (161, 164/192, 195) until one's sight goes out of focus (163/195). In this inferno everything is turned around; one's feet are stuck in the mire as one slowly sinks into the refuse (of words and myth) (165/197). Finally, one is overtaken by Maya's "black hand" because there is nothing left to do (158/188–89). And what is Maya's "black hand" but silence—a withdrawal from all human, affective, linguistic interaction—or the blank space, the refusal to play any role and the "switch off" that Chepa had earlier practiced on occasion? The self is buried in social myth and has been so driven within itself in order to protect itself that it becomes or encounters only a nonself and empty space. Part two concludes as Chepa ("one," as she has impersonalized herself) sinks into the slippery mass of disintegrating matter (note again the image of hell), the nothingness and decay that lie beneath the linguistic mask.

Like Alvaro, Chepa is trapped in a role and a need to control, possess, and make herself central in order to feel that she exists. Thus she helps "her" poor and views Maya as "hers" while noting that the grandchildren (like their mothers before them) will soon cease to need her and be hers (again, this proves to be a valid prediction, as evidenced by the final italicized section). It cannot be irrelevant that Chepa feels most needed by Maya when he is inside the controlled environment of the prison (another metaphoric fishbowl) and fears that he will not need her once he is out. In what parallels a not uncommon maternal urge to keep the child young and dependent, Chepa is ambiguous about Maya's freedom. Although she dedicates a year to working to obtain it, she also wants "him to stay in that patio forever, *enclosed* by those walls and that square of shade" (112/135; emphasis added).

At the same time, her wish to keep him imprisoned seems directly related to the desire to narrate that structures part one and the italicized segments. Chepa functions as Maya's "eyes" (127/153) in the outside world and tells him what things are like out there; that is, she imposes her vision or perspective just as literary narrators do when they describe their literary worlds. As Maya urges, she commands herself, "Tell him everything. Tell him more. . . . He's never seen. . . . Sometimes it was like talking to a blind man" (111/134). And he tells her things. In fact, her visits are described as "a whole year of Wednesdays telling her things" (109/132). But that two-way, reflexive narration is predicated on his being inside and is silenced for those outside the prison: outside, "one does not say a single word to . . . Fanny" (111/135). The outside silence is repeated at the conclusion when Chepa has withdrawn into silence, "switched off," and is scarcely visited by the grandson who had since "replaced" her with "another woman," Maman Colibrí. It is significant that this *"little old lady who scarcely spoke"* (173/205) still *listened* to the grandson's triumphs. Thus, with the exception of the year of visits to Maya in prison, Chepa is relegated to the role of listener, not speaker. She listens to the grandchildren and to Alvaro, and although she is depicted on more than one occasion speaking to him, he rarely listens to her (for example, 22–23, 109, 112–13/33, 131–32, 136–37) and would rather withdraw into his solitary world of art: books to read alone, opera to be listened to alone, a game of chess to be played alone.

"In the Fishbowl," "Legitimate Games," and "Sunday Night"

No doubt the uniqueness of *This Sunday* rests not so much in part one or part two, which seem to be the central sections of the novel both structurally and thematically, as in the subtle irony of the italicized sections, which begin and end the adult game of the text. Although the narrator of the italicized sections (unlike that of the others) is identifiable—the grandson—and although this narration is ostensibly more authoritative as it reports his personal experiences, it is in fact even more marked by invention and wishful thinking that place the narrating self (the grandson) at the center of the narrated world. Specifically, the narrator focuses on three narrative inventions: his childhood games ("idealizations" and the world of Mariola Roncafort, two renditions of the world as the children see it or would like it to be), what he would like to think about his grandfather (*"I long to believe that perhaps. . . . I think that our laughter might also have been a way of disguising"* [11/21]), and what he would like to think about his "grandmother's" house (*"I don't believe. . . . I like the idea. . . . I would prefer"* [176–77/210]). In this respect, the italicized sections are overtly structured by and predicated on the same ironies that more subtly mark the other sections.

By means of their typography (italics) and their overtly subjective, first-person narration, these sections call attention to themselves (in the way Alvaro was wont to do) and metaphorically shout: Look, this is different; neither this narration nor the narrator is like those of the other sections.

Nonetheless, both the narrator and his narration are in fact mirror reflections of those of parts one and two. The grandson, as both child and adult, proves to be as myopic and egocentric as his grandfather in spite of the fact that he resoundingly repudiates him as a role model and assures the reader (and himself) that he was determined never to be like him. I suggest that it is precisely because of his identification with Alvaro that the narrator makes his act of contrition—produces the narrative. Because he recognizes how similar he is to Alvaro, whom he considered absurd and different from other mortals, he seeks a justification for Alvaro's existence (just as Alvaro so frequently did) in the hope of ultimately justifying his own existence and again proving that he *"was not the strangest, most inept person in the entire world"* (12/22). In the final analysis, then, the grandson silences what is most important to him—that he is like Alvaro and will die like him—just as Alvaro silences what is most important to him—his powerlessness and impending death.

Most critics agree that one of the dominant motifs of the italicized sections is that of the game, but few have recognized the game's role in Donoso's project of undermining various social myths and demonstrating that narration itself is a game (in which, like all games, one temporarily assumes a mask and position of power). Parts one and two, with their games of survival, function as demythifications of machismo (erotically obsessed Alvaro uses his "potency" to disguise his fears and his sense of inadequacy) and self-sacrificing motherhood (Chepa gives in order to possess; the perceived devourer is devoured). Similarly, the italicized sections, with their children's games and games of narration, negate the myth of childhood innocence, interrogate perceptions of sameness and difference as they are related to possession, and show that both are tied to sexuality and narration.

"In the Fishbowl" begins with a subtle gesture that undermines the adequacy of language (and thus narration): *"Sunday in my grandmother's house really began on Saturday . . . ."* (3/11) As the rest of the italicized sections will attest, what the narrator remembers as the marvelous Sundays, filled with games, were really Saturdays (language has masked "reality," misled the interlocutor); for the children, Sundays were tedious social rituals (adult games) in which their parents and other visitors joined their grandparents for dinner. The narrator highlights this negative aspect of the Sunday ritual in the first sentence of "Legitimate Games": *"Why did we call them 'Sundays' . . .? Sundays were short, official, and they required our best behavior. . . . Saturdays were different because they were completely ours"* (75/93). Thus the adult-child narrator calls to the reader's attention first the inaccuracy of perceptions and then the inadequacy of naming: we called them Sundays, but they really were not; they were different. Such a bold gesture reminds us of how often language elides differences that do exist or posits differences that do not. The adult-child narrator uses his narrative to establish (create) a difference between himself and his grandfather, a difference that does exist (he is not his grandfather) but not to the degree he would like. In this manner, language (''they say'') is shown to shape perception. Thus from the beginning the reader is offered a guide as to how (not) to read the rest of the text and subtly admonished not to accept the proffered discourse (perceptions) at face value or ''swallow'' it whole. In addition, a subtle play of similarities and differences is set up in which the italicized sections provide mirror reflections of the other sections. But a mirror reflection is just that—an image, a (re)production of similarity. The image is like the original but *is not* the original (as obviously is the case with all literary worlds that pretend to reflect something external to themselves). At the same time, the sentence that begins the second italicized section, in which the narrator recognizes that Sundays were really Saturdays, highlights the question of possession that dominates parts one and two (*''Saturdays . . . were completely ours''* [75/93]), while it contradicts other ''testimony'' from the narrator. In the first italicized segments, he assures us that he had to pester his parents to get to the grandparents' house, and once there he had to subject himself to the ''ritual'' during which the grandfather played the piano and interrogated them (a ritual that he now believes served to distance the grandfather from them emotionally [9, 11/18, 21]). Thus, contrary to his assertion, Saturdays were not all *theirs* either. Possession, it would appear, is never absolute.

Similarly, the italicized sections are predicated on narrative constructs that create a world only to destroy it even as they continually prove inadequate. The seeds of destruction (like Alvaro's mole and Maya's black hand) are to be found within, for everything contains its antithesis or proves to be something else: Sundays were really Saturdays; this Sunday is really *that* Sunday; the ritual *empanadas* seem ever the same but are ever different; the punishment is reward; the children's games are deadly serious as they simultaneously do and do not reflect the adult world (they are similar but different). As a result, it is impossible to know if one is inside or outside the fishbowl of language (the possessor or the possessed) and the role playing imposed by the ''they say.'' The grandson, by means of his narration, surely hopes to prove that, unlike his grandfather, he is outside that enclosure. All he succeeds in proving, however, is how imprisoned by it he is: witness the erroneous designations that, as narrator, he continues to impose.

Metaphorically dramatizing the questions of perspective, language, and the myth of childhood innocence, the narrator shares with the reader two instances of playacting, of feigning and assuming a role, even at a very young age. In an echo of the grandfather's gestures, both of these "theatrical" performances are linked to the desire to tell, narrate, and place oneself at the center of the perceived world. Like so many other characters, the narrator (as a child) is incapable of communicating directly with his father and articulating what is really important. When it is time to go to the grandparents' house, he does not tell his father but instead hangs about—*"well, not exactly hanging about . . . but more or less putting* [himself] *at his* [father's] *disposal without seeming to"* (3/11). Already at age five or six the child is an actor, employs duplicity, and performs for the father as he performs for the reader—without seeming to (again like the adolescent Alvaro and his father). At the same time that child already experiences the sense of inadequacy, the need to reassure oneself that one exists (*"remind him that I existed"*) that he sees in his grandfather (whom he will not resemble) and that the reader will see in Chepa.

What then of society's credence in the "innocence of childhood"? To emphasize the premise of an early loss of innocence (if, in fact, it can be called a loss and not simply a lack, an absence), the text proffers a scene laden with images of violence and destruction, evocative of the passion that, according to Chepa, is soon replaced with the invention, the games, literature. The child narrator is en route to his grandmother's house. First, in a prefiguring of the images of consumption, devourer, devoured to be witnessed in Chepa, he notes that he had chewed through the thumb of his glove; that is, he had eaten, destroyed, what (like a mother) would protect him from the external and the cold. Then the child narrator images the car headlights as Christmas balls smashed against the window (the gift destroyed), indeed a particularly violent figure in the mouth (and hand) of a child. He goes on to report that he brutally squeezes (metaphorically, of course) one of the red drops on the window. The image of the red drops recalls the inadequacy of vision since the red is an illusion produced by the reflection of taillights; thus the image recalls the refracted and reflected perspectives that structure the text. Furthermore, he notes that the drop *"opens like an artery"* (4/12), a simile that foreshadows Violeta's violent death and reveals the violent nature inherent to the speaker, a child, whom we would like to imagine free from the desire to do violence.[14] As he tries to stop the "blood," he worries that his father has seen him. Again, not only does Donoso posit an inclination toward violence and destruction at an early age, but he also suggests that the child recognizes the need to disguise that proclivity and be seen as "they say" one should be. Thus the innocence (and by implication, nonviolence) of youth is doubly undermined.

The violent images created and projected by the young child continue. The river is said to roar like a caged beast. Upon arrival at the grandmother's house, the child clings to Antonia, feigning an affection he does not feel in order to hurt his father, for his father has not realized (seen) what the child wants him to see and comprehend: that he knows how to read. Foreshadowing Alvaro's interaction (or lack thereof) with Chepa, the child narrator here wants to tell but does not. Even more important, his desire to tell is predicated on his desire for centrality, his father's attention. But again, and like Alvaro, rather than using direct discourse and communication, the child relies on subterfuge and indirect speech that require active interpretation as well as associative efforts on the part of the recipient. Surely there is a message here about both life and art. In life, I may want you to know (that I know), but I do not want to have to tell you. I should be important and central enough for you to notice, to guess, to spend the time and effort required to decipher my discreet messages. The same is true in art. Do readers not frequently value the obscure message more than the evident? In both cases is not violence being done to the teller, the tale, *and* the recipient?

The child's grandmother, because of her "maternal instincts" and because of her ostensible willingness to make him central, will make the proper associations and, unlike the father, will see that the real significance is that he knows how to read. By means of this small and seemingly insignificant incident, Donoso conveys a number of messages. First, the child narrator is indeed a mirror reflection of his grandfather and every bit as egocentric in spite of his insistence that he would never be like him. Second, the male characters who demand centrality (the child narrator, the grandfather, Maya) are not only unable to offer it to another but are also unable to reach a state of plenitude. They can never be quite central enough to quite enough people and must always seek to draw more and more into their set of "personal" possessions (thus the image of devourer that is so often projected onto the other). On the metaphoric level, they devour in order to avoid being devoured, to avoid disappearing, a concept reinforced by the scene with the gelatin star. Desiring what the other has (and no doubt only because the other has it), the child demands to be given a gelatin star like the one his grandfather eats. Like Maya later, the child wants it because Alvaro has it. He is finally given the star to keep him from making a scene, but he hates it and spits it out. That it does not taste as good as it looks evokes the question of appearances versus reality that frequently surfaces in the text.

In addition, the italicized sections dramatize the links between the desire to narrate (or, inversely, the ability to read) and sexuality (a link that again points to an early loss or absence of innocence). Children apparently become conscious of the sex act around the time they learn to read. In the italicized sections, the narrator refers to the idyllic period in his life when he had learned to read and had just learned about the siesta, that *"inexplicable game of the grown-ups"* (78/96–97). Significantly, as he proudly reports (narrates, tells) the latter to his cousins, their response is, *"you're not innocent any more"* (79/97). In fact, the oblique suggestion in the first paragraph is that his father delays so in getting him into the car to take him to his grandparents' home because he is making love with the mother: *"his siesta with my mother was lasting longer than usual"* (3/11). The link between narrativity and sexuality is reinforced too by the fact that Magdalena (who tries to "do it" with another cousin, Alberto) does penance by allowing the "yarn-spinning" gardener to touch her legs. Thus penance and acts of contrition are directly linked to narration.

At the same time the narrator is explicit that although his father is oblivious to his reading skills, ones that would gain him access into the adult male world (after all, the father is preoccupied only with the *"important things that come out in the newspaper"* [6/15]), he will tell his grandmother about them *"in the warmth of her bed . . . very early so that* [his] *cousins would not have come in yet"* (6/15). Yet even then he will articulate the message circuitously, for rather than telling her he knows how to read, he *"embroiders"* a story about an elfin tomb *"to pique her curiosity"* (6/15), so she will follow him to the street and he can show her. Is this not the function and structure of the novel we read, or at least of the italicized segments—to pique our interest and encourage us to make him central?

Just as Alvaro hesitates to narrate his "death" directly, the grandson as narrator hesitates to narrate the "death," loss, nonexistence of childhood innocence directly. Nonetheless, it is pertinent that the final italicized sec-

61

tion, "Sunday Night," not only metaphorically evokes death and the end of an era with its titular reference to darkness and night (specifically Sunday, the end of the weekend), but it also continues the motifs of violence, sexuality, and narrativity so prominent in the other italicized sections. As the narrator notes, *"there was no next Sunday"* (171/203), and the "murdered" fantasy character, Mariola, had to remain dead. Similarly, the segment recounts the grandfather's death and funeral, five months after that Sunday, and the grandmother's slow physical death following her emotional death that Sunday. More important, the segment indirectly narrates the "death" of the child and the "birth" of the young man who would now play more appropriate and "grownup" games with Fernando, "other" games that are still fraught with the motifs that have already surfaced within the novel: sexuality, substitution, violence, mask, literature, and narration.

After that traumatic Sunday, the narrator forsakes his grandparents' home for the home of his friend Fernando and falls in love or pretends to fall in love with Fernando's mother (perhaps more wishful thinking). But that love is already literary in basis (a re-creation of a re-creation), since by his own admission he has read Bataille's *Maman Colibrí* and images Fernando's mother as the title character.[15] Furthermore, she substitutes for and replaces his grandmother in terms of erotic transference: they sit together next to the fire (before, it was in the grandmother's bed) after Fernando has gone to bed (before, it was before the others arrived). At that time, and again in a direct evocation of his grandmother listening to him in her bed, Fernando's mother (who is never named and has no existence except in terms of his fantasy, Maman Colibrí) *listens* to him. Nonetheless, the violence that marked the first italicized section and his journey(s) to his grandparents resurfaces in spite of the idyllic scenes of adolescence that he paints here. First he notes that he *"had to kill other things in order to leave room for"* Maman Colibrí (172/204; emphasis added). Then he acknowledges that even that "newer" world is now (in the present of the narration) as "dead" as that of his grandparents. He goes on to say that his parents gave him a gun so that he could better pursue these new, more appropriate games (perhaps of violence and killing).

Nonetheless, his newly found interest in other friends and other games is also shown to be an avoidance of the unpleasant reality of the grandparents' house—an avoidance of reality that first echoes his grandfather's approach to life as it repeats his own adult approach (or lack thereof) to the grandparents' house. In the present of the narration that house is deserted, but he will do nothing about it, an inertia that recalls Alvaro's perpetual avoidance of responsibility in all regards and Maya's refusal to take initiative, both of which are also imaged as the other side of violence. Indeed, after mentioning that several months went by before he returned to the center of youthful paradise, he states in the original, *"Por lo demás, no convenía que fuera"* (205). Although correctly translated into English as *"Besides, it wasn't convenient for me to go"* (172), this statement might also be rendered (and certainly more tellingly) that apart from this it was not advantageous or desirable to go. That is, with his grandfather preoccupied with his own death and his grandmother in an almost catatonic state (like Maya's earlier "black hand"), no one would pay suitable attention to him; he would not be central (as he apparently was with Fernando and his mother), so there was no point in going there.

Thus, although there has been a tendency among critics to focus on the self-centeredness of the adults rather than that of the children, it is apparent that the novel also highlights the egocentricity of the young. For the children, the world centers around them and their games. They would believe that nothing happens if they do not invent it. In this respect, the bourgeois grandchildren are not as different from the poor children Chepa encounters in the street as one (particularly the grandson) might like to believe. In both cases, they invent a world around her (Mariola's funeral, the "doggies" she wears around her neck), but once their games cease to center on her or she ceases to center on them, she is forgotten, and metaphorically she no longer exists (she "dies") for them; they turn their backs and do not, will not, see her suffering. And this childhood attitude is reenacted in adulthood. The adult Alvaro still exhibits the characteristics of the child Alvaro, as does his grandson. In this way Alvaro renders Chepa marginal, and the grandson's narration is an act of contrition that renders them both marginal as it centralizes him and as he turns his back on them and "kills" her a second time. His narration presents again his perceived position of centrality in her life and refuses to recognize the fiction of the same.

As if this were not sufficient, this same narrator, now fully assuming his adult position at the end of the text (perhaps because it is convenient or advantageous), goes on to invent and narrate what has *probably* become of his aunts, uncles, and cousins in a gesture that again recalls the tales he embroidered with his grandmother—fantasy recognized as such (*"I wonder," "I imagine," I don't know"* [174/206–07]). Then in what might be seen as one final tribute (or act of contrition) to that grandmother, he mingles the "they say" that surrounds the remaining house and his own wishful thinking to create the story of the house as a harbor for homeless children. He notes that he got up in the middle of the night once and *"passed the house very slowly, time and again. Until yes, through* [the] *clouded windows* [he] *did make out what seemed to be reflections of flames dancing"* (176/209–10), reflections that he concludes are children.[16] Thus on the one hand the narrator repeats the opening motif of the car, from which all is viewed at a safe distance, inside the fishbowl of warmth and through a screen of vapor or droplets. But notice the inventiveness and tentative words implicit in this. He has to repeat his gaze; to look once is not enough. Still he only glimpses, makes out (or perhaps makes up, "sees" what he wants to see), what lies behind those blurry windows, and even then what he perceives seems to be only reflections. This has been the readers' position throughout: passing by the same events over and over, trying to see through the clouded windows of the characters' perceptions, and ultimately finding just reflections. And as readers we impose our own reading on it all, just as the narrator does: *"I would prefer it to end"* (177/210).

Ultimately, then, just as Alvaro sought a *"perfect image of himself projected on the rich twilight of the bindings"* (11/20), the narrator here seeks to improve his image by doing his penance—narrating (again note the link between narration and sin, sexuality). As he watched his grandfather watch himself, readers now watch the grandson watch himself as he reinvents that universe (perfectly ordered and safe from the chaos of darkness and the storm) that was his—that of the grandmother's house, which like the traditional narrative eliminates disorder by establishing the center as himself. Thus he recalls arriving at his grandmother's in the dark, in a storm, for the chaos exists outside of that ordered, centered world, outside of the fishbowl. Nonetheless, as usual, Donoso leaves a doubt: are the reader and the narrator inside or outside that fishbowl, that laboratory flask of language and literary reflections?

Notes

1. As Hugo Achugar notes, the novel might be viewed as the evocation of a paradise lost from which the grandson had already been expelled to the extent that the paradise was the world of the adults to which he had access only through the invention of the fictionalized children's games. See *Ideología y estructuras narrativas en José Donoso* (Caracas: Centro de Estudios Latinoamericanos, Rómulo Gallegos, 1979), 207.

2. The original Spanish provides a slightly different flavor here, for the text states that when his grandfather begins (not began) to exist in his memory, he was the same age as the narrator now (no reference to writing), and that "his memory is born along with that of his old age and his absurdity" (21; my translation).

3. The mole represents decay, deterioration, and death, but it has always been there on Alvaro's chest, a fact that suggests that decay and death are always present—perhaps even in children. It is merely a question of focus and perspective.

4. The image of Chepa as a nursing dog is more powerful in Spanish than in English. In Spanish she is *una perra parida*, literally a female dog who has just given birth, but the term *perra* is also one used to refer to a woman of disreputable moral conduct.

Similarly, in Spanish there are numerous linguistic relations among the words that translate into English as teat, nipple, and teapot. Linguistically, there is no distinction in Spanish between an animal's teat and a woman's breast or nipple; both are rendered *teta*. A man's nipple (where Alvaro has his mole) is designated by the diminutive of the same word, *tetilla*. Since teapot is rendered by the Spanish word *tetera* (presumably because of its visual similarity to the woman's breast), it is not irrelevant that Alvaro is heating water in a teapot that happens to have a rough spot like the mole near his nipple (*tetilla*), while he worries about that mole, tries to recall the name of the young man who has one near his lip (Maya), and images Chepa as a "littered bitch . . . with hungry whelps . . . sucking on her teats" (22/33).

5. Although the grandson images Alvaro as partially deaf, Chepa accuses him of convenient hearing.

6. The grandson always refers to it as his grandmother's house, not their house.

7. The Spanish title for the section rendered in English "In the Fishbowl," is *"En la redoma,"* literally, "in the laboratory flask," and thus lends a flavor of scientific experiment to the novel as it highlights the question of making observations as a scientist might. In either case the title emphasizes the question of perspective, for the reader is always in doubt about whether the character (and in turn the reader) is inside or outside the container, is the experimenter or the one being experimented on.

8. For an explanation of the Spanish term *don* see chapter three, note 1. In Spanish there are two forms of address, two *yous*: the familiar *tú*, which is used with social equals or inferiors, and the formal *usted*, which is used with superiors.

On the rare occasions when Violeta did employ the *tú*, she referred to his sex organ as much as, if not more than, to him as an integral human being (52/68, 61/79).

9. Alvaro is repeatedly portrayed as a passive character (particularly sexually) who allows others to do to him: "Better to do nothing. To let her . . . do everything" (51/67). He is also apparently an expert at allowing a series of women to take care of him and exempting himself from all guilt and burden of responsibility, as he does in the case of Mirella.

10. Few critics have acknowledged this aspect of the novel, and most have accepted Alvaro's rationalizations as fact.

11. Chepa envisions herself as an ignorant woman who was not taught anything and does not understand politics or history, but who gives what she knows—how to be clean, how not to get sick (96/116–117).

12. There are continual references in the text to the various characters being metaphorically eaten or devoured.

13. Indeed, in Spanish the verb *poseer* ("to possess") is frequently used in the sense of "to make love to."

14. The plurality of the violent gestures evokes the plurality of violence in Violeta's murder. We are told that "Maya had murdered Violeta with a pillow, that he had knocked her out by punching and kicking her, and that finally he had strangled her with a cord" (173/206). The multiplicity of violent gestures would seem to be gratuitous in view of the fact that she

has been portrayed as an overweight old woman who wheezes, has high blood pressure, and is on the verge of a heart attack or a stroke (152/182).

15. Henri Bataille (1872–1922) was a French poet and playwright considered to be a master of psychological drama and analyst of love. *Maman Colibrí* dates from 1904.

16. There seems to be a typographical error in the translation, which reads, ''my clouded windows'' (176), for the Spanish edition reads, ''los vidrios empañados'' (209), ''*the* clouded windows.''

CHAPTER FIVE

Hell Has No Limits: Limits, Centers, and Discourse

In 1966 Donoso wrote *Hell Has No Limits* while residing at the home of Mexican author Carlos Fuentes and his wife, Rita Macedo.[1] At the time he was obsessed with what would be his masterpiece, *The Obscene Bird of Night,* which he could not seem to finish. In addition, he felt pressure (apparently self-inflicted) to produce a manuscript for the Chilean publishing house Zig-Zag, which had advanced him $1000 for an unspecified novel. To get beyond the writer's block that precluded the completion of *The Obscene Bird of Night* and to liquidate his debt to the publishing house, he opted to write a short novel. The result was *Hell Has No Limits,* in which he developed a scene from *The Obscene Bird of Night:* Jerónimo and his four black dogs became Alejo and his four black dogs in *Hell Has No Limits.* The novel was published that same year by the prestigious Mexican publishing house Joaquín Mortiz, and Donoso later finished *This Sunday* to pay off his debt to Zig-Zag. Thus in many ways *Hell Has No Limits* marks the dividing point between what critics have often labeled Donoso's earlier and later works. Chronologically it is related to the stories, *Coronation,* and *This Sunday.* Yet in terms of technique and thematic preoccupations, both of which undermine the status quo as they question the signifying practices in mode, it is perhaps more closely linked to *The Obscene Bird of Night* and the later works, although the seeds of those later works were already present in the earliest short stories.

Hell Has No Limits has attracted more critical attention than Donoso's early works and has been read as an allegory of the Creation and the Fall and as an allegory of the "death" of God in the twentieth century. Other critics have interpreted the novel as a satire of the Latin American socio-economic system of *latifundios,* controlled by the bourgeoisie and perpetuated since the time of the conquest (hence the insistence on Alejo's blue eyes, for he represents the Spanish conqueror just as Manuela's flamenco dress evokes the imposition of Spanish art and culture).[2] In addition, it has been read as a dramatization of ritualistic, carnival inversions and as a series of substitutions and inversions effectuated for the sake of substituting and inverting. At the same time, the novel can be read as a visual spectacle, as literature that presents itself as spectacle and theater. While all these are valid readings of the novel, the readings I propose here are perhaps more harmonious with (although significantly different from) those of Hernán Vidal and Kirsten Nigro, who have seen the novel as a literary reaction to the utopian, positivistic ideals and myths sustained by the literary schools of *criollismo* and mimetic realism, and that of Hortensia Morell, who has read the novel as Donoso's attempt to depict a world that is continually changing, always moving toward its other.[3] My readings of the novel here focus on the text as a work of art that questions the utopian cosmovision of mimetic, realistic art and as a discursive product that continually undermines its own instrument of creation. In addition, I shall demonstrate that, by means of the framing, embedding technique, the text illustrates that the characters (products of linguistic communication) as well as the instrument of that communication (language, the word) are already swathed in limitless layers of mask—frames within frames, texts within texts within texts—or as Sarduy has expressed it, inversions within inversions.[4]

Plot and Technique: Repetition, Inversion, Substitution

The frame action of *Hell Has No Limits* centers on what is probably the final day in the life of Manuela, an aging male transvestite who has assumed the clothing, role, and linguistic features of a female to the extent of referring to him/herself with feminine adjectives.[5] It begins as s/he awakens at five minutes to ten one Sunday morning just after harvest time. Thus the novel opens with the simultaneous completion of three cycles that are about to begin anew—that of the day (or night), that of the week, and that of nature, plant growth, or agriculture—as Donoso repeats the motif of Sunday as a turning point (as in *This Sunday*).[6] Both the story line and the novel conclude early the following morning after Manuela has been badly beaten, probably by the local macho, Pancho Vega, and his brother-in-law, Octavio. The novel is vague about this detail, as it is about many, and states only that "Octavio, or *maybe* Pancho first, started lashing at him [Manuela] with fists . . . *perhaps* it wasn't them, but other men" (224/132; emphasis added). Then, like the piece of meat or thing (inanimate object) s/he was perceived to be earlier in the text, s/he is left in the fields to die or to be devoured by Alejo's bloodthirsty dogs. In this respect, the novel marks the completion of yet another life cycle: Manuela's. In addition, by the end of the novel, the reader has learned that Alejo, the local cacique who seems to rule the town with an iron hand as he continually watches over it (generally from afar, like a god), is dying or perhaps has died (we know only that his dogs are unattended), and even the town itself seems destined to disappear from the face of the earth, for it will not get electricity and the road has passed it by.

Although Donoso's works are consistently in dialogue with his other works, *Hell Has No Limits* is more overt in that dialogue as well as in its ties to certain works by other novelists. Unquestionably *Hell Has No Limits* foreshadows *The Obscene Bird of Night* with its breakdown of narrative voice and literary mask. At the same time, it responds to the themes and techniques of Carlos Fuentes's *Where the Air Is Clear* (1958) and *The Death of Artemio Cruz* (1962) as it proffers what might be considered an alternative rendition of Artemio Cruz in Alejo Cruz.[7] In addition to the obvious similarities of name, both characters are powerful caciques who are, in the final analysis, unhappy men, frustrated by their own human limitations and mortality. The two novels vary in technique and in the fact that Fuentes takes the reader ''inside'' Artemio Cruz by revealing his thoughts as well as his present, past, and future. Quite the opposite is true of Alejo, who is always viewed from afar, as mask, distant from and impenetrable for the reader—a linguistic creation in the fullest sense of the word, but one whose word and influence seem to penetrate all. When on rare occasion Alejo is presented directly rather than framed within and through his words or the words of another character, he is then partially hidden in the shadows.[8] It would also not be inappropriate to view the Chilean novel's multiple perspective and apocalyptic projection for the future of the town as a prefiguration of Colombian Gabriel García Márquez's *Cien años de soledad* (*One Hundred Years of Solitude*) (1967).[9]

Still, what is uniquely characteristic of Donoso in *Hell Has No Limits* and what distinguishes the novel from the others with which it dialogues is not only the play between open and closed, limits and centers, but also the close correlation between violence and eroticism (a correspondence latent in Donoso's earlier works). Pancho's gratuitous and exaggeratedly ''macho'' violence toward Manuela is fraught with eroticism—homosexual in this case—while his outward gestures reveal a lack of inner cohesiveness (which, Donoso posits, is always lacking) as it is traditionally defined. In contradiction to his exaggeratedly masculine image/mask, Pancho had been erotically attracted to Manuela during her/his dance and in fact had tried to kiss her/him even before the violence/violation (and his treatment of Manuela is certainly a form of rape).[10] The assault scene itself is described with a figurative language that foregrounds the erotic: "like hungry animals. . . . [they] had pierced ["penetrated" in the Spanish] the thicket . . . thrown themselves upon him . . . their hot bodies writhing . . . heavy, stiff bodies . . . fused . . . moan . . . hot mouths, hot hands, slavering hard bodies wounding his, bodies that . . . grope" (224–25/132–33).

There can be little doubt that Pancho's violence is the product of a series of substitutions, erotic and otherwise, comparable to those of *This Sunday*. The previous fall, also at harvest time, when the new wine is made and the entire town reeks of wine and rotting grape residue (symbolic of both life and death, which in this novel are not mutually exclusive), Pancho's "hell raising" had been thwarted by the limitations imposed by the god-like Alejo. Pancho had sworn to return, not to avenge himself on Alejo, as might be logically expected, but rather to "screw ["mount" in the Spanish] the two of them, Japonesita and her fag of a father . . ." (150/10), a statement that highlights a significant substitution (Japonesita and Manuela for Alejo) while revealing the homosexual inclination disguised beneath the mask of masculine, erotic aggression.[11] He will do violence to, violate, "mount" (that is, place in a physically inferior position), not Alejo, who is the direct object of his anger and frustration, but rather the indirect objects Japonesita (in some respect the vicarious daughter of Alejo) and her father, Manuela, ultimately male and thus perhaps a more fitting substitute for Alejo.

Furthermore, this single, prophetic day of the frame action is presented not only as inevitable, predestined (the "natural" conclusion of a "natural" cycle of violence and eroticism) but also as the result of the absence or "death" of the "god" figure Alejo. Unlike the year before when Alejo thwarted, frustrated (in both the erotic and nonerotic senses of the word), and placed limitations on Pancho's desire and actions, this year Alejo does not "miraculously" appear to impose his will and order (again because he has "died" either literally or figuratively). After the violence/violation, Manuela cannot get to the other side, cross the Palos Canal to where s/he is sure (erroneously, no doubt) that "Alejo waits, benevolent" (225/133) with his sky-blue eyes (in Spanish, *celestes*, meaning "celestial" or "heavenly") to keep his word (224/132).[12] Ironically, Manuela has already seen that Alejo does not keep his word, that he lies; but here, as in the rest of the novel, the character tends to perceive and believe only what the superficial mask of the linguistic construct reveals, as will be discussed below.

Thus Pancho assaults Manuela, at least in part because he cannot make love with Manuela since s/he is physically male, a fact underscored during the beating: "la Manuela woke up. He wasn't la Manuela. He was señor Manuel González Astica. He. And because he was he they were going to hurt him" (223/130). The violence is also motivated in part because Pancho can neither assault Alejo nor replace him in the established hierarchy of the world. As was the case in *Coronation* and *This Sunday*, material possession is confused with erotic possession. Eroticism, gender roles, and this urge to substitution were also the primary structuring factors in the theatrical copulation between Manuela and Japonesa twenty years earlier. At that time, Japonesa was motivated to accept Alejo's bet because she wanted to own the bordello but also, in part at least, because Alejo had doubted her femininity and seductive powers (gender role). In addition, metaphorically, the script of this "play" (the "spectacle" of copulation) was written and directed by Alejo, who determined what the theater would be, when, and where. Yet in a revealing reduplication of roles, Alejo was also the spectator: he watched from the window (just beyond the "limit") while they "performed" (in both the erotic and nonerotic senses of the word) for him. And, as so often happens throughout Donoso's works, Japonesa and Manuela became so engrossed in their roles that their performance (the theater, the mask) became their "reality"; instead of pretending to copulate, as was the plan, they did. Yet this theater of representations was the product of and in turn produced a series of substitutions—roles that might have been played by other actors. Manuela not only substitutes for Alejo on a number of levels but also projects his/her own series of substitutions: s/he was "in love with" and would have liked to have sexual relations with Alejo, just as s/he would like to have them with Pancho. Indeed, early in the novel, Manuela daydreams and fantasizes that Pancho attacks her/him. It cannot be irrelevant, however, that in her/his fantasy Alejo appears in time to "save" him/her (unlike in the final moments of the text) and turns her/him over to Blanca, who will care for him/her. Thus on some level Manuela's desire to be attacked by Pancho is predicated first on being saved by Alejo (who is like a knight in shining armor—again the text dialogues with earlier literary texts and motifs) and second on being "taken care of" by Blanca and replacing her in her pink

71

bed, which is presumably frequented by Alejo. That is, as a result of a series of fantasized inversions and substitutions (recognized as such), Pancho's violence would bestow upon Manuela the female gender role s/he longs to subsume and place him/her in the position (the bed) of the object of Alejo's desire (Blanca). Nonetheless, Pancho's violence/violation has just the opposite effect—it makes Manuela inescapably conscious of her/his masculinity.

Not only are the protagonists of this erotic drama interchangeable (like their gender and erotic roles), but their erotic gestures are also interchangeable with those of violence. Pancho's aggression is an overt attempt to "prove has masculinity." Indeed, he has noted that Octavio does not let Alejo "mount" him (translated in the English as "run all over him") as he (Pancho) does (203/96), an observation that linguistically reveals Pancho's sense of inadequate masculinity as he sees himself in the "feminine" position (mounted, violated). In addition, Alejo has made him feel like "less of a man" by berating him in public, while Octavio has questioned his masculinity first by calling him *"poco hombre"* (202/94, translated into English as "coward," but the expression literally means "not much of a man") when he would not get out of the truck and later by calling him a "fag" when Manuela kissed him (a moment that echoes Pancho's childhood experience when the other children accused him of the same because he "played house" with Moniquita).[13]

Ironically, at approximately the same time that Manuela is probably dying on the banks of the Palos Canal (the same body of water in which Alejo's unwanted pups are drowned), Japonesita, unaware of Manuela's situation, resigns herself to a future of tedium (Manuela's "life" is anything but boring at that moment). As Japonesita's dreams of electricity (the metaphoric light) "die," she prepares to repeat the already often repeated cycle of the week with her ritual Monday visits to Talca and retires to her bed around five o'clock the next morning (Monday) without even lighting a candle. By means of this visual image Donoso reinforces the thematic notion that there is no light to brighten the darkness of the novelistic world, no hope, nothing to see, no "god" to worship. Life and death, heaven and hell, are indistinguishable, for the lines between the ostensible antitheses are blurred.

Although the frame action of the novel is limited to one Sunday, like that of *This Sunday,* here Donoso employs flashbacks within the consciousness of various characters or the omniscient narrator to reveal events that precede this day. Flashbacks appear early in the first chapter when

Manuela remembers the previous night (Saturday) with its bothersome sounds: the barking of Alejo's dogs and the honking of the horn. These stimuli—or the memory of them, for in fact they now "exist" only in Manuela's memory—lead her/him to recall Pancho's visit the previous year when he and his friends ripped (raped) Manuela's "famous" dress.[14] Structurally, the reader is thus presented with a distant memory framed within a more recent one, in turn framed within present events. Similarly, in chapter eight Pancho recalls, not his visit to the brothel last year (which is so significant for Manuela and Japonesita), but his youth as a peon on Alejo's estate and his relationship with the family, especially the daughter, Moniquita, with whom he played and whom he apparently infected with the typhus from which she died.[15]

Chapter eight, with its erotic undertones, immediately follows the two chapters that flashback to the alleged "paradise" (which was not as paradisaical as the characters are wont to believe) that existed some twenty years before the Sunday of the frame action. That moment of positive (rather than negative) perception (framing), of optimism rather than pessimism, was marked by the ritual celebration of Alejo's political victory (with its overtones of eroticism, carnival, theater, and excess), just as the frame Sunday is marked by Pancho's "political" victory over Alejo (he has paid him back the money, and Octavio has verbally defied him).[16] In addition, that earlier celebration occasioned Manuela's arrival in Estación El Olivo, the bet between Alejo and Japonesa, and the theatrical copulation between Japonesa and Manuela that led to the former's winning the brothel (which she promised to share with Manuela) and giving birth to Japonesita (progeny of Manuela's unforeseen potency during the "theater"). As the novel flashes back to these moments (as when the novel flashes back to the "paradise" of Pancho's childhood, before the "fall," the sin, and the death of Moniquita), that past is presented to readers in the same mode as the "present" of the frame action (also presented as past). That is, in both moments what predominates is the theater, the spectacle, directed and orchestrated (to a large degree "framed") by the gaze of the male (Alejo or his substitutes Pancho and Octavio), as shall be discussed below.

At the same time, the positioning of Pancho's flashbacks is relevant. Chapter eight, with Octavio and Pancho's visit to Alejo's estate, within which Pancho's memory is framed, is in turn framed by or embedded within the scene of Manuela's seduction by Japonesa. In that chapter Pancho's recollection of his childhood is stimulated by his "journey" through space and time, in his truck, "back" to Alejo's estate and "back" to his youthful sense of impotence (*poco hombre*) in relation to Alejo. Throughout, Pancho is concerned with the question of being able to return, be it to the paradise of his childhood, Alejo's estate, El Olivo, or the brothel. And in both the present and the past, he fears being devoured or disappearing, undesirable situations that are imaged as unmanliness or impotence. This fear is a constant that structures many of Donoso's texts, but it might also be understood as a discrete metaphor for "traditional" readers who insist on being able to return to reality (or their image or invention thereof), those who fear being "swallowed" by the fiction or discourse of the text. Like Pancho, those readers are willing to enter that other world only partially, always simultaneously concerned with a lifeline to return whence they came.

It is pertinent to this discussion, too, that Pancho's flashbacks to his youth are stimulated by his observation, through the window, of Misia Blanca, now elderly, as she is in the dining room surrounded by food. This scene evokes the plentiful kitchen of his childhood, when he could eat rather than worry about being metaphorically devoured. The latter motif puts the various scenes of the novel "in perspective," as it were, and is tied to the larger motif of Manuela's seduction, which frames chapter eight and which in turn is framed by the "present" moment in the bordello on Sunday night when Manuela and Japonesita hear the horn of Pancho's truck (183 and 207/63 and 103). In each case, to prove his manliness—and like the dogs and Alejo—Pancho must devour rather than be devoured. (Alejo's less aggressive dogs are drowned, "fed" to the Palos Canal.) Let us recall too that the scene of the copulation is similarly peppered with expressions that reflect Manuela's fear of being devoured.[17]

The framing technique in which events from the more remote past are embedded within those of a more recent past is visually repeated multiple times when characters look through windows or doors. Examples are moments such as those in which Pancho watches Blanca through the window, Manuela watches Pancho through the window, Alejo watches Japonesa and Manuela through the window, and Pancho watches Manuela perform in the center of the room within the visual frame of the candles (as he orders more food and Céspedes "sees" that they are all going to be *devoured* by time). Like the word, the window or door limits the scene and gives it an appearance of coherence it may not have, for surely both the limitations and coherence of the scenes are illusions; the scene is ever changing both inside and out. One needs only to move slightly for the entire scene to change just as the light from that inside scene inevitably "spills out" into the outside darkness and vice versa. What appears to be a limit (the frame that simultaneously marks a center, that which is framed), like artistic authority in mimetic art, is precarious and ever shifting, a product of the viewer's perspective and position (both spatial and temporal).

At the same time the framing, embedding (engulfing) technique imagistically evokes the characters' preoccupation with an existence predicated on not being devoured, engulfed, obliterated by the framing action (to a large degree linguistic). The flashback and other framing techniques are employed on the level of both paragraph and sentence. On the level of sentence, earlier enunciations or thoughts (indirect or direct quotes), either those of the narrating character or another, are embedded within a more recent enunciation, often without markers to indicate the change of moment or speaker (time or space).[18] Thus the techniques of embedding and framing function on the level of both *énoncé* and *énonciation*.[19]

Limits, Centers, and the Utopianism of Mimesis

Hell Has No Limits evinces an overt and tenacious reaction to the traditional mimetic forms of art and literature in fashion at the time Donoso began writing. Within these modes (manifested in Chile by *criollismo*), the novel and other art forms were posited as means of delimiting and finding order in a world that might otherwise be perceived as chaotic. Unlike contemporary theory (subscribed to by Donoso), the philosophical underpinnings of these art forms never question the ultimate coherence and order of the world. On the contrary, that coherence, symmetry, and order are believed to preexist both the materials and the products of art (language and the text, in the case of literature). The artist's "job" is simply to find them and represent them. According to this view, art takes a segment of the world, dissects it, discovers its coherence, and makes it manageable for the reader, all predicated on the superior perspective of the artist. To this extent the work of art proffers what I label a utopian (and thus paradoxically unrealistic) sense of both stability (permanence) and human supremacy over the unknown and the chaotic. It is precisely this traditional concept of art that Donoso's works undermine. As noted in previous chapters, the chaotic unknown lies just under the surface of discourse in his works and often bursts forth to engulf the limited, artificial, and utopian world and sense of security invented and imposed by art and society. Still, for the most part, in his earlier works order returns (or is reimposed), at least superficially, so that both social and artistic demarcations are restored after a brief eruption of the chaotic and irrational. Readers' confidence is essentially restored (although I would argue that readers are inevitably left with a sense of uneasiness), for they "know" where the fictional world ends and the "real" world begins, and they tacitly accept that the former reflects and is reflected by the latter. In *Hell Has No Limits* and *The Obscene Bird of Night* the limitless, uncontrolled, and uncontrollable threaten throughout, and the illusory utopian cosmovision of some ultimate order and structure never regains unchallenged primacy. By denying the reader the illusion of completeness, Donoso refuses to participate in the game of literature as it has been posited—that is, in the invention of utopias that pretend to reflect "reality."

Surely all Donoso's works challenge the complacency that results from the imposition of artistic limitations and illusions, but perhaps nowhere is this challenge more obvious than in *Hell Has No Limits,* whose title already foregrounds the issue of limits. Although the English translation (which draws on the epigraph from Marlowe) does maintain the titular allusion to limits, the Spanish title *El lugar sin límites* [The Place without Limits] not only refers to the question of limits but highlights the vagueness of that locale—the place that simultaneously is and is not a place since it defies the definition of "place" as a delimited space.[20] Without the presence of the external demarcations to define being (both the ontological existence of the characters involved and the literary existence of the work), the question of center emerges. Lacking outer limits to hold the parts together (Alejo's fields seem to go on forever; where do they end?) and create a cohesive whole, the search for a unifying force turns to the center. Such is the movement in *Hell Has No Limits,* although the search is frustrated, for just as hell has no limits, it also has no center.

The first traditional limitation and centralizing element patently lacking in the novel is that of a single, unique, or identifiable narrative voice. Like Humberto of *The Obscene Bird of Night,* whose narrative voice is everywhere and nowhere and refuses to be embodied in a single entity or personal pronoun, the narrative voice in *Hell Has No Limits* also wanders, resisting both containment in any one personal pronoun or character's consciousness and limitation to a single narrative mode. By definition, a novel (and particularly the mimetic, realistic novel to which Donoso is responding) is structured by a narrative voice or a narrative position from which the fictional world is presented ("seen," as it were). Theorists have

not agreed on the number of possible voices or on the various positions
from which the tale might be told, but they have generally agreed that it is
to be narrated from a specific physical and temporal position, one that is
implicitly superior. In this respect, the narrative voice serves both as a
means of delimiting a work and as a center around which the work revolves. Donoso rejects this narrative limitation in *Hell Has No Limits,*
which begins with what the reader presumes (because of narrative convention) is third-person, limitedly omniscient narration in the past tense as
it presents Manuela both internally and externally. But the narrative voice
suddenly becomes *I,* Manuela, who speaks in the present tense and whose
discourse (like that of the third-person voice) includes direct and indirect
quotations of him/herself and others in both tenses and in both persons.
The voice returns to a third-person, seemingly limited omniscience (limited to the lower classes of society, for the "narrator" never sees or understands what goes on in Alejo's mind), only to keep erupting in the first-
person voice, present tense, which is sometimes Manuela's, sometimes
Japonesita's, and sometimes even Pancho Vega's, but always mixing time,
place, and the words of one character with those of another, as one character assumes and frames (engulfs, devours) the discourse (the *I*) of another, often failing to give the other character credit for those words. As
Morell has convincingly demonstrated, even the change of narrative person does not effectively mark the voice (the fictionalized "source" of the
words), for the words of others are absorbed by the various characters.[21]
Again, the "limits" of the word break down as one's word is incorpo-
rated, possessed, devoured by another. Indeed, one of the leitmotifs of the
novel is the capacity of these words to control, change, subsume, and devour the character, not unlike their paradigmatic signifiers, the truck and
the red dress, which will be discussed below. At one point, Manuela
senses that Japonesita is "drowning him in words, slowly encircling him"
(181/60)—an image that recalls the vineyards that encircle and will eventually eliminate (devour) the town. The capacity of language to frame and
engulf will also be discussed below, but perhaps the most important aspect
of this ever shifting narrative voice, which challenges the tenets of narrative limits and centers, is that it disputes the premise of narrative
authority.

Unlike the traditional, mimetic novel, *Hell Has No Limits* proffers no
narrative position of ultimate authority from which the reader is presented
a "correct" or superior rendition. There is no definitive, reliable authority, implicit or explicit, to which the reader can turn, for even the notion

of artistic persona is debunked (a technique that foreshadows that of *The Obscene Bird of Night* and *A House in the Country*). The artist of the novel, Manuela, "sees" no better than any other character (inside or outside the novel) and is but a series of superimpositions and masks— linguistic artifice laid bare. All the reader is left with in the novel is a series of words embedded within words with no ultimate reliability or authority. Is Manuela killed or not? Is Alejo dead or dying or not? Did Alejo ever intend to bring electricity to the town? Or is it all linguistic artifice even on the level of *énonciation,* that is, within the linguistic artifice that is the novel?

Still, this oscillation between the first-person and third-person pronouns defines Manuela, Japonesita, and Pancho as both objects and subjects of the discourse, while it provides what might be thought of as an illusory movement to and from a center (ever changing and artificial, to be sure). Obviously that question of centers and limits becomes intricately connected to that of the mask (outer limit, surface) and essential personality or being (the core, the center, often hidden from view), both of which are marked in regard to gender and sex and largely dependent upon language.[22] Manuela is biologically male, but s/he is a homosexual who has assumed the feminine gender role (and linguistic features)—the mask of femininity: "They [Japonesita and the prostitutes] aren't women. She's going to show them what a woman is and how to be a woman" (212/111), not unlike how Japonesa "showed" Alejo what a woman is. Pancho Vega is also biologically male, but he has assumed a role that is the mirror inverse of Manuela's—that of super macho, another manifestation of mask, and one that may well disguise his cowardice and insecurity (presumably feminine traits) or latent homosexuality (he is attracted to "strong," powerful men like Octavio and Alejo). As Manuela says, "Let's see if he's the man he *says* he is" (173/48; emphasis added), a statement that highlights the linguistic basis of his mask. Finally, Japonesita is biologically female (theoretically, although she has not reached pubescence), yet she has not assumed the role of femininity: she does not dress or act like a woman and shows no erotic interest in men. At the same time, although she is both the daughter of a prostitute and the madame of a brothel, she is a virgin.

Thus the novelistic limitations are further rejected in that the main characters, not unlike Mudito of *The Obscene Bird of Night*, are neither distinctly male nor female but rather a juxtaposition of both. For example, Manuela's feminine name, the feminine adjectives with which s/he refers to her/himself, and the lack of a personal pronoun (which is not always necessary in Spanish) lead readers to conceive of him/her as female until s/he is directly called the father of Japonesita—a designation to which s/he vehemently objects: "don't call me father" (175/50); "don't call me, don't call me that again" (208/106). Again it is language that is at issue here, for it is the word that creates and imposes both realities and dreams. Like the characters, the reader too is duped by the word, the feminine adjective that seems to denote a female character but that effectively "masks" a male character.

In general, a word or name as a sign in nonliterary language creates a limited perception; one tends to perceive only the dominant characteristic indicated by the sign rather than the totality or complexity. The designations Manuela and father, when used under ordinary circumstances, refer to a female and a male respectively; thus when we first encounter them in a literary work, our perceptions tend to be limited to the respective perceptions of femaleness or maleness. Nevertheless, the fact that the sign "Manuela" does not refer to a female and that it is used to refer to the same character designated by "father" creates, in the words of Shklovsky and the Russian Formalists, a "defamiliarization" that at once emphasizes and derides such limited vision while leaving the reader without a sense of coherence and stability, not knowing where either the center or the limits are to be found.[23] In this sense the signs break out of traditional linguistic limitations in the Donoso text. Manuela is neither male nor female, mother nor father, while simultaneously both.[24]

In *Hell Has No Limits* the heretofore latent or secondary issues of role playing and social mask, which disguise or direct the gaze away from the inconsistency and disunity of personality, surface in all their complexity. Manuela and Pancho have assumed what seem to be diametrically opposed roles, but they are roles that actually mirror each other, although their fragile masks continually threaten to crack and expose the underlying contradictions and disunity that are only semimasked. Indeed, even Manuela's and Pancho's chosen masks evince significant similarities, for both have chosen single sign objects (possessions) that function somewhat like chosen or assumed names and with which they hope to signify themselves. Furthermore, and in what is one manifestation of numerous instances of characters' "lying" to themselves, these sign objects function as metaphoric security blankets to reassure Pancho and Manuela that they are what they would like to be: super masculine in Pancho's case, feminine in Manuela's.[25] These are the two red possessions: the truck that "symbolizes" Pancho's masculinity and the dress that "symbolizes" Manuela's femininity. Pancho's truck is meant to signal his masculinity by evoking boisterousness (through its honking; males are traditionally considered more rowdy than females), livelihood (men are breadwinners; he uses the truck for his work), independence (it physically takes him away from El Olivo and provides financial independence; "real men" are stereotypically viewed as independent). In addition, the truck is described in phallic terms or in relation to male eroticism: the horn is enough to drive a woman crazy (149/9); the snub-nosed red truck with double tires on the back wheels (149, 182/9, 62) has been seen as a phallic symbol by a number of critics. Although these images are embedded in Manuela's perception, already eroticized in regard to Pancho, the latter's perceptions of and reactions to the truck also link it to eroticism. He mentally caresses his red truck (which is *his*—again the question of possession and the interchangeability of material and erotic possession) rather than Japonesita (216/119); he can race it down the knife-straight road and "invade [in Spanish, "penetrate"] the depths of the night" (216/119). In addition, the truck is intended to evoke the violence and violent nature with which Pancho would mask his trepidation. And from his perspective, the horn will knock down and destroy what is Alejo's (201/94).

But all this fanfare and deflection of the gaze, distraction from the imagined center or the internal (Pancho is safely *inside* the truck), paradoxically can only partially disguise and protect, for Pancho's cowardice and latent homosexuality surface on multiple occasions, repeatedly emphasizing that he is not what he or others say he is. For example, in a gesture that undermines much of Pancho's bravado, Manuela recalls that as Pancho tried to hit him/her the previous year, s/he had felt him over and discovered that he did not carry the knife he was reputed to carry (159/25–26). Thus much of his masculinity is discursive invention, engendered by what he and others *say*. Similarly, he remembers playing "house" with Moniquita and her dolls and reacting strongly to the other boys' calling him a sissy (again, in Spanish, a *marica* or *maricón,* a "homosexual"), an epithet that is ironic since he was playing the epitome of the masculine role—that of father. Still, his description of Alejo's cape, when Alejo had picked him up and was carrying him, forcing him to do something (exactly *what* is never clear), is fraught with erotic terms: it is slippery and hot, soft and hot (204/97). Later he is more concerned with whether or not Octavio might perceive his homosexual desire for Manuela than with the fact that he experiences it, a situation that again draws readers' attention to the discrepancy between what he is and what he appears (or wants to appear) to be and the fact that the two are inexorably overlapping and always influx, never here nor there.[26] That discrepancy is further highlighted by the fact that Alejo repeatedly calls him a liar, and Pancho never protests the appellation; on the contrary, he internalizes it. By quoting to himself (indirectly, to be sure), "you're a liar" (204/97), he either acknowledges the validity of the designation or psychologically accepts and thus makes his what might be an inauthentic version of his personality. Again, on some level the word makes it so as it ever pursues but fails to grasp that fluid, limitless referent. In regard to language, the significant difference between Pancho and Alejo is that Alejo has managed to impose his word (veracious or not) on others (Pancho among them), whereas Pancho has not; veracious or not, Pancho's word is perceived as untrue, as a lie (not capable of grasping and limiting events), and thus is rejected or at least questioned ("Let's see if he's the man he says he is"). The inside/outside, mask/self, dichotomy (fluid though it may be) is also emphasized in the fact that Pancho suffers from an ulcer that gnaws at him from within ("an animal that roots and gnaws and tears and sucks me" [166/37]), an infirmity that suggests tension produced by the discrepancy between various aspects of mask or self-perception and a literary metaphor that signals the internal (in this case, the animal) that might burst out, eat through the mask, at any moment.

Manuela's red flamenco dress functions in the same manner as Pancho's red truck; it signals the qualities with which she would like to be associated: artistic stardom, passion, femininity, youth. Indeed, Manuela's personality changes when she dons her dress (as perhaps Pancho's does when he is safely inside his truck). In the final pages and in a direct contradiction of what the reader has been led to believe from Manuela's perspective, Japonesita tells Céspedes that Manuela frequently danced, went crazy, and left with men (228/138). She attributes this reaction to the wine s/he drank, but the dress is also a constant in these situations. In fact, although after her/his last binge, Manuela had sworn to throw the dress away in order not to repeat the escapade (s/he apparently recognized the connection between the dress and the escapades), s/he did not dispose of it but stored it in her/his suitcase for a year. Japonesita's observation that Manuela had not acted like this for more than a year signals the link between the dress and his/her behavior. At the same time, Manuela's sign object might also serve as an instrument of destruction. Just as Pancho perceived the truck as capable of destroying elements of Alejo's estate, Manuela might kill Pancho with the dress, hanging him with it (211/110). Nonetheless, since s/he never uses the dress in that manner (except as s/he inadvertently "kills" the macho in him and allows the homoeroticism to surface), the dress, like so much else, remains in the category of "might have beens."

In spite of their potential as instruments of destruction, both of these symbols are themselves damaged during the course of the novel's action. During Pancho's visit to Alejo's house, the dogs attack the shiny red truck, leaving it scratched and muddy. During Pancho's previous visit to the brothel, he and his friends ripped Manuela's dress.[27] Although the dress is repaired early in the novel, the implication is that the mask will never be quite the same again, that it will be even more fragile. And in the final scenes, that dress is muddied and torn again as it is ripped from Manuela's body.

These inverse mirror reflections (Manuela/Pancho, red dress/red truck) maintain a complex relation to each other. On some level each character needs the other to validate the chosen mask. Manuela needs Pancho's gaze and his desire to confirm her/his mask of femininity just as Pancho needs Manuela's femininity and vulnerability to authenticate his masculinity. Yet it is Manuela's biological maleness and Pancho's attraction to it/her that leads to her/his destruction, for what Pancho finally does confirm is Manuela's maleness, and as the text makes clear, that is what he must destroy.[28]

Donoso's specific use of gender or sexual roles to epitomize masks and role playing in general is revealing and intended perhaps to signal the "unnaturalness" of gender role playing. Although the social mores of the world outside the novel might encourage readers to view Pancho Vega's masculine attitude as "natural," since he is biologically male, and Manuela's feminine attitude as "unnatural," since s/he is not biologically female, the novel portrays the two roles as comparable.[29] Both are shown to be artifice, superimposed masks, and linguistic constructs. At the same time, both characters are dehumanized by their gender role playing. Pancho views Manuela as an object and wants to break her/him until s/he is just a flattened, harmless thing (221/127), suggesting that in her/his present state (that of ambiguity, without clearly defined limits) s/he can harm Pancho. At the same time, both Pancho and Manuela must be viewed as analogous to the pieces of meat Alejo's dogs devour. Alejo not only incites his dogs to attack Pancho and intimidates him with them, but he images Pancho as a dog: "you've come with your tail between your legs" (165/35). Manuela cannot sleep because of their barking, and after (or perhaps during) her/his beating—that is, after Pancho and Octavio (most likely) "fell upon him *like hungry animals*" (224/132; emphasis added)—s/he is left probably bloodied like a piece of meat, but all that is heard from the vantage point of the brothel are the dogs (heralds of death) barking. Similarly, near the beginning of the text, the analogy between the prostitutes (and by implication, Manuela) and meat is subtly established: "But drunk, at night, flesh starving for other flesh, for any flesh that's hot and can be bitten and squeezed and licked, they [the men] don't know or care what they go to bed with—dog, hag [old woman], anything will do" (152/13).

In another manifestation of role playing and inversion, the scenes of violence and aggression (both that of the dogs with the meat and that of Manuela's beating) are paradoxically imaged in erotic terms, but the ostensibly erotic scene between Japonesita and Pancho Vega (who was to violate her, "make her a woman") is anything but erotic. Although Pancho and Japonesita are supposed to be responding to each other physically and erotically, each is almost unaware of the other, for each is submerged in his/her own thoughts as each remembers a paradise lost: he, the plentitude of the Cruz home, she, the plenitude of her mother. He remembers the kitchen and foods; she recalls her mother's fragrance and warmth. In each case, the object of desire is definitively not heterosexual but rather of the same sex and gender: he thinks of Alejo and wants to caress his red truck; she thinks of her mother's warmth in bed (216–17/119–20).

Thus both sexual and temporal limitations are broken or refuted, for one overflows into the other; the past, as it is ritualistically (although not identically) repeated in the present, is and is not that present, and vice versa. Traditionally the present tense is employed in a novel to indicate the narrative moment, while the past tense is used to tell the story, report what happened. Yet in this novel the tenses fail or refuse to serve what have been considered their "normal" functions. There is often little temporal distinction between the past and the present tense. The function of verbal tenses in this novel is as much narrative as temporal. Tenses here distinguish narrative position and thus mark space (mask) as much as time, for the present tense is used to mark the limited perspective of the character whose consciousness is being reported. Since the present tense here mainly expresses the individual fantasies of the characters, it points to something of a mythic present—outside of time, unlimited, and continuous to the extent that human fantasy is continuous. Roland Barthes has noted that the narrative past tense is a mechanism that points to a security system inherent to literature insofar as it "expresses a closed, well-defined, sustantival act"; and, as a result, "the Novel has a name, it escapes the terror of an expression without laws."[30] A more literal translation of Barthes's comments in the original French would render the last phrase "the terror of a word without limit" rather than "of an expression without laws" and allow us to posit that the "Place without Limits" of the Spanish title is precisely the place of the word.

Even the setting of the novel highlights Donoso's continual challenge to traditional notions of limits, centers, and utopias. The brothel figuratively and literally rests on the border of society; it represents the maximum allowable deviation from the social norm. It does not extend beyond society's limitations—it exists with the tacit approval of society, but it does represent the last point before social bounds are overstepped. Also, in El Olivo, the brothel is physically located at the outer edge of a town that is located on the edge of "civilization," miles from the highway. The site of the brothel was once near the center of town, but that center has moved, just as the highway that was supposed to have passed through the town and link it to the outside world did not: "in better days this was downtown because of the railroad station. Now it's nothing more than a pasture divided by a line" (155/20).[31] For that reason, the final assault on Manuela, which signals the step beyond accepted behavior, takes place not in the brothel, where Manuela is allowed to live in relative peace, but out in the vineyards, beyond the limitations of the town, in the area of grapes, wine, symbolic sacrificial blood, at the boundary (Palos Canal) that marks Alejo's "place." But that line of water (again an image of fluidity) marks it ironically because this is only Manuela's perception. Alejo's "place" (like hell) is simultaneously everywhere and nowhere: everywhere since he controls all; nowhere since at this moment, when Manuela needs him, he is nowhere to be found. Only his dogs are physically present (although even their presence is signified only by sound, like the word), but they will likely attack Manuela and devour whatever remains of her/him.

The questions of sacrificial blood and Manuela's name, which in either its masculine or feminine form evokes that of Immanuel, Christ, underline the religious symbolism so prominent in the novel, which signals the cyclical ritual and has encouraged critics to read the novel as an allegory of the Creation, the Fall, and the death of God. In *Hell Has No Limits* Alejo Cruz is described as a god-like figure: "don Alejo arrived, like in a miracle, as if they had invoked him. Such a good man. Why he even looked like the Good Lord" (150/11). At another point the text notes that Manuela "knew that, thank God, Pancho Vega had other interests now, near Pelarco, where he was hauling grapeskins" (149/9). As the reader soon discovers, however, Alejo had procured the job for Pancho, and therefore, he is the "god" to thank. As an ironic center Alejo seems to control the inhabitants of El Olivo; it was he who gave (or sold) them the land, the town, and it is he who is now in the process of taking it away, as God gives and takes away. The name Cruz, meaning cross, in addition to its evocation of Christ, connotes the four cardinal points and their crossing, their center. Alejo ostensibly controls all four points, the world, of El Olivo. As he tells Pancho, who tries to escape his power, "I pull a lot of strings," (166/36) and, "if I gave you some freedom it was to see how you'd act, although knowing you like I do, I should have known better" (166/36). Paradoxically, as shall be demonstrated below, much of his power rests only in the word and in what the townspeople have chosen to believe in spite of other discourses to the contrary, for Alejo is ultimately as impotent as the rest of the characters. Although Ricardo Gutiérrez Mouat has correctly observed that Alejo is an inventor of illusions and his town is a fiction, to a large degree Alejo himself is an illusion, the text's principal fiction, created out of contradictory discourses embedded one within the other.[32] One fictional illusion mirrors and engenders another, for during the framework of the present of the novel, Sunday, Alejo's power has already ebbed. The center of the universe as it is known in El Olivo is corrupt and ineffectual. He is physically ill and soon to die. His political deals have failed, and El Olivo is never to become the town he had promised its inhabitants. He has not kept his word and has been unable to bring light and warmth in the form of electricity. The town is to be submerged in eternal darkness; it is more of a hell than the heaven Alejo had promised. The previous year Alejo arrived in the nick of time to save Manuela; this year s/he cannot cross over, leave the darkness and hell behind, and reach the illusory light and beneficence of Alejo and his heaven. The paradox is that even if s/he were to cross over, the other side is probably no different. As the epigraph makes clear, hell is everywhere; it goes with one. Thus Pancho stands outside the Cruz circle of light and idealizes it, while later Manuela decides to join the "center," the circle of light s/he observes through the doorway from her/his unpleasant vantage of the henhouse; but neither escapes from her/himself.

Although Georg Lukács has defined the novel, as a genre, as "a process of becoming," *Hell Has No Limits* defies that definition, for the characters travel in endless circles or spirals, forever doing the same things at the same time but never getting anywhere.[33] The beginning and the end of the novel are not what Lukács has called "significant landmarks along a clearly mapped road."[34] The road is clearly as unmarked and circular as the opening and closing episodes are arbitrary in terms of the "development" of the characters. The cold, dark, hell-like town, whose center has already moved, will be slowly devoured by the vineyards (nature, but nature under man's control). Limits and centers (which give the aura of stability and coherence) are created and then erased in El Olivo, just as these same qualities, which give stability and coherence to a mimetic work of art, are defamiliarized. All that will remain is language, the names of the characters, carved in stone on their graves. Even Manuela recognizes that one day they will bury him/her under a stone that will read "Manuel González Astica" (male), and eventually no one will remember "the great Manuela" (female) (182/61–62). The name, the sign, the word has the power to obliterate the self created by the name, the sign, the word.

The Locus of the Logos

Carefully considered, the characters of *Hell Has No Limits* exist only in a world of words, on both the figurative and the literal level, in the *énoncé* and the *énonciation* (to the limited extent that even that demarcation exists). "The place without limits" or boundaries is the place of language, the locus of the logos. Throughout the text it is language or the word that establishes boundaries and identity and then proves inadequate as it oversteps or blurs those boundaries. Thus the word tends to limit perception as it distracts from the center (in Donoso's terms, the self, face, or personality), which ultimately lacks the unambiguous unity and cohesion that the traditional reader expects and on which mimetic realism is based.[35] Like the traffic light in the center of town that does not work, all signs and signals fail to function in a simple, transparent fashion in this text. Nothing can be unequivocally labeled in the world of El Olivo, for everything exists pluralistically and in flux, if indeed only in words, while everything is itself and its opposite, in part because the word is never adequate to name the plurality. For example, Manuela is the epitome of a being who cannot be suitably labeled and who signals both X and not X. S/He is both and alternately male and female; her/his feminine clothing and mannerisms disguise or distract the gaze from his/her sizeable and potent mark of the male, yet that phallic signifier is made visible from time to time. Similarly, Pancho assumes the posture of the potent male and is labeled by

Manuela as a big brute (a *macho bruto* in Spanish), but at times he is nearly as homoerotic as Manuela. Japonesita is the madame of a brothel but a virgin. At the same time, her name, "Little Japanese Woman," is completely inappropriate. Diminuitive of her mother's name, it designates something she is not: a Japanese woman. Prepubescent, she is not a woman; she is also not Oriental. In fact, she even lacks the slanted eyes that gained her mother the nickname. And her mother's slanted eyes were not "natural," anatomical, genetic, but superimposed, created, part of her appearance: how her eyes looked after she became obese and after she penciled her eyebrows. In the imposition of the mother's nickname, Japonesa, one characteristic—and an inauthentic one at that, the product of appearance and artifice—is emphasized over others and taken as a sign of Orientalism while other identifying marks are elided by this name/ mask. Japonesita's eyes, like all else, are notable more for their dissimilarity from Japonesa's; as Pancho notes, Japonesita's eyes are more like Manuela's. Thus the signifier is temporally and spatially removed from its signified and must betray that signified by suggesting a coherence, a unity, and a linguistic motivation (as opposed to linguistic arbitrariness), all of which, Donoso proposes, do not exist. In some respect, then, we return to the question of limited vision and nearsightedness as discussed in chapter three, for not only do Japonesa's eyes appear to be slanted, they are also myopic (185/67). The characters (like readers) allow their "vision" to be framed or limited by the word.

The incongruities between word and referent are rampant in the text. The designator for the town created and presumably named by Alejo, Estación El Olivo, denotes an olive tree (Station The Olive Tree), but there are apparently no olive trees in the town—at least no reference is ever made to an olive tree. The houses of El Olivo are surrounded by oaks and a tall pine (224/132); there is a poplar grove (155/13); there is a pair of eucalyptus trees (155/13); there are also a pair of plane trees, an avenue of palms, and a giant oak (201/93).[36] But there is no olive tree, whose branch is an emblem of peace (of which there seems to be little in El Olivo). There is instead a multitude of vineyards, symbolic of wine, which in turn symbolizes sacrificial blood to be offered to the god, the projected or imagined creator, Alejo.

In a similar confusion of verbal designators, Japonesa is a prostitute, supposedly defined by her attraction to the male and her ability to attract the male, but in the erotic spectacle she performs with Manuela she assumes the role of the male and makes love to another "female." As is the case throughout the novel, the anatomical, sexual roles cannot change, but in that erotic scene Japonesa is the pursurer, the seducer (a male gender role).[37] And she manages to seduce Manuela (make him/her perform, in the erotic sense) only once she casts him/her in a feminine role and reacts to him/her *as if* s/he were female. At the beginning of the theatrical event Japonesa is not successful in arousing Manuela; arousal begins only once she calls him/her *mijita* (feminine) rather than *mijito* (masculine) and assures him/her, "I'm the man and you're the woman" (210/108). Not only is this theater within theater, but both of these "theaters" (their performance for Alejo and Japonesa's performance for Manuela, which elicits his sexual "performance") are predicated on language, the word. In part, at least, the words seduce Manuela, just as words "seduced" Japonesa into accepting the bet. In the first place, she accepted the bet because she did not believe Manuela's statement to the other men—"And he says he only uses it to piss" (194/81)—a statement that is already embedded discourse, repetition, quotation of a quotation. Second, she also accepted the bet because Alejo *said* that she could not seduce Manuela (194/82). At the same time, the terms of the bet are predicated on a play or manipulation of words: what Alejo "can" give Japonesa as opposed to what he is "willing" or "wants" to give her (194/82), a play on words that is imaged as a barrier that she cannot surmount (194/82).[38] Let us note too that Alejo finally accepts the bet and Japonesa's terms (which have already been shaped by his own) when she states, "they'll say you don't keep your promises. You build up a lot of hope and then, nothing . . ." (195/83). This effectively summarizes Alejo's discursive practices throughout the novel.

Like the other characters, both Manuela and Japonesa are motivated by language. The word motivates them to act and react (in the sense of both action and theater). In Pancho's case, the word that moves him to action on several occasions, including his violence against Manuela, as discussed above, is *maricón* (fag) or any comparable expression that denigrates his assumed masculinity. In an inverse but parallel fashion, Manuela finds nothing offensive about the term *maricón* but is offended by and reacts strongly to the label "degenerate" (189/72) and, as noted above, frequently reacts strongly to the word *papa* in the mouth of Japonesita. Morell has noted that in *Hell Has No Limits* the same words change value according to the character who pronounces them, but they also change value according to the character to whom they are addressed, as a result of the way in which they are interiorized and framed or embedded.[39]

Perhaps the question of language and its inadequacy to designate is most apparent in the character of Alejo. As suggested above, the reader, like the characters, is proffered significantly contradictory discourse in reference to Alejo. Although on the one hand he is viewed as a benevolent god or saviour, on the other he is imaged as maleficent, as a shady politician determined to destroy the town and as a person who does not keep his word. The question of whether he intends to destroy the town highlights the status of all knowledge in this text—linguistic creation that is always in a state of flux and self-contradiction. For example, as Japonesa first describes Alejo to Manuela, she acknowledges (albeit unwittingly) the dubious nature of his discourse: "always projects. Now he's selling us land . . . but I know him and I haven't fallen for it yet. According to him, everything's on its way up" (189/74). Yet her own discourse maintains a comparable level of ambiguity. First she offers the possibilities: "He's either a very good man or else he doesn't have time to worry about people like us" (189/74); then she openly contradicts herself: "he doesn't let himself get tied down. He has a wife, or course" (190/74). Still, it is this man they cannot categorize whom they expect to save them. As Manuela declares early in the text to Alejo, "If I die . . . it'll be all your fault" (161/29).

As one final example of this endless framing and embedding that engulfs and devours the mythic coherence and central force, let us examine the basis of Manuela's expectations of Alejo. During Manuela's final moments of consciousness, s/he demands that Alejo keep his word and protect him/her (224/131). If we examine the text, we discover that his "word," his promise to protect Manuela, which appears early in the text, actually comes from Misia Blanca, not Alejo: "Alejo is going to throw all the bad people out of town, just wait and see" (160/27). Alejo himself, on the same page, merely tells Manuela to watch out for Pancho because "they say" s/he has charmed Pancho. Of course, the "they say" proves to be "he says," but even more important is the fact that the promise of aid and salvation that ostensibly comes from Blanca is framed within Manuela's daydream and is in fact her/his own creation—an imagined script which s/he writes and directs and in which Alejo also speaks to Pancho, telling him to leave Manuela alone.

Thus *Hell Has No Limits* piles layers of words upon layers of words in a manner that undermines the traditional authority and reliability of the word (and in turn literature in general) and subtly queries, "Says who?" Both limits and centers are erased as Donoso posits that the linguistic masks that engulf and devour the self are our hell.

Notes

1. Carlos Fuentes is one of Mexico's foremost novelists. Most of his novels deal with the social and historical situation of the Mexican people today. His best known works include *La muerte de Artemio Cruz* (*The Death of Artemio Cruz*) (1964), *La región más transparente* (*Where the Air Is Clear*) (1958), and his recent *Gringo viejo* (*Old Gringo*) (1985), which was made into a movie in the United States.

2. The *latifundio* is a large estate, owned by a wealthy landowner but worked by the local peasants.

3. See Hernán Vidal, *José Donoso: Surrealismo y rebelión de los instintos* (San Antonio de Calonge, Spain: Aubi, 1972); Kirsten Nigro, "From *Criollismo* to the Grotesque: Approaches to José Donoso," in *Tradition and Renewal: Essays in Twentieth-Century Latin-American Literature and Culture*, ed. Merlin H. Forster (Urbana: University of Illinois Press, 1975), 208–32; and Hortensia Morell, *Composición expresionista en 'El lugar sin límites' de José Donoso* (Río Piedras: Universidad de Puerto Rico, 1986).

4. See Severo Sarduy, "Escritura/Transvestismo," *Mundo Nuevo* 20 (1968): 73.

5. Throughout this chapter I refer to Manuela with pronouns that simultaneously evoke both genders—s/he, his/her—to emphasize the character's duality, which is fundamental to Donoso's message, and to avoid privileging either the male or the female facet of her/his characterization.

6. Although contemporary thought and usage, as evidenced by calendars, mark Sunday as the first day of the week, biblically it is the seventh or last day of the week, the day on which God rested. This analogy can be carried one step further to the extent that the novel can be read (as it has been) as an allegory of the Creation and Fall. Just as God rested on the seventh day, Alejo (god figure in Estación El Olivo) "rests" and fails to come to Manuela's rescue (although the irony is that by the time s/he is dying, it is Monday, not Sunday).

7. Donoso had read and admired both novels by the time he wrote *Hell Has No Limits*.

8. For example, when Alejo is about to take leave of the brothel, where he has just tried to con Japonesita, he stands up only to have the shadow of his hat partially hide his face (180/58).

9. Colombian Gabriel García Márquez won the Nobel Prize for literature in 1982. His best known novel, *Cien años de soledad* (*One Hundred Years of Solitude*), allegorizes the history of Latin America in a masterful blend of realism and fantasy.

10. Donoso has been adamant about the fact that the novel concludes with Manuela's rape, but critics as early as Sarduy have tended to see Pancho Vega's violence toward Manuela as a substitution for the act of physical possession (72).

11. The expression used in Spanish, *montar* ("to mount"), dehumanizes Manuela and Japonesita since it is generally used with animals. In fact, it is the verb don Céspedes uses in chapter ten in reference to the four dogs and their repetitive reproduction (215/118), a description that bears significant similarity to the description of Pancho and Octavio's assault on Manuela. The verb also foregrounds the notions of space so prominent in the text as well as the hierarchies implied by those notions: he who mounts is up or above and superior or preferable to those down below, a position which is inferior or less desirable in Western thought.

12. A number of critics have pointed out the significance of the name of the canal, Palos, which translates into English as "sticks," a homonym of Styx, one of the five rivers of hell. What has not yet been noted, however, is that Styx is specifically the river of hate (from the Greek *stugein*). At the same time it was also the medium for oath-taking. An oath taken by the Styx was considered inviolable. In some myths the river also is connected to the god of wine, Bacchus, whose mother was destroyed as a result of the inviolable oath his father took at the river.

13. The similarities between these two moments are more apparent in the Spanish since similar epithets, *marica* and *maricón* (both referring to homosexuals or effeminate males), are used rather than the English translations of "sissy" at one point and "fag" at another (which suggest a differentiation that is nearly nonexistent in Spanish).

14. In rhetorical terms, Manuela's dress is ripped, raped, as s/he will be.

15. The nature of Moniquita's illness is ambiguous. Pancho calls it typhus, but there are sexual innuendos, especially in the Spanish: "I approach and I *touch* her and from the *tip of my body* with which I was *penetrating* the forest of *maleza* [which might be understood as undergrowth and thus symbolize her or which might be translated "pus" or "rotting substance"], fleeing, that *tip of my body drips* something and *wets me* and then I get typhus and she does too" (my translation of pages 97–98 in the Spanish edition and my emphasis; a slightly different translation can be found on page 204 in the English edition generally cited in this chapter).

16. Lost in the English translation is Octavio's play on words at the conclusion of his conversation with Alejo. His enunciations, "Con tanto fresco. . . . Frescos . . . tres . . . ." (99), which are translated into English, "There's a lot of fresh air here. . . . Tons . . . of fresh air . . ." (204–05), are also a reference to Alejo's brazenness and link him to Octavio and Pancho—as a *fresco*, a fresh or brazen person who defies social mores and decency and misbehaves in a daring way.

17. Some of the terms of engulfment or obliteration include "warm body surrounding me . . . me smothered in that flesh . . . woman's mouth searching . . . the way a pig roots . . . hunger for my mouth . . . biting . . . her heat devouring me . . . mutilated, bleeding inside of her . . . [that "you" no longer exists]" (208–10/106–09; bracketed words are my translation from the Spanish, omitted in the English edition).

18. This framing process that distances the source and by implication the authority is exemplified in Japonesa's description of current events to Manuela: "*dicen que decían*" (75), not rendered in the English translation (190) but literally "they say that they said."

19. I use the French terms *énoncé* and *énonciation* to distinguish between the linguistic act and the product of that act. *Énoncé* refers to what is said, the message conveyed, while *énonciation* refers to the act of expressing that message and the terms used to communicate that message.

20. The epigraph of *Hell Has No Limits* quotes some lines from Marlowe's *Doctor Faustus*. In them Mephostophilis [*sic*] states, "Hell hath no limits, nor is circumscribed / In one self place; but where we are is hell, / And where hell is, there we must ever be . . ." (149).

21. See *Composición expresionista*.

22. I make here the standard distinction between gender and sex. Sex is biological and is revealed by genitalia. Gender is social, learned, and often revealed by external dress or mannerisms, all of which are relatively easily altered.

23. See Victor Shklovsky, "Art as Technique," in *Russian Formalist Criticism: Four Essays*, trans. and ed. by Lee T. Lemon and Marion J. Reis (Lincoln: University of Nebraska Press, 1965), 3–24.

24. Indeed, Manuela's relationship with Japonesita is more like that of a mother than that of a father. They sleep together (a situation that society would deem intolerable were Manuela a "normal" father), s/he fixes the daughter's hair, s/he wants her to "find a man," etc.

25. If the reader accepts Japonesita's words in the final chapter (although there is probably no reason to privilege her words over any others), Manuela has lied (to others and him/herself) about being trapped in El Olivo and never leaving there. Her/his perception that s/he is dominated by Japonesita may be as unreliable as Pancho's perception of himself as a macho and Manuela's of herself as a woman.

26. I concur with Antonio Cornejo Polar that in this novel the permanent confusion between appearance and reality renders the dichotomy absurd. See Cornejo Polar, "José Donoso y los problemas de la nueva narrativa hispanoamericana," *Acta Litteraria Academiae Scientiarum Hungaricae* 17 (1975): 219.

27. In Spanish the verb employed is *rajar*, "to rend, cleave, or split," a verb that calls attention to the question of split personality and cracked mask.

28. As Kirsten Nigro notes, Pancho is threatened by the awareness that behind Manuela's feminine mask "there is a man as potent as he." Nigro, 224.

29. I concur with Morell (*Composición expresionista*) that the hell of the epigraph is not a moral condemnation of homosexuality. Instead, the term evokes the social structure within which all human beings function. Obviously, gender identification is one aspect of that structure.

30. Roland Barthes, *Writing Degree Zero and Elements of Semiology*, trans. Annette Lavers and Colin Smith (Boston: Beacon, 1967), 32.

31. The word in Spanish that means downtown also means center.

32. Ricardo Gutiérrez Mouat, *José Donoso: Impostura e impostación* (Gaithersburg, Md.: Hispamérica, 1983), 133.

33. Georg Lukács, *The Theory of the Novel*, trans. Anna Bostock (Cambridge, Mass.: MIT Press, 1971), 72.

34. Ibid., 81.

35. Although many of Donoso's texts predate those of many of the poststructuralist and postmodernist theoreticians, he shares with them their refutation of the humanist concept of subject or subjectivity (self), which presupposes "an essence at the heart of the individual which is unique, fixed, and coherent." Chris Weedon, *Feminist Practice and Poststructuralist Theory* (New York: Basil Blackwell, 1987), 32.

36. The Spanish *alameda*, which is translated "poplar grove," might have also been translated "town park" or "promenade."

37. Again I remind the reader that gender roles are learned, not innate. In Western society the male is taught to pursue and seduce the female.

38. Although the translation states, "There was no way of breaking him down. Forget it" (194), the Spanish says, "There was no way to *break the barrier*. Better not to think" (83, my translation; emphasis added).

39. *Composición expresionista*, 37.

CHAPTER SIX

The Obscene Bird of Night

Kaleidoscopic. Labyrinthine. Chaotic. Carnivallike. Nightmarish. Grotesque. These are just some of the terms that have been used to describe Donoso's masterpiece, *The Obscene Bird of Night,* a fantastic novel in both the literal and the colloquial senses of the word. Some eight years in the making, the book was completed only after Donoso's experiences under morphine during an ulcer operation. He claims to have written forty drafts of the novel before the final, "definitive" version, which appeared in 1970.[1] Although it was to be published by Seix Barral publishers of Spain and was expected to win the prestigious Biblioteca Breve prize, that coveted prize was eliminated before the novel's release. Then, just before the gala affair to launch the book, government censorship intervened, and no books were available for signing at the party. The novel was released in Spain after Donoso deleted a few sentences with double meanings.[2]

Unquestionably, all the terms listed above describe the novel to some degree. *The Obscene Bird of Night* is frequently difficult to read because of its hallucinatory nature and because it can (indeed, must) be read on a number of levels: one can (and should) look for profound meaning and at the same time, one can (and should) approach the novel as a game to be enjoyed (although the game is no doubt deadly serious).[3] Indeed, the diversity of critical interpretations the novel has inspired attests to both its greatness and its plurality. Just as Donoso claims to have written thousands of pages en route to the final version of the novel, it is probably no exaggeration to state that thousands of pages have been written about the text. I shall summarize some of the possible readings of the work and point out the strengths and weaknesses of each. Ultimately, no one of these readings can be conclusive since any single reading is necessarily only partial. The text not only encourages but demands multiple readings, all of which, even when taken as an opus, still cannot encompass the totality and complexity of Donoso's masterpiece.

Story, Plot, and Structure

As most critics have noted, *The Obscene Bird of Night*'s fantastic, ostensibly unstructured, and self-contradictory quality makes it difficult to summarize the novel. Everything metamorphoses and metaphorizes into its antithesis and yet paradoxically remains the same. The text is a compendium of contradictory discourse and literary modes, some ostensibly mimetic, others overtly figurative. Thus whatever one says about the novel is necessarily a simplification of the text's complexities. At the same time, any summary inevitably sets up a hierarchy and privileges one segment of the novel over others, a privileging that is nullified by the work itself. Within the novel no segment, no metaphor or image is privileged over another. Similarly, because the text continually questions and contradicts itself, the reader is given no reason to conclude that version *A* is more valid, truthful (or any of the other privileging adjectives one might use in reference to discourse) than any other. With that in mind, let us examine some of the story lines.

On the one hand, the novel juxtaposes the stories of two ostensibly separate but parallel spaces: the Casa de Ejercicios Espirituales de la Encarnación de la Chimba (The House of Spiritual Exercises of the Incarnation of the Chimba, hereafter referred to as the Casa) and the Rinconada (*rincón* + *nada* = "corner" + "nothing," the corner for those who have no place in the world or perhaps the corner that is not really there, that is really nothing). The Casa is an old convent that was the glory of the aristocracy in days past. Owned by the Azcoitía family, it was apparently built to house (enclose, protect, and imprison) one of the family's female ancestors, Inés, protagonist of both the legend of the child witch and that of the child saint. Since its foundation the convent has been bequeathed to the male descendants of the Azcoitía family. At the opening of the novel, the Archbishop is about to have the dilapidated Casa torn down. He had acquired control of the Casa when Jerónimo, the last male in the Azcoitía family line, signed the title over to the Church. He did so in part for want of a male descendant to inherit it but also, perhaps, to "punish" his wife (Inés) for her endeavors to have their mutual ancestor (also named Inés) canonized, or perhaps simply to prove he had the power to do so. At the start of the novel, the Casa has evolved into a maze of closed-off corridors and patios filled with the surplus possessions of wealthy families, things no longer desired nor desirable. All that remains in it are a handful of nuns; a group of old women (former servants of upper-class families who can no longer serve); a group of orphans with nowhere else to go; and Mudito, whose name means "little deaf-mute" and who works there serving the servants.

The story of the Casa is apparently narrated by Mudito, but his perspective, his narrating *I*, frequently metamorphoses and incarnates itself into and onto the place and perspective (the locus and the logos) of other characters. To call him a center of consciousness in the traditional sense, or even the narrator, for that matter (as readers have been wont to do), is therefore to simplify and to impose a structural hierarchy that does not exist in the novel. Sometimes the narrative "voice" is Mudito's, but sometimes it is Mudito's repetition or imitation of the voices of others; at yet other times it is impossible to discern the "origin" of the words.

The other spatial center of the novel is the Rinconada. That story seems to be narrated by Humberto, who may be a younger incarnation of Mudito or even his invention, though it is also possible that Mudito is an invention of Humberto. Nothing in this text of phantasmagoria ever unequivocally *is* or can be stated. The story of the Rinconada may either precede the story of the Casa or may simply be an invention. On the other hand, the Rinconada story may be "fact" and the Casa story invention, but it matters little, for one of Donoso's points is that this is a novel.[4] It is all invention, and our insistence on establishing a hierarchy among fictive inventions is absurd: one fiction cannot be more or less true than another.

The Rinconada also belonged to the Azcoitía family and was the first home of the oligarchic couple Jerónimo de Azcoitía and his wife, Inés Santillana, who is distantly related to the Azcoitías through the maternal line. It was the scene of their initial marital bliss (which, as might be expected, was not as blissful as appearance would have it). It was also the scene of their repeated attempts to procreate the much desired progeny to continue the male line of Azcoitías, which otherwise would die with Jerónimo. When that heir is finally born, if indeed he ever is and all is not just a figment of someone's imagination, the Rinconada (like the Casa) is converted into an asylum to protect and imprison him; for Boy, the son apparently engendered by the (magical) copulation between Inés and Humberto, or Peta (Inés's nanny, and a witch) and Jerónimo, or Inés and Jerónimo, or Peta and Humberto, is a monster.

Before that birth, Jerónimo, a member of the country's upper, ruling class, had lived a perfect, organized life that comfortably conformed to preestablished canons and structures; in many ways he might be seen as the emblem of classicism with its symmetry, order, and idealized forms. When Boy is born a monster, deformed in every way and a product of nature's chaos (or disregard for order), Jerónimo must face, perhaps for the first time, the "other side" of things, the possibility that one's natural inheritance is disorder, nonorder (as the epigraph posits). In an impressive reversal predicated on his desire to impose his power and convert disorder into order, he constructs a "new" world at the Rinconada and populates it with monsters. That is, not unlike the landlord in the legend of the child witch, he spreads his metaphoric patriarchal poncho and hides the chaos that does not conform nicely to the world as he has fashioned it (or would have it fashioned). He surrounds his son with levels and layers of other deformed beings (a structure that simultaneously mocks the world outside the Rinconada and proffers a distorted mirror reflection of it) so that he will grow up believing (indeed, "knowing") that monstrosity is the norm. To reinforce this idea he has all the statues, plants, and architecture at the estate deformed, inverted, or twisted to defy and deny classical form and symmetry.

In addition, Jerónimo places Humberto in the Rinconada to serve three functions. First, he will write the story of the Rinconada so the world will know how Jerónimo conquered the unconquerable, ordered the chaos, imposed art upon nature. That is, the world is to witness a double inversion not recognized as such, for Humberto will convert the chaos of monstrosity (paradoxically, in this case, already contained, planned, and structured) back into the ordered, symmetrical, classical forms of literature. Indeed, Humberto's failure in this project may well signal a commentary on the artistic project itself and its attempts to impose structures that may not preexist the literary/artistic gesture—a project Donoso has struggled to overcome in this text (with a significant degree of success, I would add). Second, Humberto, a humble would-be writer who admires Jerónimo and would like to be (just like) him will *be* Jerónimo at the Rinconada: he will administer in his place and be treated as if he were Jerónimo (as his incarnation). Third, he will be there to epitomize or incarnate the exception to the rule. He will be the only being who is not deformed, and thus he will embody (be) the abnormal, the monster.[5] In this way Donoso again dramatizes that everything is (embodies) its opposite: my monsters may be your beauties.

The tale of the Rinconada ends as Jerónimo dies, despised and mocked by the monsters whom he has afforded a "normal" life. The way he dies is significant: he drowns in the reflecting pool of his own creation while trying to rip from his face either the mask he donned to attend the monsters' masquerade party or the mask that is simply his own face (his monstrous role), reflected and then distorted in the monstrous Diana's reflecting pool—that is, distorted in the "mirror" of art. And, despite all the careful planning, structuring, and rewriting of the script so that abnormality is figured as the norm, Boy nonetheless has discovered his deviance from the (other) norm, as well as love and a fear of the outside world (which still threatens in spite of all the protective layers). To escape the pain of this knowledge, Boy will undergo surgery to extirpate from his brain all memory of his father and the outside world. The result will be a permanent state of limbo, but one that Donoso obliquely suggests may well mirror the one in which we all live as we refuse to recognize the artificiality of the constructs that shape our "world."

In the final chapter of the novel, Mudito is miraculously (re)born as an incarnation of the long-awaited savior baby. Then, wrapped and sewn into a burlap sack, he becomes smaller and smaller. In this respect, the fictional space of the novel—the burlap sack that contains the ostensible narrator and was earlier figured as an oppressive creation or creative space of the mind (199/245)—becomes smaller as the physical space of the novel (the number of pages to be read) becomes smaller. Thus content and form mirror each other. Finally, as the old women and orphans are about to depart, believing that they are going to heaven because they have been saved by the progeny of that immaculate conception and miraculous birth, hundreds of pumpkins are delivered. In the excitement (chaos, disorder) of the "gift," the burlap sack is forgotten, left behind in a corner of the Casa. Mudito (or some narrative voice) tries to escape from the sack into the outside world (tries to escape from the space of creation into the "real" world, which is another creation), where someone is waiting to tell him his name (to empower him and ensure his existence). His repeated attempts are frustrated as an old woman's hands sew up the holes as fast as he opens them. A few minutes, hours, days, or centuries later in this text in which time is ever expanding and contracting, never measurable by external standards, an old woman (perhaps the same one, perhaps not) makes her way through the jungle of pumpkin plants, whose seeds have miraculously propagated and proliferated, and "journeys" to the bank of a river. There the burlap sack and all its contents (perhaps Mudito or his manuscripts or the manuscript of this novel or just trash or society's discursive constructs) are burned; the ashes float away on the wind as the narrative voice metaphorically kicks not the bucket but a little tin cup that rolls away.

Such are some of the main threads of the novel. Clearly the problem with trying to speak of the novel is that everything self-destructs, disintegrates, or becomes its opposite: normal becomes (is) abnormal; religion becomes (is) demonic or pagan. Time also breaks down as past becomes present and present becomes past, and eventually it is irrelevant whether the action is past or present, whether an action precedes or postdates another, for it is all mythic, repetitive, the same yet ever different. As presented, both the present and the past exist only as narrative events and thus are equally fictitious. Similarly, the first-person pronoun no longer holds the position of authority traditionally accorded a narrator, for it ceases to designate *the* (a) narrator or center of consciousness. Indeed, the narrative first person is a compendium of voices; it is everywhere and nowhere, refusing to settle and be identified as it appropriates and juxtaposes the discourse of others (generally without benefit of the quotation marks that would signal the appropriation). In this manner the novel challenges the tenets of our epistemology and the basis of our knowledge as it proposes that narrators, both veritable and fictitious, inside and outside the novel, have always been creators of and created by discursive edifices—linguistic, grammatical, or syntactical. In this novel the narrative voice has overtly been disenfranchized and "knows" no more than the reader, in a discursive gesture in which one voice envelopes another (the words, knowledge, quotations of another), who in turn has done the same with yet another, ad infinitum.

Structurally, the text begins and ends with death, fire, and rhetoric. It opens with the death of Brígida (imaged as a "little flame that flickered out") and a telephone conversation that prefigures many of the novel's principal concerns. As might be expected, these motifs also prefigure the novel's ending—or endings, because it might be said that the novel has at least three endings. One is marked by the delivery of the "gift" (the pumpkins), promised by Raquel at the time of Brígida's death, and the exodus of the inhabitants of the Casa, who go off to what they believe is heaven but is really just another "home."[6] Yet this "ending" is followed by several more pages of text, narrated perhaps by the narrative voice (Mudito's?) enveloped in burlap sack and left behind at the Casa. While one narrative thread (that of the old women) ends with the exodus to a place that is other than what the characters believe it to be, another (that of Boy) had concluded two chapters earlier. Thus the narration continues beyond the two ostensible endings as time structures disintegrate, and the reader is left unable to fathom the quantity of time that passes between the various endings.

Even more significant is the fact that the narrative voice, traditionally the textual center of control, is here enveloped in the sack (the predominant motif of enclosing) and subject to outside control (the old hands that keep sewing up the holes—perhaps reminiscent of the traditional mimetic modes of literature that would feign to align themselves with some external reality). Finally that outside force, imaged as an old woman (epitome of the storyteller, the creator), obliterates the narrative voice as the contents of the sack are burned in the fire (another little flame that flickers out).[7] Thus the destiny on a rocky riverbed under the bridge that Mudito had foreseen for himself more than three hundred pages earlier (120–23/ 154–56), a destiny that follows his clamor for water (perhaps to put out the fire) (117/149), is finally realized: " . . . to depart without leaving a trace . . . [. . .] . . . without casting a shadow like a paper cutout" (123/ 156).[8] Even here, however, the narration and a narrative voice continue for five more sentences after the presumable destruction of the narrative voice. Who or what is narrating at the end as the fire consumes itself (438/ 542)? Is it the voice of an old woman that, as we were told at the beginning of chapter two, "slowly die[s] out, like the embers" (23/34)?[9] Are we to conclude that Mudito was right all along, that the old woman—the witch Peta—not only pursued him but also always controlled everything, including the tale we read and the tales interspersed among the tale we read, which like all else in the Casa have already and always been wrapped in infinite layers of packaging and discourse, layers that have lost their distinctions and hierarchies, for the old woman had already sewn or threaded them together?[10] Throughout, the reader is repeatedly warned about Peta's "narrative" powers and capacity to twist time and events as if in a prism (284/356, 181/222–23). Is the reader to understand that Mudito's voice, power, authority, like that of all the other male characters (and many of the females), is merely that afforded him by the female—the witch Peta?

The question of power requires a discussion of the sociopolitical as a thematic and structural thread. Before beginning that discussion, however, I would note that throughout this work Donoso, consciously or not, has embraced many of the premises of contemporary thought and philosophy proposed by poststructuralists and deconstructionists. As the discussion will demonstrate, Donoso echoes the theories of contemporary philosopher Jacques Derrida, as he first questions the artificial structures and hierarchies imposed by the binary nature of language and perception and then acknowledges the role of discourse in establishing and perpetuating those false hierarchies.[11] At the same time, and like both poststructuralists and deconstructionists, Donoso views the self or subjectivity as an ever fluctuating series of identities, produced by discourse and reconstituted each time the subject speaks. Thus being or self is a mask, but a mask that covers a void as it continually threatens to disintegrate.

The Sociopolitical Thread

The sociopolitical thread of the novel is frequently privileged by readers and critics who have interpreted it as a commentary on the sociopolitical situation in Chile or as the dramatization of the demise of an oligarchic, feudal family or society.[12] Certainly the novel does comment on the privileges of the aristocracy and their tendency to abuse those privileges. At the same time it questions the alliance between that socioeconomic class and the Church, a coalition which allows that class to "play god" and its members to compete among themselves for a terrestrial power that eventually projects itself (and is perceived) as a divine power over others and over life and death. What is fundamental, however, and what has frequently been overlooked by the novel's readers is that the external "reality," the sociopolitical structures that the novel supposedly mirrors or "represents," are already shown to be fictive constructs, engendered by discourse and the word. Thus, unlike the traditional mimetic novel, which posits "the existence of a reality to portray" (197/242), *The Obscene Bird of Night* recognizes that "reality" and the world are already repetition, discursive construct, rhetoric, and fiction. Indeed, chapter three of the novel, with its "history" of the chaplaincy, highlights the artificiality of "reality" and the duplicity of the discursive antitheses on which it is based and which are posited as demarcations between the spiritual and the worldly. For example, although the Casa is used by the Church, it remains the property of the family; and although the family *appears* indifferent to its existence, no father ever forgets to bequeath it to his son. In fact, the novel repeatedly emphasizes that things are never what they appear to be and that the smooth, ordered surface of things merely masks the chaotic underside. The reader is ever reminded that the ordered surface of "reality" is also an artificial construct (perpetuated by literature, discourse, rhetoric) designed to mask or distract the gaze from that "unsubdued forest" of the epigraph.

Similarly, Jerónimo's uncle, the Reverend Father Clemente de Azcoitía (the same Clemente who ends his days running naked through the Casa and terrifying the old women, who later pray that his clothes be returned to his ghost), highlights the rhetorical foundations as well as the alliance of Church and State (represented, in this case, by the politically-minded, aristocratic Azcoitía family). Making full use of the available rhetoric, Clemente assures Jerónimo that the latter's lack of interest in the politics of his country is a "blasphemy" that will "upset the foundations of society such as God created it, when He vested authority in us," making "us His representatives on earth" (141/174). He continues, further twisting and intertwining the political and celestial in a way that leaves no doubt about the power, authority, and divine right of the aristocracy: "We have to defend ourselves and defend God. . . . To defend your property with the help of politics is to defend God" (141/174). Note that the traditional hierarchy and priorities (God first, then man) have been discretely, almost imperceptibly, inverted: defending ourselves and our properties is placed before (above) defending God. Yet no one questions these statements, uttered as they are with conviction and authority. Obviously, such statements subtly underline the use of discourse or rhetoric to perpetuate the world as one would have it. The discursive gesture here mirrors and appropriates the order and authority that are presumably God's.

In this manner Donoso dramatizes the Church's role in politics while demonstrating that both institutions employ rhetoric (a distortion and reinvention of empirical reality) to position themselves as (mythic) centers of the universe and to impose a perception of that universe that is favorable to them, their position, and their further exploitation of that position. In this respect, both the aristocracy and the Church are presented as creators of fiction (authors), and surely the reader is to comprehend that what Jerónimo attempts at the Rinconada parallels what the Church and aristocracy have long accomplished: they have constructed a world in their own image and proffered themselves as the ideal or the standard while assuring themselves and others that all that does not reflect or belong to them is abnormal. The success of this project is manifest in Humberto and his father, who want nothing more than to assume Jerónimo's role or mask, never recognizing that it too is a fiction, a role he had been forced to assume, as is apparent in chapter ten. At the same time, chapter ten hints that Jerónimo mirrors Humberto, who would mirror him, in that he too had been seeking an identity—that is, to be somebody by finding a group to which he might belong—and had returned from Europe to his uncle's home and to conversation "more political than ecclesiastical, more worldly than mystical" (135/167) to find that place.

The novel's sociopolitical message is thus far less simplistic than might be imagined. Even in their positions as creators of a world of artifice, the upper classes lack the idealized existence (another artifice) imagined for them by the lower classes, for they too have been forced to assume a mask, a role. As Mudito notes, the people with faces and status were almost like those of the "faceless" lower classes and, like them, ate onions and sat in ugly chairs (78/102). Paradoxically, however, his father "knew" that such was not true because he read otherwise in the newspapers (78/102). Here, as later when Mudito mocks Damiana and Iris's belief in an external reality (102–8/131–38), he does so precisely by highlighting how their perception of the world is formulated by what they read in newspapers or hear embedded in the "they say." In this manner, Donoso continually destabilizes the authority of our knowledge and unmasks the shaky foundations (the vacuity or ellipsis) of all that we "know."

Nonetheless, the novel demonstrates that this distorsion of the world and the layering of fictions upon fictions by the powers that be (Church and aristocracy) produce monstrosity—to wit, Boy, in all his incarnations: young Jerónimo, Humberto, the monster son, all of whom are called Boy at some point. This multiplication and layering of fictions is predicated on maintaining others in ostensibly inferior positions (both economically and sociopolitically), but that exploitation disfigures and makes metaphoric monsters of both the users and the used. As early as his first days back from Europe, Jerónimo recognizes the monstrosity of this artificial edifice that presents itself as "natural" (as a product of nature rather than of society and discourse), for he wishes to leave the "New" World (an imitation mirroring the artifice of the "Old" World) and travel as far as possible away from these people "and from this world *which wants to convince me that I am nothing more than a monstrous figure, perhaps a dwarf, perhaps a hunchback or a wordy [blurred, obscure, extended] gargoyle"* (142/175; italicized portion omitted in English translation). A parallel image of the interdependence of exploitation and monstrosity is evoked several times in the repeated descriptions of the stained glass window in the Casa. In it the aristocracy surrounds (encloses, frames) the saints while the feet of the Immaculate Conception crush "the head of the *monster* holding the sphere of the world in his claws'' (257/324–25; emphasis added). Again the aristocracy (re)creates the world as it would have it (with them existing side by side with the saints), but paradoxically that world is held up and held together by monsters.[13] Earlier Humberto/Mudito assures the reader that he and Peta, "*grotesque monsters,* carried out our mission of *supporting* that new medallion, *holding it up* . . . like a pair of magnificent heraldic animals'' (186/228; emphasis added). In both cases the image is essentially unchanged; the social edifice is supported by the lower classes, imaged as monsters (deviants from the norm of aristocracy). Only the value judgment afforded the support system has varied. In the second example, the grotesque monsters are figuratively linked to magnificent heraldic animals. The monstrous and grotesque have become (are) magnificent and heraldic (announcing, proclaiming and making it so).[14]

In addition, the social structure (artificial and arbitrary though it may be) is sustained and perpetuated by means of possessions, given or stolen. Thus, after Brígida's death, Raquel's prime concern is for material goods: the nightgown she interjects into the opening phone conversation and the bicycle for which she detains the funeral procession. Even in death, Brígida will be ''used/employed'' by Raquel to preserve her space in the family mausoleum, ''keeping it warm . . . with her remains'' (6/15). When the possession cannot be attained ''naturally'' (that is, given or willed through the patrimony), it is stolen as Jerónimo (like the monsters) ''steals'' Humberto's wound and blood.

Similarly, all the characters desire to devour or engulf the others, to rob them of their possessions and, by implication, of their essence or being. The quest for the accumulation of material goods (often simply for the sake of possession, as evidenced among the old women) reaches its apogee in the question of the face and the name. The belief is that if one accumulates a suitable stockpile of material goods, one will be able to fashion a face, a mask, an identity—that is, one will ''be somebody.'' To be somebody thus is not only a question of role, having a niche in society, but also of economics and possession. A ''proper'' (in both senses of the word) name proves that one has been born into a ''proper'' family. In a sense it is a possession that indicates that the family has material goods as well as a social position to be inherited and later bequeathed to one's son. In the society portrayed, neither the name nor the material goods can be possessed by nor bequeathed through the female line. Only males bequeath or inherit properties, while the women are "possessed" (both sexually and in terms of ownership and control) by the men. Indeed, male power/potency is demonstrated by that possession: Jerónimo is more of a "man" if he erotically possesses Inés and other females as often and as potently as possible; he is more of an aristocrat if he marries someone suitably beautiful and wealthy, whose body and possessions will become his.[15]

In this sense women are presented as the servants are, as another group of the dispossessed. What they do "possess" and pass along to their daughters, however, are their "womanly" arts such as cooking and sewing, their stories (which perhaps are just the reverse side of the fictions men perpetuate), and their capacity to procreate. But, unlike the males' properties, which belong to someone and thus are truly "proper," the women's properties (arts and stories) belong to no one; the name, the author (but not the authority), is elided by and disappears into the "they say." And, unlike the males' endeavors, which produce wealth and material goods to be accumulated, the female arts produce consumable goods—foods to be eaten, household items and clothes to be used and worn out.[16]

As depicted here, the only other product or possession of the woman is the child she bears, but in the society portrayed even this is not "proper," that is, not hers. The child will bear the father's name and in this respect "belong to" him and his family.[17] Furthermore, the child will eventually be taken away from the mother: taken off to war or business, in the case of the male child; married off to a male, in the case of the female child. Thus *The Obscene Bird of Night* portrays the "monstrous" attempt on the part of the women to "repossess" the child.[18] This female response is manifested in two forms: the Immaculate Conception and the *imbunche*. Although one is officially endorsed (at least ostensibly) and the other is not (in a mirror reflection of the stories of the child witch and the child saint), both are products of the same drive to possess. In the Immaculate Conception, as modified and rewritten by the old women, the male's role in procreation is negated (elided); his name cannot be passed along. Without his name, the child cannot be considered the father's possession, and he (the child is always figured as a male) cannot be taken away from the mother and her cortege. On the contrary (and here is where the "new" Immaculate Conception varies most significantly from the official version), rather than abandoning the women for heaven and God (as Christ did the Marys), the child will take them with him. To some degree, then, the concept of the Immaculate Conception (especially as exaggerated and rewritten in this novel) is a response to the males' tendency to elide the females' role (property) once the birth has taken place.[19]

On the other hand, there is the *imbunche,* a mythic being with all orifices sewn up and without the use of its limbs. Predicated as it is on women's sewing skills, this myth allows the woman to "steal" back the child and promises one of two things: either that the child will forever be the female's possession, forever in her care and totally dependent on her, or that she might "graft [herself] onto the child . . . rejuvenating . . . and living a life other than the one [she had] already lived" (48/64)—perhaps a male life of possession rather than a female life of dispossession or rebirth instead of birth.[20]

Surely the central issue of the sociopolitical motifs is power in all its manifestations. Among other things, the novel must be read as a struggle to power. Bourgeois Humberto aspires to the power and prestige of aristocratic, oligarchic Jerónimo. The servants, in the form of the old women or Mudito/Humberto, aspire to the power of their masters. The females would seize the power held by the males. The old women of the Casa would invert the power of the Church (male dominated) and its rites by feminizing those rituals and establishing a strictly feminine society that excludes male participation except as the totally dependent (savior) child.

More closely examined, however, the text unmasks the inadequacy of traditional concepts of power along with its implicit dichotomies. Throughout, the powerful, the enfranchised, are less powerful than might be assumed, while the disenfranchised, the disempowered, are less powerless and impotent than might be concluded. Anticipating the theories of Michel Foucault, Donoso's text demonstrates that power is ubiquitous, multifarious, and always other than where or what it appears to be.[21] As is dramatically revealed, society is not simply divided into those with and those without power, as some groups would have us believe in order to shore up (fabricate) their own (dreams of) power. On the contrary, the power is everywhere, always plural and interdependent. In fact, Donoso posits that both power and powerlessness are masks that disguise either their antitheses or the vacuities that underlie them. Thus Mudito dons the mask of powerlessness (he says) to escape the demands of Peta and Jerónimo, while the female descendants of the Azcoitía family keep their eyes lowered "over the multicolored silk threads in the embroidery frame" and pretend to understand only unimportant things, effectively hiding their power (37/50).[22] Powerlessness is a disguised form of power, and vice versa.

As portrayed in *The Obscene Bird of Night,* each individual possesses and employs power, but at the same time each depends upon another to validate or ensure that power. Like all else in this text, power surges and ebbs, is and is not, is more and is less. Jerónimo needs Humberto to ensure his power and potency (both creative and procreative), as Humberto needs Jerónimo to ensure his. Servant of the servants, Mudito in some ways (but certainly not all) becomes the most powerful of all (50/66–67). Similarly, Raquel uses (has power over) Brígida, who in turn uses (has power over) her and makes Raquel the slave of her greed while seeming to maintain her role of subservience and impotence.

The novel emphasizes the ubiquitous and *masked* nature of power by opening precisely with the motif of Brígida's funeral and leading the reader (like the old women) to believe that Raquel had kept her word and underwritten the cost of the funeral that Brígida had craved (and, as we discover, planned down to its last detail). Ironically, however, in a gesture that mirrors the text's status as a series of wrappings, discourse piled on top of discourse, threads interwoven among others, Raquel's "word" proves to be Brígida's word (disguised as Raquel's, to be sure) as possession is openly inverted. "Raquel's word" or "promise" (4/5, 12/13) is Brígida's discursive invention (that Raquel would provide the funeral) and her imperative (she "ordered" or forced Raquel to see through the plans she had made).[23] Only much later in the text do we discover that the text (the word) has (mis)lead us, (mis)directed our gaze, and elided the important fact of Brígida's wealth (possession) and power over Raquel. Thus, Brígida not only financed her own funeral but also lied; she said that Raquel would do so and in the process created a complex narrative structure. As a result, readers enter a novelistic world in which the word is not to be trusted, in which the word makes us "see" things that are not there. In turn, we are reminded once again of the duplicitous nature of any discursive product: be it the "they say," novels, or even the newspapers and history books, which, as Mudito assures us, did not record the facts of Jerónimo's wound (164/202, 166/204). As the text repeatedly demonstrates, no one's word (not even that of the figure of authority—the historian or novelist) is to be trusted since the authority vested in one is already based on a power structure that is artificial and other than what it seems, other than what we have been told it is.[24]

Nonetheless, this version of Brígida's fortune and funeral may itself be the erroneous one. Although it is the version the reader tends to privilege (probably because it comes later—that is, follows the others spatially and temporally), the format and framework within which it is presented renders it suspect.[25] This version of Raquel as Brígida's victim appears in chapter nineteen, some 250 pages into the text. Ostensibly narrated by Raquel, it is framed by and embedded within what appears to be the discourse of Madre Benita, but, as is so often the case in this novel, the quotation marks are missing. If they were present, those quotation marks— conventional indicators of property and repetition—would locate the version's origin in an authoritative other (Raquel).[26] But since they are not, we cannot be sure whose discourse this is. What we do know is that it is surrounded by and interwoven with other threads of Madre Benita's discourse (which ultimately may be Mudito's or even Peta's) that are self-contradictory and hail back to the other major topics I have been discussing. The surrounding discourse focuses on the chapel that is to be deconsecrated (what was *said* to be sacred no longer is), Brígida's obsession (to put all the other servants to shame, to prove her superiority— mask and power), and theater/simulacrum (the funeral that was overly showy, theatrical).

At the same time, the two paragraphs call into question the vision of Madre Benita, the speaking subject. Madre Benita seems to be dreaming, daydreaming, hallucinating, imagining, but we are not sure. First she sees Menche trying to steal (again the question of possession) the lamp ("heartbeat," core of the Casa, which is soon to be a void). Menche, however, proves to be Father Azócar (who looks like Iris—a series of semblances and masks). Finally he is literally toppled from his elevated position (metaphoric power, authority) as he utters an expletive (discourse not proper to his role that should and will be excised, silenced). The question, then, is whether Madre Benita's appropriation of Brígida's words is any more proper (acceptable, correct) than Father Azócar's expletive or stealing of the lamp, whether her words are any more reliable (authorized, authoritative) than her "vision" of Menche, and whether yet something else has been elided, (censored, excised), as in Humberto's/Mudito's operations. While on the one hand this scene ties together the various threads of the text, it still refuses to privilege one version of the contradictory discourse over another since this rendition is ostensibly filtered through (interwoven into, enveloped within) the discourse of a character who "sees" what may not be there or who may be dreaming. What it does, however, is call both versions of Brígida's funeral into question by leaving open the possibility that something has been left out of both, that this story too is a product of multiple wrappings around a void.

Further inquiry into this apparently gratuitous fabrication on Brígida's part must be preceded by a consideration of the psychological thread of the novel.

The Psychological Thread

Because the division between the psychological and the sociopolitical threads of the novel is tenuous, the two areas frequently overlap, particularly in regard to role playing and power. When critics have emphasized the psychological, they have read *The Obscene Bird of Night* as a novel of vengeance or as the history of Mudito's resentment and frustration. Alternatively, the novel has been interpreted as an individual's search for identity and subsequent fear of obliteration or effacement—that is, as Mudito's/Humberto's (and by analogy Jerónimo's) struggle for survival and their denial of death, a denial and subsequent survival (immortality) that would be realized in the creation of either a son or a work of art. While not without merit, such readings implicitly privilege Humberto/Mudito, variously viewing him as crazy, resentful, frustrated, or vengeful but nonetheless as a mirror of a human being and as a center of consciousness through which the novel is filtered. Clearly this is a potentially dangerous critical stance since, as noted above, the novel refuses to privilege any one voice. Furthermore, to speak of characters in the traditional manner, as mirrors of human beings in the extratextual world, is to presume a unity and coherence of subjectivity that, as the text demonstrates, exist neither inside nor outside the novel.[27]

In *The Obscene Bird of Night,* each character reconstitutes itself each time it "speaks." In fact, Humberto/Mudito's *I* incorporates a series of other *I*'s, voices (discourse, words) or masks that are momentarily assumed and then discarded but are always interdependent: "you're what you are only for as long as the disguise lasts" (122/155). This appropriation of the voice (mask) of another to which I have already referred in the discussion of Madre Benita's appropriation of Raquel's words surfaces again in the telephone and dog track games in which Inés overtly assumes the voices and masks (clothing) of others. Thus the text vividly dramatizes the fluidity of subjectivity (self) that metamorphoses with each new, discursive mask, each new "exterior." Nonetheless, in the world of *The Obscene Bird* this exterior does not simply hide the former self or even some "interior"; on the contrary, it replaces it, becomes it as both inside and outside, container and contained.

In this respect, the dichotomy of inside and outside upon which any psychological study is implicitly based is invalidated in the novel. Outside is merely a projection of inside, which overlaps it, and vice versa, since both are linguistic constructs with no distinct line of demarcation. So the burlap sack, perhaps the final mask and permutation—security yet entrapment—is simultaneously both inside and outside, container and contained. As the text notes, prefiguring the final pages,

> he didn't know which of the two was reality, the one inside or the one outside, whether he'd invented what he thought or what he thought had invented what his eyes saw. It was a sealed world, stifling, *like living inside a sack* and trying to bite through the burlap to get out or let in air and find out if your destiny lies outside or inside *or somewhere else.*" (199/245; emphasis added)

The pronoun *he* here overtly refers to Jerónimo, but it might equally well apply to the reader, the author, or any character once one acknowledges the artificiality of the spatial metaphors "inside" and "outside." As the quotation proposes, reality is what we have been told it is; we see (perceive) what we have have been told is there ("they say") by some "authority" whose authority is another linguistic construct, ad infinitum. Those linguistic constructs give us a sense of security and safety, but they imprison us. Nevertheless, even our vision or what we "see" is not to be trusted, for as in earlier Donoso works, it all depends upon the light (hence the lengthy scene of Inés/Iris forever changing in the modulations of light in the chapel [409–10/509–10]) or the framework of previous discourse (all the inhabitants of the Casa "saw" Brígida's funeral; all the witnesses "saw" Jerónimo's wound).

In spite of the reservations I have expressed, the novel might still be said to proffer a thematic and structural thread that evokes or is analogous to the psychological, without privileging any character, without perceiving that character in the traditional sense, and without presuming some unity of subjectivity. The novel might be read as a dramatization of desire, which, as shall become apparent, is directly related to the question of power as discussed above, equally ubiquitous, multidirectional, and formulated on an absence or void.

What all the characters and the text itself have in common is unfulfilled and unfulfillable desire. Each wants, needs, quests for something in the present, past, or future (words that may simply represent different incarnations of desire). Thus, on the one hand, the desire/nostalgia of Humberto/Mudito to "be someone," to "be" Jerónimo, to possess Inés (erotically and materially) might be seen as one incarnation (metaphor) of the desire implicit in all discourse, signifiers, enunciations (and by implication in all speaking subjects) as they seek first to substitute the word for the thing and vice versa, and second, to "represent," to make present, what in fact does not exist in the present if it ever did exist and is not just an imagined ideal (often imaged as beauty), that is, more words: "decrepit images of beauty my longing creates and my desire destroys" (344/431). In another context, Mudito declares that he had created Inés so that he could touch beauty (378/470). Significantly, then, the Inés Mudito desires (like the Jerónimo he wanted to be) is already an artistic (re)creation, "luminous, unchangeable . . . the one you preserve in the photographs in the trunks you keep in your cell" (345/432), enclosed (imprisoned) in successive containers. Relegated to another time frame, the ideal is necessarily ever unattainable.

Like the world dramatized in the text, a world of discourse intertwined with more discourse, such a desire is based on an absence, that blank space that Madre Benita keeps finding at the "core" (which, of course, is another fiction) of Brígida's packages and that blank space readers keep finding at the "core," at the "truth," of the text and the legend of the child witch. In this respect, the text images desire as a drive, a quest (impossible though it is), to fill that emptiness, that blank which (like the scene behind the father's poncho) is the essence of all our discursive constructs, all our knowledge, indeed at the heart of our being (death, that ultimate void already latent in each living being). As a result, the emptiness and desire to fill it are frequently imaged as an insatiable hunger or as a fear of being devoured, swallowed up: "I'd pounce on him with the fury of a starved animal to sate myself with his things, to devour him until I had my fill" (365/456). Never satisfied, that desire succeeds only in shrouding the emptiness of the core by accumulating successive threads of invention, but it never fills or displaces the void. The text posits that our narrative constructs (the novel, the legend, the rhetoric of Church and State) are (to borrow the text's own organic metaphor) growths, like a cyst (36/50), like a Monster with polyps (286/358), which disguise the central vacuity, the elision that desire would but cannot fill or represent. The monster Boy would, in fact, eliminate his desire by cutting out part of his brain so that "the truth that was invented for [him] will be *the* truth" (389/485; Donoso's emphasis).

On the other hand, the text depicts the notion of triangular desire as developed by René Girard and links the question of desire to that of possession and power.[28] Each character desires (wants to possess or steal) what is another's, not for want of the thing itself but because the other has it, because it belongs to (is possessed by) the other. That is, object *X* is desirable not in or of itself, but because it is possessed by *Y*; the illusory value of the possessor is conferred on the object possessed. And, Girard adds, the character expects to be radically changed by the act of possession, for this triangular desire is ultimately a desire to be the/an other: Humberto expects that by/in possessing Inés (imaged as both desire and beauty incarnate) he will *be* Jerónimo.

The Donoso text takes Girard's theory of desire one step further, however, and demonstrates that, like the question of power, desire, too, is more complicated than it might appear. Here not only is the "illusory" value of the object of desire dependent on the possessor, but in turn the possessor's value, desire, must inversely be validated by the desire/envy of the dispossessed. Jerónimo depends on Humberto's desire/envy (frequently imaged as the empowering gaze) to maintain and perpetuate his own desire (and potency) and thus the desirability of the object of desire, hence the need for witnesses to assure us of our existence, for "everything will vanish if there are no eyes to watch us" (155/192). But as the story of Humberto's "stolen" wound suggests, things may vanish even if there are eyes to see. Witnesses do not always "see," or they may steal the power, appropriate with their gaze "the most important part," the imagined capacity for fulfillment.[29] Desire is not unidirectional and parasitic, as we have believed, but rather multidirectional and symbiotic (like the structures and webs of power). It is for that reason that Mudito is imaged not only as one who desires and perpetuates both Jerónimo's desire and the value of the object of desire (Inés), but also as the object of desire (Peta's) himself.

By virtue of its nature, desire is ever deferred, never fulfillable (the object is never attainable), as it feeds itself, ever imag(in)ing new objects, for "the greedy monster will bare its claws again to demand more and more and more" (59/79–80). One always desires what the other has and by implication what one does not have. Were one to possess the desired object, it would no longer be desirable; it would lose its value, thus the endlessly redoubled movement in the text: when one is outside one wants to be inside, and vice versa. Even the *imbunche,* visualized as the absence of desire (346/433) and into which the narrative voice would convert (has converted) itself at the end of the text, still paradoxically desires, needing (435/539), longing and wanting (436/540). The only difference is that now the desire is made concrete in the physical act of chewing through the layers of burlap. But here again and as always, the desire is frustrated. It is perhaps for this reason that desire is imaged as hell: "the hell of an existence where desire's compulsory . . . but I've never satisfied any desire" (410/510–11). Nonetheless, the possibility of fulfillment (freedom) is also hell: "I'm going to sate myself. . . . I'm free before this free woman: this is hell" (410/511). Desire is eliminated only with the destruction of the voice (the speaking subject, discourse) itself, only in silence and death, which are precisely the void it longed to fill.

Or is it? Brígida's desire and power continue after her death. Her lie, her discursive construct (like society's discursive constructs) outlives her. Thus we return to the power of the disenfranchised to make others "see"(with an envy or desire that validates one's own desire) what is not there, a simulacrum that again elides, effaces, the epigraph's "essential dearth into which the subject's root are plunged." But like the other forms of desire and power discussed above, Brígida's too must produce monsters: as Raquel complains to Madre Benita, the maid wanted "to convert me into the monster of love I'm not, that was the luxury she bought herself with her fortune" (250/316).

The Thread of Art and Narration

The Obscene Bird certainly manifests sociopolitical and psychological threads or messages, but those threads still depend on discourse and the word, not only in form (the word is used to communicate the message) but also in content (the message is about the word). Thus Donoso highlights the artifice upon which traditional literature (especially mimetic realism) has been based as it has elided the void it would disguise. Indeed, the reader might understand Brígida's packages as a metaphor for traditional literature: all wrapping with nothing, no univocal reality, no prior and privileged presence, at the core, a package that is viewed as "like" something else but that is ultimately only itself with no meaning beyond itself. Traditional literature is aptly described in the novel as "a world lost beyond other lost worlds beyond other lost worlds, one perfection supplanting the other, superannuated, perfection" (119/151), invented by an author (Humberto as a youth) who writes, for example, about women precisely because he does not know any. Although they pretend to reflect or stand as metaphors for something, his writing and the product of that activity are the materialization of a desire to displace a void.

As depicted in *The Obscene Bird of Night,* literature and the work of art offer smooth, ordered surfaces and present themselves as mirrors (as mimetic art has long done) as they hide the void, the underlying chaos, that lack of rhyme and reason (essential dearth) on which the universe is structured: "everything hidden just below or just beyond eye level" (18/28). Furthermore, the text posits that readers fail (refuse) to see and accept this void, lack, disorder, because like Madre Benita we do not want "to face this other unofficial [side], the one [which does not leave itself] open to view" (18/29), for we are all "tied up in these packages [we] want to force a meaning from because [we] respect human beings" (19/30). The text proposes that, like Madre Benita (often the imagined interlocutor), we seek (impose) correspondences and meaning (inside and outside the work of art) that may not be there. Thus, Iris/Gina models herself after the protagonists of cheap love stories and comic books (9–12/18–22), while the old women of the Casa see her in terms of the full-color picture of the Virgin (in Spanish, "that virgin," less specific than *the* Virgin) that Madre Benita has in her office (55/72). In both cases, supposed reality is viewed as a simile or metaphor for some earlier art form (already simile or metaphor).

As obliquely posited by the text, one of the principal desires, bidirectional as we shall see, on which all literature and art are based is that of the metaphor. Numerous critics have noted that in *The Obscene Bird of Night* everything is a metaphor for everything else, and everything becomes its opposite. The mirror reflects only the image already reflected in yet another mirror, and the distortion is endless. At the same time Solotorevsky has accurately viewed the novel as an endless process of "literalization."[30] Throughout the novel, what is first presented as simile becomes metaphor and then is accepted literally, *as if* it were fact, in a three-step process in which the "like" that forms the basis of the simile (and in turn the metaphor) is elided: Iris is pregnant *like* the Virgin Mary (46/61, 55/72); Iris is metaphorically the Virgin Mary (104–05/133–34); Iris is perceived literally as the Virgin Mary incarnate (258/325).[31] Similarly, Jerónimo is *like* a monster (142/175, but omitted in English translation); Jerónimo is metaphorically a monster (327/410, 397/493–94); Jerónimo is literally a monster and sees himself as such (399/496–97, 403–07/502–06). In this way Donoso demonstrates how art is based on metaphors and similes that are eventually elided or forgotten or simply disappear as we take art as an exact replica (the same thing, no longer just "like") of that entity. At the same time, because of the tendency of rhetorical tropes to emphasize similarity, significant differences are elided and effaced as we see only similarities. We forget that X is (or is like) Y only in terms of certain qualities. We forget that the differences outnumber the similarities and see only the latter. Thus the crowd saw only the similarities between Jerónimo's and Humberto's wounds, not the *significant* differences. And the text indirectly implies the most significant (and perhaps for that reason most frequently elided) difference may be precisely the difference within, for in this text everything "contains" and is a part of its opposite.[32] There is something monstrous about "normalcy"; power includes impotence; life includes death and in fact is a process of dying; beauty always carries the germ of ugliness and is dependent on it: Peta, the ugly old witch, had "always existed there, deep in the young Inés's beauty" (378/471).

Perhaps nowhere in this text is this intermingling of apparent antitheses more apparent than in chapter twenty-one. This chapter, like parts of chapter two and chapter twenty-five, functions as a guide and offers some of the possible ways in which one might read specifically the legends of the child saint and the child witch and by implication all texts. It shares with the rest of the text a number of repeated (and significant) motifs. What is known, the "truth" of the story, is based on the "they say," discourse that is embedded and encircled within, devoured by, the discourse of another and another, and without the authoritative (and authorizing) benefit of quotation marks. "Truth" becomes a composite of conflicting discourses that contain grains of "truth" (although where is never clear) but that cannot be reconciled (she was a saint; she was a witch) unless or until we accept that all is multifaceted and pluralistic and incorporates its own antithesis. At the same time, the legends (like all else) are predicated on absences: the coffin that cannot be found, the scene behind the poncho, the center (original patio) of the Casa that housed the earlier Inés. Like the legends, the novel, and Brígida's packages, the Casa, built to imprison the witch/saint, has continued to grow and proliferate around that absence, that void.[33] Ironically, and to reinforce the notion that everything here contains (and is contained by) its opposite, chapter twenty-one proffers just the kind of mimetic, realistic interpretation of the legend (the daughter's pregnancy) that Mudito had mocked in Damiana and Iris (102–08/ 131–38). Yet the text is specific about the fact that reality is art, art is reality, and both are structured around an inevitable void or abyss: "Yes. Victims. Protected by us . . . by our monstrosity, your son is king. We're the props: the painted backdrop, the flies, the papier-mâché heads, the masks. If they're withdrawn from around the central character who was born a king on stage . . . well, he'll be swallowed up by an abyss'' (394–95/491–92). Thus Mudito speaks for us all as we continue to ward off the abyss from our papier-mâché sets.

Notes

1. See Ronald Christ, "An Interview with José Donoso," *Partisan Review* 49, 1 (1982): 39.

2. It appears, however, that several thousand copies of the unexpurgated version were sent to Latin America prior to the intervention of the censors.

3. The less than orthodox discourse I employ throughout this chapter is (im)posed by the novel itself. Whenever readers encounter an expression similar to the one in the previous sentence, they should understand that the discourse is both posed by the text and imposed by it as a result of the text's own alternately surfacing and disappearing, independent and interconnecting thematic and structural threads.

4. Jerónimo notes that he gets the two places mixed up, for "they're all the same" (141/175).

5. Even this may not be valid since at another point in the text Raquel refers to him as deformed (318/395).

6. Here the reader will recall the question of the gift as discussed in chapters three and four.

7. Donoso seems to have taken another untraditional stance here by recognizing and imaging the storyteller as female. Although contemporary thought tends to envision authors and creators (including God) as male, it is, of course, the female who literally gives birth, creates, and who is charged with passing "knowledge" and other collective memories of her society on to her children, frequently by means of stories told around the fire or hearth—an image repeated multiple times in the novel, even at the conclusion.

8. The ellipses are both mine and Donoso's. I have included both to emphasize how the discourse structurally (indeed visually) reflects the message of the text, for the narrative voice here attempts to efface itself, elide itself, and disappear into the blank space of the ellipses.

It should be noted that Mudito's "end" is foreshadowed at other moments in the text. For example, in chapter two he talks about crossing the bridge, dropping down to the river and the slippery rocks where he cuts himself on a tin can and the wind swallows his voice and leaves him mute (33/45–46). At the same time, one might make an interesting comparison between Mudito's desired end and that of Andrés in *Coronation*, who is cutting out paper figures at the end of the novel.

9. In the Spanish, although the specific words employed are not the same as they are in English ("embers"), the images are similar. In both cases the voice is compared to a dying fire.

10. My suggestion, that this old woman who repeatedly mends the jute sack and prevents the voice's escape may be Peta, is encouraged by the references to her warty hands and gummy eyes and the observation that she "mends it as carefully as if she were embroidering initials on the finest batiste" (436/540). Earlier, when Jerónimo first met Peta, she was imaged as a heap of rags with warty hands, and she presented him with handkerchiefs of the finest batiste, embroidered with his initials (146–49/182–83).

Although this indeterminateness of layers and levels is most apparent near the end of the novel as the old woman joins the various levels by sewing up the holes the narrative voice has chewed in the jute sack, it is also present as early as the first chapter in the text. At that time, Madre Benita and Mudito enter Brígida's living quarters and unwrap the packages they find under the bed, which are a series of wrappings that make it impossible to distinguish what is wrapped and what is the wrapping. The image is repeated when, in a defiant gesture, Madre Benita clutches the shreds of tinfoil and restructures them into a ball—the wrapping or the wrapped, container or contained? The same is true in terms of the text as a whole in that what we have is not a story within a story so much as a series of stories, partially contained in others but not totally, for they overlap and their thematic and structural threads wind in and out of other stories, neither encompassing nor excluding them.

In this discussion I employ the notion of thematic and structural threads to avoid using the terms "layer" and "level," which imply a hierarchy of the container over the contained, or vice versa, a hierarchy I believe Donoso specifically intends to render null and void. At the same time, the text resorts to the image of thread or yard on more than one occasion, tying it to the notion of discourse: "Our voices, the endless ball of yarn that is our talk" (55/72); "the thread their voices are rolling into a ball that never grows" (32/44).

11. Jacques Derrida is one of the foremost philosophers of our time. His works, most notably *De la grammatologie* (*Of Grammatology*), propose a new way of thinking of, speaking about, and perceiving our world, which he sees as constructed on hierarchized, binary oppositions.

12. Although certainly not without some value, this interpretation is marked by its own mythic, wishful thinking since there is little reason to believe either that oligarchic families have died out or that the Chilean sociopolitical situation has changed significantly.

13. This artistic depiction encourages the perceiver to conclude that the two groups exist on the same hierarchal level. At the same time, however, it also underlines the mythos surrounding both groups, dependent upon written "history," repeatedly shown to be unreliable in this text.

14. Significantly, however, both images, that of monsters and that of magnificent ("sumptuous" in the Spanish) animals imply excess and variation from the norm, while the term heraldry is etymologically related to the question of power, authority, and force (the head of an army).

Later, however, Mudito declares that he and Inés are the heraldic beasts (379/471).

15. This situation, as proposed and portrayed in the novel, is somewhat less exaggerated in "real life," in which Spanish-American women may well be heirs to family properties that never become the property of the husband. The novel presents an exaggerated model, seeing the production of female progeny as a "curse" (37/50) and "incapable of passing on the family name. . . . The family was in danger of dying out and, with it, prebends, rights, properties, powers" (37/51).

16. The exception to this generality is Brígida, who has learned to play the "male" game, as it were, and amass a fortune.

17. Again the image presented in the novel is exaggerated, for Spanish-American women may well keep their maiden names, hyphenating them and passing them, along with the father's name, on to their children.

18. The reader is reminded here of Chepa's exaggerated need to be needed in *This Sunday* and of our discussion of motherhood in that chapter.

19. Inés is elided in the story of Boy's upbringing (perhaps having died in childbirth). The landowner's daughter is motherless. Humberto's mother is effectually portrayed as a shadow, sewing (producing practical but consumable goods) on the sidelines as the father and son dream center-stage. Mudito would eliminate Iris's body or "shell, that useless container" (101/129), once Boy is born. (See also 58/76 and 71/95 for references to the expendability of all but the issue of her womb.)

20. Chilean folklore, as cited in the novel, has it that witches steal babies and turn them into *imbunches*. Curiously, however, even the folklore cited in the novel is dependent on a linguistic inversion or elision; in earlier traditions the *imbunche* is the witch who steals the

children and sews up their orefices. Thus, in the contemporary tradition cited in the novel, again the female role as agent has been elided, and the term has come to designate the product not the producer.

One might carry the notion a step further and posit another association and a reversal of the elision: if Mudito is the *imbunche* in the end, he is also the witch and therefore another incarnation (invention) of Peta.

21. French philosopher Michel Foucault has studied the ubiquitous nature of power in Volume One of his *History of Sexuality,* trans. Robert Hurley (New York: Random House, 1978).

22. A similar portrayal of the disguised power of the Azcoitía women is proffered later in the text when the narrator posits that generations of them, all forgotten by the history books, wove a protective net around the Casa and prevented their husbands from disposing of it (302/376–77).

23. Here as in so many other places in the text, Donoso evokes the dictatorial power of the word, its capacity to impose a will or vision.

24. As William Rowe has noted, "Jerónimo's power as a member of the oligarchy [is] dependent on the system which disguises social power by making biological features its symbols, thus providing it with the alibi of nature. Illusion-creating is power. To be excluded from power is to find that someone else controls the 'reality principle.' " William Rowe, "José Donoso: *El obsceno pájaro de la noche* as Test Case for Psychoanalytic Interpretation," *Modern Language Review* 78 (1983): 591.

25. Western philosophical thought has taught us to view both narrative and history as linear and progressive; what comes later is an improvement on what preceded it.

26. A number of quotations (appropriations of the discourse of others) are included here without benefit of quotation marks: Father Azócar's, the old women's (collective "we"), Raquel's, that of the "I" who speaks to Raquel (perhaps Madre Benita). In this manner the discourse is presented as several times removed from its source.

27. As I have repeatedly insisted in my other articles on the novel, the characters of *The Obscene Bird of Night* are presented as such, that is, as groups of words only tenuously, if at all, connected to anything (such as people) outside the novel.

28. Contemporary French philosopher and literary critic René Girard proposed such a theory of desire first in his *Deceit, Desire, and the Novel,* trans. Yvonne Freccero (Baltimore: Johns Hopkins University Press, 1965). See especially pages 17, 53, and 83.

Pamela Bacarisse also notes the presence of desire à la Girard in "*El obsceno pájaro de la noche:* A Willed Process of Evasion," *Forum for Modern Language Studies* (Scotland) 15, 2 (1979): 114–29.

29. Humberto claims to have stolen the "most important part," Jerónimo's potency, his sex organ, in a metaphoric castration that is repeated near the end of the text when Inés/Iris castrates Mudito. Yet this castration too is immediately inverted, making her the victim, not the agent. Similarly, Mudito's potency is also imaged in his eyes, and he repeatedly insists that he has no sex.

At the same time, the castration scene might be read as another rendition of the relationship between Jerónimo and Inés, whose "obstinate menstrual blood has been denying" (154/ 190) him the offspring he desires. In this later scene, Iris's menstrual blood, imaged as Mudito's castration, also signals Mudito's past and future impotence: she is not pregnant, and the long-awaited baby has not been and cannot be born. Thus, Mudito is neither its father, as he believed, nor the son, the baby, as he has enacted. Here the dreams, the visions, of the metaphoric Oedipus are patently inventions of his self-inflicted blindness.

Many critics have insisted on imaging Iris's pregnancy as "hysterical," but all she is doing, like a child with a doll, is playing the role assigned to her. The episodes with Iris and the "virgin pregnancy" might be viewed as a contemporary reenactment of the legend of the saint/witch, a legend in the making.

30. See Myrna Solotorevsky, *José Donoso: Incursiones en su producción novelesca* (Valparaiso: Universidad Católica, 1983).

31. Curiously, Iris's image as the Virgin Mary is simultaneously affirmed and refuted: "But Iris isn't the Virgin Mary, it's an ordinary miraculous birth" (104/134; note the contradictory discourse within—ordinary, miraculous) and " 'Is Iris a virgin, then?' 'Why shouldn't she be one, Amalia? Brígida said so' " (105/134).

32. The term "difference within" is borrowed from Barbara Johnson, *The Critical Difference* (Baltimore: Johns Hopkins University Press, 1980).

33. The presentation of the Casa repeats this gesture of enveloping, engulfing. Originally located outside of town in the country, the Casa grew and expanded around the original patio (blank space, void no longer locatable), and the town grew and expanded around the Casa, devouring the farm lands (like the vineyards in *Hell Has No Limits*) and surrounding the Casa, making it the center of town, enclosed "like a cyst, mute and blind, in a very central section of the city" (36/50).

CHAPTER SEVEN

Sacred Families: Reading and Writing Power

Although *Tres novelitas burguesas* (*Sacred Families,* literally "Three Bourgeois Novellas"), published in 1973 by Seix Barral, returns to the shorter genres of Donoso's earlier career, it nonetheless proffers a prolongation and amplification of the themes and preoccupations of *The Obscene Bird of Night.* As was the case in his masterpiece, the major concerns of the trilogy are art and discourse, their power, and the effect they exercise on bourgeois society. In these works Donoso probes the instruments of representational art and shows them to be the same instruments by which our social structures are created.[1] Paradoxically, however, *Sacred Families* has elicited and surely will continue to inspire readings that perceive the text only in terms of social realism, for in it Donoso has abandoned, at least superficially, much of the overt fantasy and linguistic play of *The Obscene Bird.*[2] To the extent that *Sacred Families* has met readers' demands for an ostensibly realistic, representational portrayal of society, it should delight the casual reader and the student of history or sociology. Nonetheless, I suggest that the work's ostensible realism and mimesis are masks that undermine the representational mode they seem to support. In fact, Donoso spotlights the art and language that bring the text (and most of our social and psychological structures) into existence, challenges them, and undermines our belief in their ability to re-present. And more important, he subtly examines how those media lead us to perceive power where little exists, where, underlying the mask of power, there lies only an intrinsic impotence from which our attention has been diverted. Thus, like the works discussed in previous chapters (particularly *The Obscene Bird of Night*), *Sacred Families* must be read for its aesthetic as well as its psychological and sociological messages, for the trilogy of novellas again underscores the interrelations among art and society (social structures) while it highlights the inevitable, if at times disguised, artificiality of them all.

119

Donoso's preoccupation with language and art is already underscored in the titles of the individual stories; each refers to another work of art—linguistic, musical, or pictorial. "Chatanooga Choo-choo," the title of the first story, refers to a North American song of the big band era and thus to both a musical and a linguistic work of art. As Charles M. Tatum has noted, the song evokes the postwar evasionist period; that evasionism is reflected in both the words of the song and in the society portrayed.[3] "Green Atom Number Five" is the name of a painting by the protagonist of that story, and "Gaspard de la Nuit" refers to the musical composition by Ravel and indirectly to the prose poem of the same name by Aloysius Bertrand.[4] In each novella Donoso examines the status and nature of another work of art while he indirectly considers his own creation and being. At the same time each artistic creation to which he alludes is characterized by the fact that it is distanced in both time and mode from any "origin"; it is overtly artistic re-creation. Mauricio whistles "Gaspard de la Nuit," which repeats the musical composition for orchestra, which imitates the prose poem by Bertrand based on the work by Hoffmann. Anselmo and Ramón repeat the "Chatanooga Choo-choo" number performed earlier by Sylvia and Magdalena, which copies the 1940s creation, already conspicuously artificial and unconnected to a social reality. Similarly, the title of Roberto's painting highlights the fact that it is the fifth variation on the same theme. The additional fact that he had considered naming it according to its weight underscores the nonreferentiality, its distance from what we might label sociopolitical reality.

Plot and Technique/Being and Power

The setting of the stories of *Sacred Families* has moved from Chile to Barcelona and given the work a more cosmopolitan, international flavor. Although each narrative is autonomous (at least in terms of plot), each relies on the same cast of characters in that Barcelona setting. With the exception of Sylvia, a major character in both the first and the last narrative, the protagonists of each story are the secondary characters in the other stories, as each is placed in a slightly different context and viewed from a different perspective. Nonetheless, all the stories address the theme of possession and how individuals define themselves by means of possession or appropriation, socially, sexually, or linguistically.

"Chatanooga Choo-choo" recounts events of a week in the life of two Barcelona couples: Ramón and Sylvia, Magdalena and Anselmo. The action of the story (although not the narrative itself) begins at a social gathering, where Sylvia and Magdalena, identically dressed, perform a song-and-dance number to the North American tune "Chatanooga Choochoo." The story concludes a week later at a similar gathering when Anselmo and Ramón, also identically attired, perform the same song-and-dance number, demonstrating that the former controllers are now the controlled. In the interim we learn that Sylvia's face may be erased at any moment (reducing it to a blank, white ovoid) and repainted according to the desire of the man at hand. A night at the weekend home of Sylvia and Ramón leads Anselmo to have a brief affair with Sylvia, during which he paints and then erases her face and she steals his penis or makes it disappear. During the week that separates the two performances of "Chatanooga Choo-choo," Sylvia teaches Magdalena the technique of dismantling her husband when he becomes vexatious or superfluous. Thus in this narrative the identities of the characters—their existence, form, and personality—are directly and immediately dependent on the whim and will of another, while inversely and paradoxically each is responsible for shaping another, for providing the other with the "possessions" or features that mark being and personality. In this respect, power shifts according to context.

The males, who seem all-powerful early in the text as they erase and re-create Sylvia's features, prove less powerful than the reader may have imagined. In fact, our initial perception of their power is based to a large degree on our (mis)perception and unquestioning acceptance of the first, unilateral rendition of a situation that proves bilateral or even multilateral. Although the narrative technique proffers at least two narrative voices (Anselmo's and that of a more omniscient narrator who tells what Anselmo cannot), the beginning of the story is narrated by Anselmo. Because of the naturalness with which he paints the scene and presents his "point of view," it does not occur to the reader to distrust his rendition, his "superior" vision. Furthermore, since at the start we have no access to information other than Anselmo's narration, we accept his version and view him (and by implication Ramón) as powerful because he says he is. The suggestion is that as "readers" in the world, we tend to react the same way; we are deluded by the discursive spectacle of power and presume that power to be unilateral and unidirectional: we accept someone's rendition of events as fact because it has been presented as natural and indubitable, because someone has *said* that is how it is. Thus, paradoxically, while Donoso's characters and plot may not be totally representational, his technique is; that is, it accurately reflects how discourse functions in the world as it leads us to erroneous conclusions and perceptions of power. As we are afforded more information, however, we learn that the power is far less unilateral than Anselmo (and by implication we, as readers) had imagined. On the contrary, we soon discover that the women have the power to deprive the men of their penises (the emblem of manliness and being), to dismantle those men, and to pack them away until they have further need of them. What at the beginning of the story seemed "natural," an unalienable truth proffered by a reliable narrator, not only proves questionable but finally undermines the realistic deceit. In this manner Donoso leads us to question all our knowledge and sociopolitical "givens." Nonetheless, the overt "unnaturalness" of the final version (the dismantling of the men) precludes our facilely falling into another perceptual trap. It is not merely a matter of power's being inverted or changing hands (from male to female) in this story. Instead, our basic assumptions about power and being are challenged. Power is not either/or but and/also.

In terms of technique, it should be noted that while Anselmo narrates (that is, controls the discourse), he governs our perception, leading us to view him as all-powerful as he creates Sylvia by projecting his desires onto her, as Ramón did earlier, thus making her a mirror of their desires—paradoxically a reflection of the self. But even then their control is not absolute, for although she is their creation, Sylvia still exhibits some degree of autonomy and challenges their control. As a result she must be continually eliminated, erased (or at least her appendages, mouth, and facial features must be), so they can try again to (re)create the ideal embodiment of their desires, an embodiment with no desire apart from theirs. This task proves impossible. At the same time, although Anselmo thoroughly enjoys what he perceives as his absolute power, Sylvia's quasi powerlessness and helplessness necessarily convert him into her slave, for he must perform for her the tasks she cannot. Still, once her mouth and, by implication, her power of speech are returned to her, she begins to take control of the discourse and command him to perform menial tasks (close the curtains, repaint her face as she wants it), ever more demanding and less subtle. Eventually she fully "repossesses" the discourse when she "steals" his penis, and he is forced into relative silence (he cannot tell Magdalena about it and thus isolates himself from her), while she and Magdalena converse at will.[5] It is also at this point in the narrative that the other, ostensibly more omniscient narrator enters to supply a perception of power that differs significantly from Anselmo's.

In the next narrative, "Green Atom Number Five," Marta and Roberto, a childless upper-middle-class couple, have installed themselves in their "definitive apartment." They have gone to every expense and effort to surround themselves with perfect and carefully selected objects, which, they believe, reflect their unique personalities (like Sylvia's face). The irony, of course, is that these personalities are not "individual"; they are merely vacuous reflections of others' masks, for the rooms have been created and the objects combined with considerable influence from others, much as Sylvia's features were created by others and reflected their desires. As soon as everything in this apartment is finally and definitively positioned, various items begin to disappear or are stolen (like Anslemo's penis), beginning with Roberto's painting, "Green Atom Number Five." As the objects continue to vanish, Roberto and Marta discover that, after fifteen years of marriage, neither of them possesses anything that belongs to him or her alone; everything is shared (not unlike the male organs in "Chatanooga Choo-choo"). What they never realize is that not only is everything communal property, shared between the two of them, but that, in turn, all (like their language and aesthetic taste) is shared with the rest of their society: neither of them has anything that is unique, proper (belonging to the self), not shared with the rest of their group. Again possession and uniqueness are shams; a comforting mirage of proprietorship is provided by art and discourse. Furthermore, although Donoso focuses here on the theme of possession already predominant in some of his earlier works, in this novella he highlights the vacuity of possession for the sake of possession. Roberto's painting is of no value, but both characters want to be able to declare it theirs. Similarly, Roberto insists that the extra room *belongs* to him. Empty and thus devoid of any intrinsic or extrinsic value, it is nonetheless his mirror, for it metaphorically reflects his own emptiness and the fact that he has (possesses) nothing, not even a unique personality.

On the thematic level, the story concludes as the two have gotten lost in the streets and alleyways (a labyrinthian setting reminiscent of the conclusion of *This Sunday*) they entered in search of the painting. Having assaulted and robbed the taxi driver, they attack each other and are left naked, glaring at each other, "lacking memory of past or thought of future, possessing only this narrow present of violence in the midst of empty space'' (137/187). Deprived of their possessions (masks), they are reduced to emptiness and gratuitous violence.

Technically, however, the conclusion of the novella is significantly more complex and more open-ended than is immediately apparent, for discursively it reflects a desire for definitiveness, closure, and possession (like the apartment and life style of the bourgeois couple), while it underscores the lack thereof as it proffers multiple and perhaps self-contradictory alternatives (again in a reflection of "Chatanooga Choo-choo"): "like two animals that separate in the moment before pouncing on each other to destroy or to possess, or turn their backs and flee . . . into the vast, empty space'' (137/187–88). What stands out in this plot resolution is that it resolves little, for the ostensibly omniscient narrator fails to authorize a single, unequivocal explanation of events. Instead he offers a series of alternative, antithetical possibilities (signaled by "or") that would appear to be mutually exclusive. First, he states that the couple is *like* animals—a simile that calls attention to itself as it reminds us that the couple simultaneously are and are not animals. Surely, one characteristic that separates people from animals is that the latter cannot possess. Marta and Roberto are acting like animals—without possessions—but all along they have presented themselves with the mask or veneer of polite civilization—with possessions, which, like art and discourse, disguised their animal nature. But specifically, they are like animals that either separate only briefly before coming together or flee in separate directions, not coming together. If we opt for the first conjecture, that they will eventually come together, we are faced with yet two more alternatives: they come together to destroy or to possess. Ultimately, however, the ostensible antitheses here are conflated and dissolve, for their results are identical. Whether they hate and destroy or love and possess, they each metaphorically devour (dispossess) the other. And whether they devour the other or turn and flee they still find themselves alone, vulnerable, always surrounded and threatened by that vast, menacing other(ness), all that is outside the self and threatens to dispossess one of the possessions that mark and define self.

Mauricio, the protagonist of the final novella, "Gaspard de la Nuit," handles the problem by actively seeking dispossession before he is passively dispossessed. He has recently come to live with his mother, Sylvia (of the first narrative). Unconcerned about the things that interest other boys of his age, he passes his days whistling the Ravel composition "Gaspard de la Nuit" and wandering through the streets trying to entangle others in his tune: "it was audible music . . . halting the woman and proving to her that she wasn't free, that she was dependent on other powers; and from the frontier of her consciousness, Mauricio at last plunged into her . . . calling to her, commanding her" (159–60/215). The story concludes when Mauricio exchanges clothes and identities with the nameless street urchin (who looks like him) after their respective symbolic baptisms in the swamp and waterfalls. The unknown boy returns to Sylvia's apartment and proves to be the ideal son Sylvia needed to complete the cast of her bourgeois mother-son comedy (147/198). Thus Mauricio is freed of all identity and ties, free to pursue whatever it is he seeks, significantly freed of all artistic impulses as epitomized by his whistling. (After he exchanges identities he can no longer whistle "Gaspard de la Nuit.") One of the problems that Sylvia had sensed all along with Mauricio was his lack of desire to possess. He does not want anything (155/209). The "new" Mauricio (the street urchin), however, desires possessions and thus can be defined by Sylvia.

Although the reader might be inclined to view this conclusion as the most positive of the three, careful consideration of its language challenges such a perception. At the final encounter of the old Mauricio (now the nameless street urchin) and the new Mauricio (formerly the nameless street urchin), the latter recalls Sylvia's words "I don't know how you could stand life before, living there . . . " (205/273; Donoso's ellipsis). As he whistles his (in)famous music, that same "there" is recalled in the thoughts of the old Mauricio, who recognizes that he no longer needs to whistle and that he cannot limit himself, but should leave. Specifically, he is going to leave by *going down* to the *other side* and continuing to walk (beyond *there*) toward other things. But is it not precisely from there and those things (social possessions) that he was trying to escape? Has anything been achieved here other than the bidirectional illusion of possession/dispossession?

Like that of "Chatanooga Choo-choo," the narrative technique of "Gaspard de la Nuit" is predicated on a displacement of power as it subtly proffers more than one narrator or narrative position. At the same time, the text proffers numerous (often overlooked) narrative corrections which suggest that the situation might vary from what the discourse has initially posited. Although the opening words of the text take us back to the first novella as they recall Sylvia's artificiality (mirror, tweezers, *Vogue*), we soon learn that the ever changeable and malleable Sylvia is about to assume yet another "mask"—that of mother, a role still imposed by a male, this time her son Mauricio. Ironically, although the narrator notes that the latter's arrival threatens to fix Sylvia and Ramón's life into an artificial routine, his ensuing description of their present life specifically highlights its routine and artificiality; contrary to what the reader has been told, Mauricio would have no real effect on it. Later the narrative correction is more overt when the reference to "Ramón's ex-partner's wedding" is rectified to "Jaime Romeu's *daughter's* wedding" (141/192; Donoso's emphasis), a modification that subtly emphasizes the role of perspective in relation to possession: whose wedding is it, anyway? Similarly, because the tale opens with Sylvia and initially focuses on her (although she is not the narrator), we are likely to view her as the powerful, "castrating" mother who will metaphorically devour Mauricio, the innocent, dull, powerless son. But the narrative technique undermines this perception too; soon after we discover that although such is precisely his fear, in fact, his music is described as an aggression against her (and others) and threatens to devour her: "the circle Mauricio's music was tracing would conquer and devour her" (151/204). Power is indeed in the eyes of the beholder.

The narrative power play continues as the reader accompanies Mauricio on his walk and sees from his perspective. Now he is the powerful one who attempts to violate others with his music until, in an unexpected inversion of power, the man in the brown suit, whom he had believed he was stalking, stalks him. Mauricio becomes a "frightened boy running home to Mama" (165/222) when that man proves to be only a "counterfeiter who had made him believe he [Mauricio] was powerful" (165/221), that is, until the man he was about to execute in his music and imagination stares at him with sad eyes and indicates the rest room sign. Note that it only takes a look (and a reasonably impotent one at that) to "reawaken Mauricio's childlike vulnerability" (165/221). Again power shifts quickly and easily.

Perhaps even more significant in regard to the question of power in this narrative is the presence of Sylvia. Throughout the three narratives, the characters who believe they have power generally do not. Sylvia is the character in the first narrative who initially allows Anselmo and Ramón to believe they are powerful, when in fact she controls them as much as they control her. Might not the same be the case here? Has Mauricio accomplished anything at the end of "Gaspard de la Nuit," or have the covert powers of Sylvia merely led him to believe he is choosing a new life? After all, as the story concludes, she finally has the son she wanted (one in her own image). Again Donoso dramatizes the difficulty of identifying the source of power and the impossibility of finding it fixed and stable.

As in *The Obscene Bird,* then, two of the thematic concerns of *Sacred Families* are being and power. As has been demonstrated, being proves to be ever precarious, inherently superficial, and structured by the other person (who does or does not allow the self to continue to possess), while power inevitably proves to be other and differently located than what appearances had suggested. Thus the perfect object woman, the mannequin-like Sylvia of "Chatanooga Choo-choo," who can be dismantled and re-created at the whim and to the specifications of any male, proves to be far less helpless and controllable than was first suggested by the males' dreams of domination. In "Chatanooga Choo-choo" not only does she metamorphose from a silent, helpless blob of raw material to a potent being who gives orders and controls Anselmo's acts and "creativity" (as he paints her face), but she even manages to deprive him of his manliness and by implication his personhood by taking "away the thing that endowed [him] with gravity and unity as a person" (35/54)—his penis. In fact, in the first story she is literally the castrating mother/female that she is only metaphorically or covertly in the last. In either case, the reader is left to wonder how much of her castrating power is genuine (even within the fiction) and how much of it is imagined, a fear projected by the male characters (Mauricio and Anselmo). Donoso proposes that it may all be a question of point of view, of discursive structures and strategies imposed on society and supposed reality.

Indeed, all three narratives might be read as the literalization of the sociopsychological desires and fears already outlined in Donoso's previous works. "Chatanooga Choo-choo" dramatizes, first, the male desire for and fantasy of the object, adjective woman, pure decoration and dependency, created in his own image, fashioned for the whim of the moment. That dream of power, however, is followed by the dramatization of a fear of castration. Since the male organ is envisioned (imagined and imaged) as the center and essence of being or personhood, castration leads to that loss of personhood and individuality so feared in *The Obscene Bird of Night.*[6] What is particularly interesting about the novellas, however, is the fact that the males' fears, literally and figuratively realized in the first narrative but only potentially plotted in the last, are but inversions of their desires. "Green Atom Number Five" similarly literalizes the desire for something definitive and unchanging in a world of constant mutation but terminates in a frightening drama of loss, dispossession, and the metaphoric defrocking of the trappings of culture and civilization. Finally, "Gaspard de la Nuit" simultaneously dramatizes the desire to invade and violate the other (Mauricio's music) coupled with the fear of invasion and violations (Mauricio's perception of Sylvia's relationship to him). In this sense, the final novella circles back to the preoccupations of the first and demonstrates that desire and fear are predicated on perspective (thus the importance of narrative technique): one's desire to control another is the inverse (and by implication a mirror reflection) of the other's fear of that control. Similarly, one's "power" depends on another's "impotence," and vice versa. At the same time, "Gaspard de la Nuit" juxtaposes the dream (desire) to be someone and the dream (desire) to shed one's social role/mask and disappear into the freedom of nonidentity. Again it is all a question of perspective, point of view, where one is located or locates oneself in relation to power. And power is frequently imaged here in terms of the erotic, particularly in "Gaspard de la Nuit," in which Mauricio repeatedly seeks to "penetrate" or "plunge into" others but sees their relation to him as penetration of the reverse type: as violation or rape.

Reading the Writing

While students of naturalism or sociology may be offended by the "unrealistic" dismantling of the literary characters in "Chatanooga Choochoo," they will no doubt attribute it to a *representation* of a Freudian dream of power. On the other hand, we must not neglect the importance of Donoso's analysis of language and representation themselves. In this text the literary character, a linguistic entity recognized as such, is overtly portrayed as a more or less arbitrary conglomeration of signs—signs, words, elements of meaning, which can be joined, separated, or erased at will. In many respects this novella underscores Sylvia as the literary character par excellence, an artificial repetition of an artificial repetition. Just as any literary character can never be more than an arbitrary grouping of nouns, adjectives, and verbs, Sylvia is overtly just that. Her creators, like the author, work with her blank white face as they would use a blank sheet of paper (or in the pictorial arts, a blank canvas). The creators write or paint, with other materials, on that blank space and create the character and personality they desire (or so they believe). As her creator puts on her cosmetics, he formulates her and assigns her qualifying signifiers. Inasmuch as she is even called "the woman-adjective" (46/70), there obviously is little difference between the symbolic act of painting her face, making her up—and in this sense, providing her with specific modifiers—and that of fashioning her in language, again supplying her with adjectives that restrict and specify.

The individual facial features selected from *Vogue* magazine have no relation to Sylvia until they are grouped and labeled "Sylvia." Donoso here emphasizes that the literary character is a mere assembly of words and that, contrary to our traditional manner of viewing the literary character, the group of signs from which each character's signifiers are chosen is finite and shared. His metaphor here is not different from the one in *The Obscene Bird of Night* when the old women are left alone among the ruins of the desecrated chapel. In the rubble they find pieces of statues of saints, pieces that postdate earlier artistic creations that no longer exist in the same manner. Much like Anselmo and Ramón, the old women join these preterit particles and components to fashion new saints, new characters. In both cases what varies and what gives significance to the conglomeration is the context, the juxtaposition (the interrelation of the signifiers), as much as the signifiers themselves. Although the characters of the Donoso text naively seem to believe that these groups of signifiers are unique, the text emphasizes the nonunique nature of them and the entities that result. Because adjectives are finite in number and must be shared and repeated, the result is an entity that is neither distinctive nor unique.

Furthermore, the novellas in many ways might be seen as self-reading; that is, Donoso seems to be perusing and interpreting his own work as it progresses. Closely related to the detective novel (which he will pursue more overtly in *La misteriosa desaparición de la Marquesita de Loria*), in which the protagonist's primary function is to find the clues and "read"or interpret them, "Chatanooga Choo-choo" at first focuses on Anselmo, who, like the detective, repeatedly tries to discover the significance of various events and of the words of others. He finds as he "reads," however, that the words are not directly related to a single, specific referent and signification; instead, each group of words allows for multiple interpretations (again it all depends on context and perspective). For example, the story's beginning pages examine Anselmo's attempts to interpret the words of Sylvia:

> As she passed [the chops], Sylvia persisted. "And Magdalena's taste is so marvelous . . . [literally, "Magdalena has such good taste"]"
> Had she tasted it, [in Spanish, "her"]? Maybe because she was passing the meat as she said this, it flashed through my mind that she meant a "taste" of Magdalena's that only I knew; the idea made me retreat before the anthropophagous Sylvia. But of course she meant a different kind of "taste": the "taste" that governed our visit to the houses that afternoon, providing us with a com-

mon language; a "taste" related to aesthetic judgment, ordained by the social milieu in which we lived. (4/13)

As the detective-like story concludes, Donoso demonstrates that Anselmo has become both the narrator and the detective (reader of clues) as well as the murderer (to the extent that he "erases" Sylvia) and the murdered victim (to the extent that Magdalena disassembles him).

With a similar emphasis on the act of reading and interpreting clues (detective story motifs), "Green Atom Number Five" culminates in the events that result from the reading of a small piece of paper on which the title of the painting and its weight (Pound-Ounces 204) are written. The words are (mis)read as the address at which the painting will be found, and it is this (mis)interpretation that leads to the destructive chaos of the conclusion. What becomes clear, then, is that Marta and Roberto's problem is not just social (as critics have suggested) but also linguistic or semiotic. The couple has failed to see the arbitrary and ephemeral relation between the signifier (both in the sense of words and in the sense of objects, possessions that they want to "reflect" their personalities) and the signified. They have simplistically found a one-to-one relation between the signifier and signified and have overlooked the fact that the attempt to capture a definitive signifier is but the first step in the erasure of the signified. They have buried themselves in signifiers as the significance has disappeared, and they have failed to understand that their signs must be the essence of plurality insofar as each is shared not only by more than one referent but also by more than one speaker, writer, or reader. In this respect, it cannot be irrelevant that the title of the story, "Green Atom Number Five," signals the nonreferentiality (vacuity) of art. Roberto's painting of the same name (art within a work of art) is abstract, art for the sake of art. It does not pretend to "reflect" reality, to represent or "say" anything. It cannot be "read" because it has no message. Ostensibly its only functions are related to its context(s)—temporary at that. It functions as a possession and thus a mark of power and individuality, or it functions as the final touch that marks the completion of the apartment (again possession and individuality). But Donoso's message is clear: as a potential symbol, the painting is inevitably "misread" like all else in this world of surfaces and masks.

"Gaspard de la Nuit" evinces interesting similarities in regard to the question of reading. When Mauricio first arrives in Barcelona, Sylvia struggles to establish a relationship with him, only to discover that there is something about him that makes her uncomfortable. That "something," in fact, is that she cannot find the words with which to label him and describe him, words that would limit and define him. She cannot "read him." Similarly, Mauricio views her efforts to find signifiers that are applicable to him and will define him as violation, which he hates but which he simultaneously tries to inflict on others through his music. To this extent and in connection with the other two stories, Donoso presents Sylvia, in this novella, as the realistic, naturalistic writer or reader. She seeks the right words to name and describe events, people, objects, emotions, and sensations; but Mauricio, like Donoso himself, objects to this limitation.

Thus, while *Sacred Families* unquestionably portrays bourgeois society and its fantasies, it is simultaneously and equally concerned with its own existence and status as well as those of any linguistic or artistic creation. If Donoso were attempting only to portray society, there would have been no need to make the stories so closely interrelated. Surely the correspondence of characters in the narratives underscores a linguistic concern. The characters, groups of signifiers united by a proper noun or name, are repeated in the three novellas just as all signifiers, all adjectives, are inevitably repeated, shared, and exchangeable.

Concurrently, the format of separating the text into three stories rather than joining it into one more or less unified novel emphasizes the isolation of the literary sign. While superficially shared and repeated, like all signs, each character is nevertheless isolated and distinct due to the context in which he or she is presented. Ultimately the Sylvia of "Chatanooga Choochoo" bears no more resemblance to the Sylvia of "Gaspard de la Nuit" than if they were two distinctly named characters placed in similar social milieus. The mask worn (or face presented) by Sylvia in the first narrative must differ from that of the last narrative in spite of the repetition of the name and other signifiers because the context is different—in one she plays the femme fatale and in the other, the mother.

Surely Donoso's texts should not be understood simply as descriptions of external events. Instead, the trilogy is a self-portrait and a self-analysis—a text that reads itself as it is written. The author shows not only that language masks and violates but that it is ever interchangeable and supplemental because it can never be unique or proper (in the sense of possessed). Donoso is not just seeking the right words to describe what he has experienced; he is also trying to analyze an experience that is neither separate nor external but ultimately a part of and dependent on the process and the medium (language and discourse) itself. It is not a question of a transposition into words but an analysis of those words. In *Sacred Families*

Donoso has shown creation and commentary to be synchronic and indivisible.

Notes

1. As Griselda Pollock has noted, "[Art] is one of the social practices through which particular views of the world, definitions and identities for us to live are constructed, reproduced, and even redefined." Pollock, *Vision and Difference: Femininity, Feminism, and the Histories of Art* (New York: Routledge, 1988), 30.

2. Hortensia R. Morell's *José Donoso y el surrealismo: Tres novelitas burguesas* (Madrid: Pliegos, 1990), which came into my hands after the writing of this chapter, is an intelligent exception to the general rule. In it she focuses on how the text is in continual dialogue with the precepts of surrealism, thus suggesting, both implicitly and explicitly, that the goal of the text is not realism but rather an ironic questioning of bourgeois values.

3. Charles M. Tatum, "Enajenación, desintegración, y rebelión en *Tres novelitas burguesas*," *The American Hispanist* 2, 16 (1977): 13.

4. Aloysius Bertrand is the pseudonym of Jacques-Luis-Napoléon Bertrand, a French author born around 1807, from whom the French composer Maurice Ravel "borrowed" his title and the three sections of his composition for "Gaspard de la Nuit": Ondine (Water Nymph), Le Gibet (Gallows), and Scarbo (Beetle). Apparently, however, the Bertrand work had already been "borrowed" from German writer E. T. A. Hoffmann. For a detailed analysis of the relation among the works, see Hortensia R. Morrell, "El doble en 'Gaspard de la Nuit': José Donoso à la manière de Ravel, en imitación de Bertrand," *Revista de Estudios Hispánicos* 15 (1981): 211–220.

5. There is the suggestion that one of the reasons for the initial dismantling and erasing of her face by Ramón is that she talked too much in the presence of the two men. At the same time, Donoso seems to be mocking here some of the contemporary psychoanalytical theorists who view discourse as a phallic activity.

6. Donoso takes an almost feminist, perhaps tongue-in-check attitude here in regard to the sociopsychological value placed on the male organ by psychoanalysts such as Jung, Freud, and Lacan.

CHAPTER EIGHT

A *House in the Country:* (Up)Staging the Realist Deceit

During the five years that elapsed between the publication of *Sacred Families* (1973) and that of *Casa de campo* (*A House in the Country*) (1978), Donoso was living in Spain and working on a film script for the Italian producer Antonioni. Displeased with the script when it was completed, he began another, which developed into *A House in the Country.* He claims that the idea for the novel came to him during siesta hour on September 18, 1973, as he listened to the radio and discussed the September 11 military coup that had overthrown Marxist president Salvador Allende and imposed the military dictatorship of Augusto Pinochet in his homeland.[1] Juxtaposed with reports of the horrors of the dictatorship were the sounds of his and Vargas Llosa's children playing games forbidden at siesta hour.[2] The conjunction of the two "realities" cast political overtones on those "innocent" games, and *A House in the Country* was born.[3]

Although in the eyes of some readers *A House in the Country* may be less innovative and literarily adventurous than *The Obscene Bird of Night,* it is a logical continuation of Donoso's preoccupations, especially those concerning the ostensibly realistic or naturalistic modes of literature. As much as anything *A House in the Country* is about the "literature" we live, "literature" we pretend is reality/realism. In it Donoso overtly attacks and undermines the traditional realistic novel with its "good taste," the ornate *preciosismo,* or affectation, of Spanish-American modernism, *modernismo,* and the modern novel with its mask of narrative freedom that distracts attention from its underlying rules.[4] At the same time, Donoso's commentary on the "politics" and conventions of literature critiques the politics and conventions of society and history on a more grandiose scale (those of modern Latin America as well as those more universal), as he scathingly (if metaphorically) exposes the social and psychological structures that allow one group of people to exploit another and remain blind to that exploitation.

Story

A House in the Country encompasses several stories and narrative levels. On its most literal level the novel tells the story of an exaggeratedly wealthy family, the Venturas, who spend three months each summer at their *casa de campo* (country house).[5] The family, comprising thirteen adults and thirty-three children (two have died before the novel opens), visits the summer house each year for two reasons: to oversee the production of gold mined and hammered into thin laminas by the local natives (often labeled cannibals) and to preserve and strengthen familial rituals and bonds (mostly based on eroticism and betrayal). During the summer in which the novel opens, the adults of the family (*los grandes*) have decided to take a day trip to a mythical site in their vast lands, a paradisaic glade where the "waterfall plung[es] in rainbow wreaths to the lagoon, the pads of giant water lilies [are] strewn like lacquered islands over the water" (25/44).[6] The site is endowed with everything exotic and beautiful that nature might offer, but it has been idealized and decontaminated of any "natural" imperfections, unpleasantries, or ugliness. As will be discussed below, the invented site bears more resemblance to stylized artifice (especially *modernismo*) than it does to reality, perceived and imaged as it is in terms of paintings or painted designs (9/22, 140/203, 315/445). The children are left behind at the country house while the "army" of servants accompanies the adults to attend to their every need and protect them from hypothetical attacks by hypothetical cannibals. When the parents have departed, the only remaining adult, the supposedly crazy Adriano (husband of Balbina and father of Wenceslao), is released from the tower where he has been held since the deaths of his daughters. Once free, he enacts a series of reforms that violate the previous highly structured, inflexible oligarchic order: he promotes friendly relations with the natives and equality for all. Although Adriano's intentions are good and his ideals praiseworthy, his lack of practicality and inept leadership produce a "government" that fails dismally: hostile factions struggle for dominance; individuals are incapable of working together for the common good and, like the absent parents, are interested only in personal gain, survival, and power.

On their way back from the outing (at the end of the day that apparently is simultaneously a year), the adults encounter two of the children, Fabio and Casilda, who had earlier tried to escape with the family gold but had been outmaneuvered by another child, Malvina. After incisively negating the existence of the baby born to Casilda and questioning the credibility of their "confession" (which "confesses" what the parents want to hear, not truth or anything external to their closed, self-reflecting, and self-perpetuating world), the adults conclude that that cannibals *may* have taken over the country house. To quell the disorder (which even to their minds may not exist) and to (re)establish the previous order, theirs, "the one true order" (188/269), they send the "army" of servants to the house while they proceed to the city, postponing their return to the country until the following year.

Back at the house, the servants use suppression, terror, and torture to reestablish order and the family's traditional way of life. In this respect the "return" to the former order is artifice, a thin veil or disguise superimposed on the violence. The adults finally return to the country house (later that summer or the following summer) in the company of some foreigners to whom they plan to sell the property. After a short period of feigned elegance among the ruins and pretense that nothing has happened or changed here, the foreigners and family are joined by Malvina, who had earlier escaped with the family gold during the parents' "day" in the country. She and the foreigners beat the family at their own game of intrigue and betrayal, appropriate their possessions, and flee into the plain (perhaps never to be heard from again, but the reader cannot be sure). Many of the adults and the remaining servants also escape into the plain in pursuit of them, but according to our narrator "we know" that they all perished. The rest of the family (adults and children) is abandoned to what appears to be a sure death by asphyxiation in the thistledown that inundates and suffocates the area each year. The novel ends as the elegant and efficient ("discrete" in the English translation) figures in the trompe l'oeil of the ballroom, the optical illusion that epitomizes realistic art, step down from the fresco to "make sure they didn't die."

The Sociopolitical Reading

There can be little doubt that among the various interpretations one might afford *A House in the Country,* the least disputed is the political. Averse as he is to the oversimplification of his novels, even Donoso labels the work a political novel although he stipulates that it encompasses many levels.[7] As the early critic Ignacio Valente noted:

The allegory is obvious. The Ventura family is the dominant class. The servants are the military, the natives the proletariat, the myth of cannibalism is international communism. Uncle Adriano has points of contact with Allende, the entrance of the natives into the mansion signifies the triumph of the *Unidad Popular,* the resulting chaos is his three-year reign, the victory of the servants represents September 11; the Majordomo is a reference to General Pinochet, the foreigners point to the imperialism of the North, the successive episodes refer to the current regime with interrogations, torture, executions, disappeared.[8]

While there can be no doubt that *A House in the Country* does allegorize the Chilean sociopolitical situation, there are several problems with reading the novel strictly as a parable of Chile during the 1970s. First, the world of the novel is conspicuously exaggerated and presented as artifice, openly created and mediated by the whim of the ever-present narrator who insists on his godlike control over his imaginary creation. More important, while Adriano and his proposed reforms have points of contact with Salvador Allende and his government, as Valente noted (other critics have been more adamant and seen him as a symbol), the literary character demonstrates little similarity to the political figure when the former savagely kills his daughter, Mignon, after she has slaughtered her sister, Aída, in a "childish" and "innocent" imitation of the natives' ritualistic slaughtering of the pig.[9] And although, like Adriano, Allende may have been idealistic and in some respects politically ineffectual as a result, he was never presented (nor did he present himself) as a God/Christ figure (although others may have wanted to perceive him that way) in the hyperbolized manner in which Adriano is portrayed at the end of part one: "a resplendent figure draped in long robes, white-bearded. . . . 'God the Father Almighty' " (166/239). Furthermore, to insist on a one-to-one relationship between the novel and the political events in Chile during the 1970s is to ignore the novel's plurality and more universal implications and to fall into the trap of a realistic reading in the style of the eighteenth- and nineteenth-century roman à clef (a novel in which historical people and events are portrayed in a veiled manner, almost like a puzzle), so deplored by Donoso himself.

First, the sociopolitical system delineated in *A House in the Country* is surely not limited to Chile of the 1970s.[10] On the contrary, the novel should be read as an allegorical rendition of generic sociopolitical situations: revolution, counterrevolution, and repression in any place at any time, and perhaps more significantly, in any realm (whether national politics, interpersonal relations, art, language). To highlight the universality of the novel's events, Donoso treats time and space with ambiguity: Marulanda is not specifically located geographically; and temporal references to this century, the last, or others of the past are mingled.[11] Furthermore, while some of the speeches in the novel are almost literal transcriptions of speeches of Pinochet, many evoke those of any dictatorship or group trying to impose its point of view. In fact the following statements recall the Argentine military regime of the 1970s as much as the Chilean: "Disappeared, as in disappeared? Impossible . . . because there are no magicians around here to make him vanish in a puff of smoke" (242/344); "we are here to aid and protect you. Our mission is only temporary" (202/288).

Second, the text metaphorically evokes its own plurality. Indeed, it proffers a program for reading when it refers to the lances and accentuates their potential for multiple arrangement and interpretation: "When all of them had been freed from the mortar (how? when?) and had become separate units, inexchangeable elements that could nevertheless be grouped and regrouped in a thousand different ways" (78–79/118). The lances might be viewed as symbols of artistic elements, and their previous imprisonment in the mortar as a metaphor for rigid interpretation. Furthermore, Donoso dramatizes the relations of domination and, by implication, repression that are encountered within and among social classes or groups, however those groups might be constituted. As is illustrated in this novel, domination and repression are not solely the results of revolution or a change in the locus of hegemonic power; on the contrary, they are always present. Think for example of the ever-present Majordomo and his ubiquitous role in acts of repression (and at times violence) in spite of his changing individual features. Other examples of repression or undue cruelty that predate the "revolution" include Balbina's "repression" of Wenceslao's sexuality by dressing him like a girl and Olegario's rape (and blinding) of Celeste, who in turn exerts her more covert power over him by forcing him to attend to the menial details of her grooming ceremonies (a motif that posits an enigmatic link between the mask of machismo and underlying femininity reminiscent of *Hell Has No Limits*).[12] Even among the children there is an elite group that represses or performs acts of cruelty against the others.

At other times the potential for violence or cruelty is not carried to completion. In the opening pages Melania wants to burn Wenceslao. Olegario pretends to shoot Juvenal, but only in jest (94/139–40). Similarly, the parents' loving admonitions to their brood are tinged with threats of or wishes for violence: the children will go up in flames, crack their heads, or have to have their legs amputated (9/22). Thus Donoso demonstrates in *A House in the Country* that the coup d'état in Chile was not a unique, unprecedented, or fortuitous suspension of an institutionalized democratic order. On the contrary, as Carlos Cerda has noted, it was a form of exacerbated repression whose goal was to reinstitute the daily repression without which not even the most "democratic" way of life could function.[13] Repression is not the result of an order threatened; it is the fundamental principle upon which order is based. And it would appear, if Donoso is correct in his assessment, that none of us is immune to the allure of power and the exercise of repression and violence.

Furthermore, Donoso proposes that the urges toward domination and repression are the outgrowth of a struggle for power that is never original or unilateral but always imitative, repetitive, and multilateral. The power may change hands, but the oppressive structure remains constant as it does when either the children or the servants take over and repeat the power patterns (and often even the words) of the parents. For example, the game Mauro and his brothers play with the lances (which simultaneously is and is not a game in the traditional sense of the word) is a calculated assault on parental authority: their only purpose is to do something forbidden, against their parents' wishes (68/103). Still, as he discovers after they dig up (free) thirty-three lances (a number that corresponds to the number of children at the country house) and find the rest of them already freed, the "cause . . . far from marking him as an individual . . . would merely identify him with the preceding generations" (83/124). Similarly, at the conclusion of the novel Malvina forms a new elite that echoes the earlier parental one as well as that of the children. Yet the imitation is never simple or unidirectional, for although the Majordomo imitates the adults, he in turn is copied by Juan Pérez ("his frog voice imitating the Majordomo's booming tones" [216/306]), producing a simulation, though not a very good one, of a simulation (as so much of the world of Marulanda is). Perhaps for this reason all attempts at "revolution" (political or artistic) are destined to failure in the Donosian world, based as they are on the repetition and reproduction of the old patterns.

As a result, games and their manifestation as theater are especially significant, and indeed threatening, in this novel. In their games in which they would empower themselves, the children mirror the adults and repeat their repressive structures even though, as children, they may not comprehend why they do what they do, why they emulate the adults, any more than Mauro and the other children comprehend the frantic (and perhaps pointless) activity of pulling up lances (84–85/126–127). Furthermore, in the children's principal game, *La Marquise Est Sortie à Cinq Heures* (discussed in more detail below), they imitate the intrigues and power of the adults; they play at being grown up, when they will, they imagine, cease to be vulnerable to doubts (62/95).[14] In this game of mimesis they rehearse for the roles they will assume and the power they will exercise when they replace their parents at some future moment. But at the same time, their game functions as a segment of life (a shield) they can place between themselves and the parental laws and thereby not have to rebel against their authority (62/95).[15] In other words, the game, play (in this case, a form of theater), duplicates parental structures while providing a buffer to them, allowing the players to believe they are not dominated by those structures that, paradoxically, they copy. The game allows them to assume (pseudo) power and pretend/believe they wield the power that is in fact wielded over them. The game, then, not unlike the children themselves, is anything but innocent as it serves a bidirectional function and reproduces the repression even as it would nullify it. Still, the fact that the game (*La Marquise*) is referred to as life highlights how little difference there is between life and a game, how artificial and theatrical "life" is at Marulanda.

Within this framework, Mignon's ritualistic slaying and roasting of Aída takes on a poignant significance, for it is a game-like reenactment of the ceremony she witnesses. And the girls are more accurate than they (or we) realize when they play with the pig before it is killed and shout, "We're cannibals" (51/81), or earlier when Mignon tells Aída that the cannibals are coming to eat her and then sets her on fire—that is, metaphorically attempts to consume her (45/72). When the family attributes the death of the two girls to the influence of the cannibals, it fails to recognize that the "cannibal" (potential for violence, cruelty, and metaphorically "devouring" the other) is within each of us. For example, Juan Pérez, so trenchant in his campaign against the natives, is actually one of them (Agapito, his brother, tells Wenceslao that his mother was the daughter of a woman from there [270/382]). Even more revealing, Mignon's replication of the sacrificial ceremony echoes the children's game in that it is at least partly the result of her earlier double exclusion. Because she was ugly, she was loved by neither mother nor father, and when the pig's head was served, her father, Adriano, excluded her from the ceremony because of her sex: "Wenceslao and I, *who are men*, will eat" (53/83; emphasis added).

Much of the intrigue, betrayal, repression, and violence dramatized throughout the novel originates in the individual's sense (valid or not) of exclusion: because Malvina was excluded from the family wealth (ostracized because of her illegitimacy), she plotted their overthrow; because Casilda was excluded from the vault of gold and from her father's affection, she engineered the theft; because Adriano was excluded from the intimate elite of the family, he attempted to overthrow all they symbolized; and because Juan Pérez could not get Adriano to acknowledge his existence, he felt excluded from the latter's world and supported the counterrevolution. The irony is that in each case the "overthrow" of the norm reproduces the same hegemonic structure; the only difference is that the previously excluded person is now included, indeed made central. Is Donoso not proposing that sociopolitical and historical events are motivated precisely by the very human, if indeed petty and ignoble, sense of exclusion and disenfranchizement and by the sometimes violent need to perceive the self as central? And are our narrator's rebellion against literary "good taste" and his overt exercise of power not endeavors to centralize himself?

As presented in *A House in the Country*, revolutions are motivated less by ideological positions than by petty emotions, envy, and desire for personal gain. As Juan Pérez recognizes, the Venturas posit the conflict as an ideological confrontation in order to regain what they fear has been taken from them (210/298); that is, it is the discursive reformulation of greed (envy and desire for possession) and exclusivity (which would include the self by excluding the other) in the name of ideological differences. Although each character has a different motive for supporting the revolution or the counterrevolution, all are egocentric and ignoble. In addition, the characters join the action in part to have a role. As Donoso so frequently underscores in this mise en scène of theatricality which is the novel, neither the children nor the adults can long tolerate being spectators rather than actors, preferably protagonists (156–57, 179/226, 256). In this way, they mirror the narrator, who will not remain quietly in the background observing; rather he must continually thrust himself into the foreground and assume a visible, central role.

Even Adriano, whom the reader might like to perceive as something of a hero with his idealistic goals, reveals himself to be as power-hungry as the rest. Viewed by the family as an eccentric outsider, he is treated as a god or savior by the natives. Nonetheless, he is forced to admit his less than noble motivation when Balbina accuses him of eating the natives' ritual food only to fulfill his range of possibilities as a god and not risk his power (53/83), words which, not unlike the knife that slit open the pig's belly (52/82) or Wenceslao's knife that slit open his straitjacket (29/50), "slit open his secret arrogance . . . exposing . . . the viscera of his messianic ambition" (53/83). Similarly, much later in the text, our narrator assures us that Wenceslao's disillusion with his father stems from his realization that Adriano is tormented not so much with finding a suitable solution to their problems as with "his own tarnished image" (327/462).

Still, the system portrayed in *A House in the Country* is even more complex than is immediately apparent. As is the case in *The Obscene Bird of Night,* not only is the power (source of repression) multilateral, but it is often other than what and where it seems to be. The lines of power are rarely straightforward and visible; on the contrary, they are diffuse, multifarious, and polymorphous. When power is absolute (or so appears, like the Majordomo's), it is only temporary (he has power only after curfew). In the same vein, who really controls or represses the other: Wenceslao or his mother, Balbina or Adriano, Lidia or Hermógenes, Celeste or Olegario, the narrator or his character? If even the Majordomo, with his ostensibly absolute power after curfew, is still subject to the frown of the adults (190/272) or the bribery of the children (24/42), the adults to the new power of the foreigners, and the family to the whims of "nature," to whom or what is the narrator still subject? What is he repressing or what is repressing him?

Furthermore, the repression and violence themselves are frequently exercised not by the person with the ultimate authority (if such a person exists independent of a discursive construct) but by overly zealous intermediaries who emulate the authorities. The parents do not directly repress the children; that "dirty work" is left to the servants (both before and after the "revolution") and is not "seen" (like what exists behind the dark curtain so often dropped) by those who actually wield the power and would pretend that they do not have to repress others to maintain their power and position. In turn, the Majordomo seldom performs the killing and torture that take place after the reconquest; he leaves those tasks to his lackeys (Juan Pérez among them), just as Adriano leaves much of the "enforcement" to the overly fervent Mauro.[16]

Thus the power, if indeed frequently disguised by appearances or hidden by the dark curtain, is anything but unilateral. While the adults' power and role in the repression of the children may not be immediately visible, the fact that the repression is left in the hands of the servants confers power on them. In turn, by considering the children a threat or in need of repression, the parents indirectly acknowledge that they may not be as powerless as they appear: "what if, down deep, the children *didn't* love them?" (9/21– 22; Donoso's emphasis). To some degree the parents' repression of the children, enacted by the servants, is a result of their fear of them, based on the children's potential to wield power and exclude them rather than allowing themselves to be excluded—a potential to wield power that will be realized in time but that meanwhile must be kept both hidden and repressed.

Naturalism (Mimesis) and *Modernismo*

In spite of Donoso's obvious interest in the questions of revolution and counterrevolution in the sociopolitical realm, those are not the only revolutions and counterrevolutions, nor is the sociopolitical the only repressive, rigid structure he addresses in *A House in the Country*. Of equal concern to him are the revolutions, counterrevolutions, and repressive structures of art, particularly literature. As students of literature soon discover, literary schools or movements are generally imaged as a pendulum that swings from one side to the other as one set of rules or standards is rejected in favor of another (usually antithetical) set, also replaced in due time as the pendulum swings back to its "original" point (just as the sociopolitical counterrevolution restores, superficially at least, the prior status quo).[17] Donoso posits in this novel that literary "revolutions" are as unproductive and superficial as the sociopolitical, for they are necessarily based on recurring structures, artificial antitheses between reality and fantasy, form and content, and repressive (if disguised) politics.

More specifically Donoso has chosen to utilize the techniques and forms of two twentieth-century Spanish-American literary movements generally considered diametrically opposed: *modernismo* (with its inherent *preciosismo*) and naturalism or realism.[18] Spanish–American *modernismo,* not to be confused with non-Hispanic, twentieth-century modernism, was made popular at the turn of the century by Nicaraguan poet Rubén Darío. Newmark defines it as "a reaction against naturalism in literature, against bourgeois conformity and against fossilized standards. It strove for new values and for a renewed spirituality. Creativity, individualism and subjectivity were its hallmarks. . . . [It began] under French influence with an ivory-tower esthetics of art for art's sake."[19] It was characterized by its exoticism (swans, princesses, nymphs) and detailed, sensuous descriptions. Realism, on the other hand, rejected the exoticism, subjectivity, sentimentalism, and idealism and painted the everyday world and familiar experiences with verisimilitude, often with the goal of correcting social wrongs. Its cousin, naturalism, also decreed that works of literature should project an accurate and objective picture of reality, but it focused more on the sordid and the ugly or unpleasant (censored or repressed in other art forms) as well as on the forces of nature (often imaged as malevolent) in society and human beings.

In *A House in the Country* Donoso juxtaposes and intricately interweaves the two modes of literature, both thematically and stylistically. He demonstrates first that the two are not as antithetical as they might seem and second that they are often employed in contradiction to their express goals.[20] The differences between the two modes are not so much a question of essence as of combination, the manner in which the integral elements are joined (style). Think, for example, of Casilda and Colomba, twins endowed with the same features, harmoniously combined in one and clumsily in the other, making Colomba beautiful (perhaps like *modernismo*) and Casilda ugly (perhaps like naturalism). It is all a matter of style, combination, or context, like the lances from the fence, signifiers whose signifieds have changed with time: from instruments that protected the natives, to symbols of protection from the natives, and back to protection of the natives, endlessly. Thus Donoso suggests that the same elements can be used for many ends and that the basic ingredients of seemingly antithetical artistic schools differ little. In fact, the more "artificial" forms might communicate a social message lacking in some more realistic or naturalistic products in which we might expect to find that message. Although the choice of form is ethical as well as esthetic, Donoso demonstrates that those ethics may not be as predetermined and clear-cut as we have believed.

Similarly, although the Venturas pride themselves on the "sane realism that governed their lives" (182/261), their world is exaggeratedly artificial, an imitation of artistic modes and described in terms of *modernismo*. Think, for example, of the description of the country house, filled with refined and exotic detail as it mirrors art more than life: "its broad lawns where peacocks strolled, the miniature rocaille island in the *laghetto* . . . the leafy green theatre peopled with commedia dell'arte figures . . . the marble nymphs, the amphoras—all copied only the noblest models, banishing any trace that might compromise it with the indigenous" (34/57). The passage highlights the decorative (that is, nonutilitarian) character of the park while it subtly underscores the implicit masking gesture as the Venturas disguise the native, the natural, and superimpose on it the exotic, all in the name of good taste—that is, in obedience to some artistic rule (that is, repression). And surely the Venturas' primary concern is for good taste and the esthetic. Think, for example, of the guard located near the steps of the house, placed there not to guard (note the misnomer) anything but to lend a splash of red to contrast with the green of the park. Not unlike the artist of *modernismo,* the family reduces a human being to a decoration (194/276), while failing to perceive the oppression implicit in the gesture.

Indeed, the world of the Venturas and Marulanda of the first part of *A House in the Country* is an elaboration on and imitation of (thus marking it as doubly artificial) two poems, "Sonatina" and "Era un aire suave," by Rubén Darío, the father of *modernismo,* an art form paradoxically considered uniquely American even though it was to a large degree an imitation of the French Symbolists (with some New World enhancements added). The first poem speaks of a sad, lonely princess in her palace. Like the garden in Marulanda, hers is filled with peacocks, and, like the Venturas' lackeys, her clown in red performs somersaults. Still, her life is empty and meaningless; she is enveloped in luxury, surrounded by guards to "protect" her (an ambiguity between confinement and security also present in *A House in the Country*). The second poem, whose title, "It Was a Gentle Wind," contrasts with the final, devastating wind of Marulanda, also presents a world of exotic beauty and calculated harmony. The protagonist is a marquise (think of the children's game), Eulalia, who, like the unfaithful Eulalia of the novel (mother of the illegitimate Malvina), has two lovers: an ecclesiastic (echoing Anselmo's propensity for the religious) and a blond viscount. She is imaged on the terrace, surrounded by gardens and classical statues. Meanwhile, the "sweet violins of Hungary sing" (like Juvenal's rendition of Liszt as Celeste thinks about her own and Melania's "erotic" relations with Olegario) while the blue-eyed marquise, ever frivolous, laughs and laughs, oblivious to her surroundings (again not unlike the various Venturas).

"It Was a Gentle Wind" concludes with a series of rhetorical questions that foreshadow the multitude of rhetorical questions that punctuate the Donoso novel. Only at the end does the poet/narrator indirectly acknowledge the artificiality of the marquise, who belongs to no historical time or space (not unlike the Venturas and Marulanda, whose fictionality is repeatedly affirmed by the narrator): like the narrator of *A House in the*

Country, Darío's poetic voice wavers between knowing and not knowing, telling and not telling, as he concludes, "I do not know the time and the day and the country/but I know that Eulalia is still laughing,/and her golden laugh is cruel and eternal!" (my translation). Thus Darío eternalizes the artistic creation and brings it to life in much the same way as Donoso concludes his novel with the artistic, unreal figures of the fresco that "come to life" and become as "real" as the other characters, if not more so—a paradox that underlines the fictionality of them all, including the narrator. Also evoking the openly artificial world of Darío, Donoso proffers, in the final chapter of *A House in the Country,* a series of questions about the future of the characters (and by implication himself as narrator) (347/490–91) but concludes that to answer these question he would have to write (invent) that future which, like all else, would be artifice. Clearly, Donoso openly evokes the artificial, exotic, and frivolous world of *modernismo,* which (like the Venturas) intentionally excises and excludes anything common or ugly, while he simultaneously underlines the universality (in time and space) of such an attitude (structure, form, style).

Unlike Darío and *modernismo,* however, in *A House in the Country* Donoso combines the *preciosismo* with a realistic bent. After his series of interrogatives, the poet of *modernismo* leaves his frivolous marquise laughing eternally. Donoso's text forswears this lightheartedness and continues until all characters disappear into clouds of thistledown or the fresco. Then his questions merge *modernismo* and realism, wondering as he does if Melania built a luxurious mansion beside the waterfalls and lilies and what the final gestures of Juan Pérez and the Venturas might have been as they perished on the plain: "their clutching fingers, the terror in their eyes" (347/490–91), surely not the normal fare of *modernismo.*

Also in contrast to *modernismo,* Donoso questions beauty and esthetic judgment, demonstrating that the term beauty is (1) relative and not absolute (like power) and (2) a tool for domination. Among the Venturas, Celeste has the "power" to determine what is the most esthetically pleasing, yet she is blind, unable to see what she judges beautiful. Similarly, because Melania has been declared beautiful by the rest of the family (in spite of the fact that other cousins might well be considered as pretty or even prettier), she is afforded certain privileges (62/96). To designate Melania "the most beautiful" is one more example of the Venturas' imposition of their will, vision, and in turn power, through language and rhetoric (in a manner reminiscent of the realistic, mimetic artist). Nonetheless, arbitrary though it is, the morpheme *pretty* or *beautiful* goes unchallenged, becomes the "official version," and thus appears self-evident ("natural"), like any official version (56/88).

The irony is that although the Venturas exemplify *modernismo,* they have nonetheless repressed, erased, and nullified its express goals. *Modernismo* was against fossilized standards, but its forms and techniques as employed by the Venturas (the lake, the peacocks, swans, statues of nymphs) have become as fossilized as what they replaced, just as the new "political" regime probably would have, had it survived. *Modernismo* strove for new values, but the only "new values" the Venturas will allow are their own (old values). *Modernismo* was against bourgeois conformity, but the Venturas utilize the artistic forms precisely to ensure that conformity. Furthermore, the creativity and individuality heralded by and implicit in the art form are precisely what the Venturas would forestall.

Nonetheless, the world of exoticism and decorative detail (art with no apparent utilitarian goal) à la *modernismo* is counterbalanced, indeed in many ways negated, in *A House in the Country* by the very realistic, indeed terrifying and ugly, world of torture, death, hunger, and greed for power portrayed in part two, a world paradoxically brought into existence, to some degree, by the Venturas' endeavors to repress that reality. Thus Donoso demonstrates the interdependence of the two art forms and the two mind-sets, showing them to be inverted mirror reflections that pretend not to be; he proposes that they are motivated by the same "politics" of repression. Although readers may often feel more "comfortable" with the realistic and naturalistic art forms, especially if they pride themselves on having a social conscience, the "reality" of the realistic modes is artifice to the extent that it is the product of the perception of the observers (narrators, writers, reporters, poets), subject to language and the limitations of the dark curtain of their previous experience. Thus, in the mode of *modernismo,* the Venturas' metaphoric dark curtain is drawn over the utilitarian and the ugly; anything that is not harmonious or beautiful (by their standards) is rejected. Inversely, in the naturalistic mode the curtain is drawn over the beautiful while the pragmatic, often imaged as disharmonious or ugly, is emphasized. In either case, something is left out, suppressed and repressed, rendered invisible, disenfranchized. One might in fact understand the garden at Marulanda as a metaphor for the changes that artistic form undergoes. First imaged as a green emerald, filled with roses and peacocks, it is later converted into the most practical of gardens, producing food for the community, while the formerly purely decorative *laghetto* becomes an irrigation tank.[21] After the reconquest, it becomes a wasteland, providing neither beauty nor function. At the end, it is slowly invaded by the neither beautiful nor utilitarian thistledown in what might be understood as a symbolic, if indeed ironic, return to nature and origins, that is, to nonart. Is Donoso's point that we have lost sight of both artistic modes and "buried" art and the world in thistledown, a blinding cloud of choking irritants that make it difficult to swallcw and breathe?

The Appearance of the Natural

Whether the artist opts for the overt fantasy of *modernismo* or the feigned reality of the naturalistic modes, the (re)creation of that world still depends on the instruments of the trade, the word or language that shapes perception. We know that *modernismo* is artifice; we often forget that realism is equally so. The confusion is related to the artistic form and our confidence in vision, our sense of sight. Indeed, as Griselda Pollock states, "realistic modes of representation present the world *as if* total knowledge is possible through empirical observation . . . positioning the viewer/reader in a specular relation, *as if* in a mirror, to what is seemingly revealed by its transparent textual devices. Denying the fact of being a construction, being produced, the realist text offers itself as merely a picture of the world which does not depend for its sense on any other text, references or information" (emphasis added).[22] As a result, Pollock notes, dominant realist modes naturalize bourgeois ideologies as fact or common sense. What Donoso successfully demonstrates is that it is all a trompe l'oeil, an optical illusion, and that the vision itself is an artistic invention. Think, for example, of the number of times the Donoso narrator alleges "as we have already seen" or "naturally," when in fact we have "seen" nothing; what we have before us is a novel, not real life, as the narrator repeatedly insists, and what is perceived as "natural" is anything but.

Ostensibly, "nature" (the thistledown) dominates at the conclusion of the novel and will perhaps the destroy the remaining Venturas. The thistledown, the greatest threat to the survival and perpetuation of the Ventura way of life, is presented as natural—that is, predating and antithetical to the cultured *preciosismo* of the Venturas' garden. Yet such is not the case, as the text will correct itself to inform us: "Contrary to appearances, it was untrue" that the thistle had always been there (34/57). Not native to Marulanda, it was imported by the Venturas in their alteration of earlier "natural" forms. It was brought there at the encouragement of a "foreigner" who had assured them it would bring greater profit than agriculture or mining. Released on the plain, the seeds spread rapidly, and the thistle plants "devoured" all the beneficial plants (just as the *preciosismo* of the Venturas metaphorically devours all). Still, time has erased the memory of the origins of the thistle, so they *appear* natural, part of the original, "natural" world outside the scope of human intervention. It is merely a question of where the narrator of the (hi)story arbitrarily elects to situate the point of origin, for it is in relation to that origin that we determine what is "natural" as opposed to what is modified or supplementary, added later by the metaphoric clothing (investment) of "civilization" (and our narrator assures us that he chooses the crucial, central present of the history [3/13]).

Similarly, the nakedness of the natives appears natural, that is, culturally and temporally more primitive than the "civilized" donning of clothes, when in fact the opposite is the case. As we learn, the natives wore clothes before they began to go naked; they began to go naked (and thus appear more primitive) only after the Venturas stole their sumptuous vestments. Significantly, the "di-vestment" occurred concurrently with the Venturas' theft of the natives' control over the salt, when they were forced to abandon the salt (whose value they understood) and mine the gold (whose purpose they did not comprehend). By dispossessing the natives of their autonomy and thus of much of the threat they posed, the Venturas altered history and "nature" (247–48/349–50). In other words, the "natural" inferiority of the natives (and by implication the "natural" superiority of the Venturas) is a creation of the family, but as is typical throughout the novel, this fact is soon forgotten, and "history" is rewritten in a gesture that would posit itself as realistic and naturalistic.

Indeed that world of "realism" and the "natural" (created by the Venturas' word) is frequently demythicized in the text. For example, although not a particularly reliable narrator himself, given as he is to inventing (hi)stories that fit his purposes, Wenceslao notes that because the adults could not admit that the picnic site was an invention, they had to conduct themselves *as if* it were real; and without realizing it, they ended up "on the other side of the mirror they themselves had invented, where they became prisoners" (89/133; emphasis added), like the princess of the poem. Similarly, Donoso suggests that the perpetuators of realism (like the manipulators of political rhetoric) enter their world and forget it is a creation, based on ideological premises that, because they remain just out of sight, hidden from view, endow that creation with an aura of the "natural."

In addition, the suggestion is that realistic (historical) narrators capture only the surface, those appearances that become the crux of the novel. "Appearance is the only thing that never lies" (5/16), states one of the child elite. True, but only if we acknowledge it as appearance, surface, and nothing more than that—something we rarely do. For example, when the narrator describes the house after the "revolution" in terms of paintings by Robert or Rosa, he continues, "But on closer inspection [literally, "looking better" or "looking more carefully"] an observer would have discovered ["could discover" is a more literal translation]" (204/290–910). Thus he suggests that we rarely do look better, closer. Although our sense of sight gives us access only to an appearance (the superficial or the optical illusion), we seldom recognize it as such (as how one person sees something) or understand that a change in angle or the care with which one looks might alter that appearance significantly.

The mutability (and perhaps nonreferentiality) of appearance is illustrated by the children's game/theater *La Marquise Est Sortie à Cinq Heures,* which has the power to transfigure everything into (the appearance of) something else (25/43). The name of the game comes from Paul Valèry, who opposed realism and sought new ways of expression that might go beyond appearance, the ostensible referent.[23] For him the statement "La Marquise est sortie à cinq heures" ("The Marquise left at five o'clock") and ones like it are in bad literary taste and should never be used, for they epitomize the mimetic that would attempt to capture some extratextual referent. The irony, of course, is that in spite of its status as the epitome of both the realistic mode and bad literary taste, the phrase functions in the Donoso novel as a signifier that has assumed a new meaning because it has changed context (like the lances). First, because the Ventura children are the offspring of their parents, they presumably have good taste, not bad (a debatable point, to be sure). Second, as contextualized in the Donoso novel, the sentence/game becomes the emblem not of the mimetic but of its opposite, the nonrealistic, for it embodies the fantasy of the children and the extravagant adventures of its characters with no thought to verisimilitude. Thus the game is linked to the double artifice of realism that pretends to portray its referent objectively without the artistic imposition of other art forms, yet is already doubly alienated from its origins: "that masque that concealed the masquerade" (101/149), a double covering.[24]

History, Truth, and Discourse

The question of realism and the word leads to the other central issue addressed by Donoso in *A House in the Country:* history, historical discourse, posited as the most "realistic" of discourses. Throughout the text, the narrator refers to his tale as an *historia,* a term that translates as both "history" (in the sense of fact, reality, verifiable truth) and "story" (in the sense of fiction, artifice). Donoso proposes that the two are equally fictitious invention, arbitrary renditions of the extratextual referent, and dependent on narrative technique and discourse, both of which inevitably respond to an invisible agenda that makes the artificial seem natural. Donoso repeatedly stresses the relativity of truth as posited by language (or by our limited senses) and at the service of the hegemony; for example, at one point the Chef wonders "which truth [the Majordomo] had in mind, among the many that power commands" (228–29/325). Indeed the novel opens by emphasizing the distance between discourse and reality: what the grownups had said many times, that they would leave at sunrise, they did not put into practice. Let us recall too that the mythic site for the picnic was a linguistic creation that originated we know not where, but apparently with help from Wenceslao. The irony must not be missed, however, for even as Wenceslao assures the other children that the site is an invention and that the adults had been caught in their own creation, he must ultimately admit that he is not sure if it does or does not exist (89/133). Even in his role as one of the assistant creators (perhaps not unlike our narrator), he is as uncertain as the adults where the mirror (fiction) begins and ends.

Even the most casual reader cannot be oblivious to the number of times the characters or the narrator employ the expressions *true* and *it was true* when in fact it was not true at all. One example of this insistence on truth comes from a page in the chapter "The Assault," where the morphemes *true* and *truth* are used five times in one paragraph (six times in the English translation) (196–97/279). To prove that he is telling the truth here, Juan Pérez echoes the procedure of a realistic narrator or would-be historian; he assumes the stance of observer and reports what he has seen (that presumably no one else has observed). The underlying premise (as in realism and naturalism) is that truth can be reached by observation. But as the reader of *A House in the Country* soon discovers, more often than not what one sees is theater, the optical illusion of the ballroom, appearance. After Juan Pérez's initial report of his observation (credible within the self-contained world of the novel), he asserts that it is true that (1) a year has passed, not one day, and (2) the children are rotten to the core. While the first proposition might be viable (although the reader cannot be confident), the second is not entirely accurate, although it does contain a core of truth. The children are not as innocent as some might think, but they are probably not as corrupt as some might postulate either. Then he adds that it is also "true that in Marulanda anarchy and mayhem reigned supreme," a statement that again evokes a partial truth, but one doubtlessly exaggerated. It is also true, he assures his listeners, that at Adriano's instigation the cannibals have taken over, an assertion that cannot be accurate (in the closed world of the novel), for there are no cannibals and therefore Adriano cannot instigate them. Juan Pérez concludes by declaring that the servants (1) will now defend the one true cause (apparently the Venturas and the reimposition of order) rather than (2) simply perform a decorative function as they have until now (like the lackey in red against the green of the park). Again, while the second proposition is tenable, the "one true cause" he cites is never specified; it is left in the vague realm of some generic truth, neither provable nor disprovable. Thus Donoso demonstrates the fluidity and relativity of this thing we call truth and posits that sometimes its referent is indeed irrefutable, sometimes only partially valid, and sometimes not at all—like any discourse (historical, novelistic, realistic, *modernista*). Realistic, historical discourse, not unlike the optical illusion of the ballroom, does not just reflect or reproduce reality; it is its own form of reality. Paradoxically, however, not all the doors of the optical illusion are fake or trap; some do lead somewhere and proffer depth and insight into reality (just as the fictitious world of the Venturas offers insight into both sociopolitical and artistic repression), but not all of them. The challenge is to discover which is which.

In that it is the epitome of the process of abstraction, Juan Pérez's harangue in the above-cited paragraph recalls much political discourse that would rewrite history or historical events to portray the group in power in a more favorable light. To establish his credibility, he begins with a report of what he has seen, then moves through half truths, and ends with abstractions ("the one true cause") that are accorded the adjectival quality of truth. That is, the abstract statements seem credible, not because the message or supposed referent is verifiable, but because of syntagmatic contiguity; they are located in proximity to other bona fide statements and thus the adjective "true" overflows onto them, endowing them with the aura of truth. Also reminiscent of historical or political discourse, one of these invented "truths" is repeated a few pages later in a matter-of-fact manner by the narrator as if it were absolute truth and thus not debatable: "the children so recently saved from the clutches of the cannibals" (208/ 296). In this manner, the act of stating or writing something (as is the case with history) lends a note of credibility, an aura of truth that in time causes it to be repeated as truth (note the role of time here as throughout the novel). Is this not the basis of the historical process? Does this process not mirror the political underpinnings of any realistic, historical endeavor? Indeed, the series of rhetorical questions that Wenceslao asks himself after he has been shown the chicanery of the library (the source of much knowledge for most people), whose books are merely well-wrought and carefully crafted covers that hide the emptiness inside, are the questions Donoso would have us ask of all "truths" we receive or observe: "where . . . did Arabela get all that learning . . . *is it true* that she knows so much? Or do I only think so because I know so little myself, and do the grown-ups only think so . . . because it suits their purposes that she should?" (17/33; Donoso's emphasis). Readers might wonder if we ought not ask the same of our omniscient narrator, who "knows" so much.

Surely one of the questions Donoso poses here is what happens when either art or historical discourse falls into the hands of the unscrupulous—which is not to suggest that any hands are scrupulous (indeed the novel presents most of them as gloved, masked). Thus all renditions of history become suspect, reflecting and incorporating as they must the "vision" of the group in power. Indeed at several points Donoso discretely attacks historical renditions of the past by utilizing the standard historical motifs (salvation, foundation, conversion) in an ironic mode. Think, for example, of the family's "crusade" against the natives, frequently imaged with a religious terminology that recalls the crusades of the Middle Ages and the conquest of the Americas, both of which may have been little more than convenient charades in which religion masked imperialistic impulses. The credibility of vision takes center stage again when, like a historian trying to "rectify" misconceptions of the past or an artist trying to redo, retouch, an old art form, Juan Pérez and the other lackeys try to repair the optical illusion of the library. What they produce, however, is a different work of art. Reminiscent of the transition from *modernismo* to realism, Juan Pérez and his lackeys convert the goddesses of the original fresco to harpies, the rosy clouds to thunderheads (228/323), suggesting that no art form can do other than project the perspective, the limited and limiting psychological framework, of its artist (observer). In either case the depicted world is exaggeratedly unilateral, metaphorically too black or too white, something Donoso consciously and overtly attempts to avoid by combining the goddesses and rosy clouds (*modernismo, preciosismo,* the esthetic and beautiful) with the harpies and the thunderheads (realism, naturalism, the ugly or darker side of life) and overtly placing himself and his control at the center for all to see. Such a gesture, the fact of making himself visible (rather than invisible, as controlling powers so often are), however, does not mediate or lessen that control/authority. It just makes it visible, converts it to appearance, part of the product (like the children's game), and perhaps helps him avoid being devoured by his characters. Nonetheless, the liar who tells us he is lying is still a liar.

Narrative Technique

The narrative technique in *A House in the Country*, with its perpetual interruptions, makes us ever conscious of that authoritative liar (artificer), the narrator, and his control while it emphasizes the unnatural (artificial) quality of any fictitious world. Donoso similarly wants his reader to question history and historical discourse with its authoritative and authoritarian "official versions" and convenient memory of events. To those ends he employs a mixture of narrative techniques. On one hand, the fictional world, the history of the Venturas and Marulanda, is presented through a narrative technique that mimics the historical mode of discourse. That is, the narrator generally begins in the present (if indeed mythic and eternal), but that present (origin) is arbitrarily chosen, as it is in any historical document. After selecting this moment of origin, the narrator then regresses in time and reports earlier events to explain how the present came to be, why the present situation is the "natural" and logical result of the events of the past. As a result, events of the past are perceived through the screen (dark curtain) or visual frame of the present. In addition, the narrator selects and metonymically links (in a cause-and-effect chain) those events judged pertinent, while he omits mention of those not considered part of the cause-and-effect chain. As a result, the reader receives only a selection of events that responds to and depends on the perception and goal of the narrator. On a larger scale, Donoso's technique implies that historical selectivity may not differ greatly from artistic selectivity—for example, that exercised by *modernismo* and realism as they include or omit according to their purposes.

Because of this insistence on establishing causal links, the (hi)story of *A House in the Country* is anything but lineal; the text is structured like a spiral that circles back on itself as one event from the past influences more than one present event and necessitates ever more complicated digressions. Because of the emphasis on cause and effect, the chapters of the text are organized by topic rather than by time span and overlap chronologically although the chapter titles are frequently misleading (as perhaps is the novel's title). For example, the chapter entitled ''The Gold'' is more about Casilda and her relations with others (Fabio, Colomba, Higinio, and Malvina) than about gold per se; ''The Natives'' focuses more on the prehistory of Balbina and Adriano and their family than on the natives themselves.

In addition, the novel's discourse seems designed to confound readers: predication is complex and confusing while digressions often produce or enclose other digressions. Some examples from the first chapter of the text will illustrate the point. After alternating among fictitious present and immediate or remote past (equally fictitious, to be sure) for several pages, the narrator returns to the present (the day the adults desert the children) and Wenceslao's thoughts as he heads for the tower (17/32–33). But the narrator soon abandons Wenceslao and narrates the history of the library, a history only tangentially connected to Wenceslao's thoughts (17–18/33–34). Then he digresses even further to tell the history of the natives before he finally returns to the events of the night preceding the excursion (19/35), which is still not the starting point of this series of digressions. All of this happens in five pages. At the moment the gloved hand apprehends Cipriano, the narrator again leaves the reader ''suspended'' as he defers the action and digresses to tell of the ''absolute'' power of the servants after curfew (20/37), a digression within a digression that eventually entangles the reader in a web of discourse and events, confused about the chronological sequence of events as well as cause and effect. To further exacerbate our sense of confusion or abandonment (not unlike Wenceslao's), the text does not return to the moment of Cipriano's ''capture'' until several pages later (24/42) and not to the present (the day of the expedition) for two or three more pages (26/45). A similar pattern structures chapter twelve, in which, instead of telling what happened when the parents arrived (after the children had devoured Amadeo), the narrator digresses to tell of his imagined interview with Silvestre as well as the latter's interview with Lidia and Hermógenes and then describes events at the country house from Juan Pérez's perspective. Only after this digression of more than twenty pages is the reader brought back to the present of the end of the previous chapter, when the adults arrived at the country house.

Furthermore, the narrator overtly exercises his power to cover or reveal, a power wielded more covertly by a realist narrator. The result of this succession of masking and unmasking, appearance and reality, is that readers are never sure which is which and thus are ever disoriented, always at the mercy of the narrator. In fact, one of the first confusions created for readers by the discursive masking and unmasking is the sex and gender of the characters. Indeed the novel early addresses the motif of (eccentric) sexuality: although Wenceslao left his mother's bed to go to Melania's (thereby evoking his promiscuity but also masculinity), he is soon after described as female and as a doll (also female). The confusion (and layering) is even greater when he reveals a "respectable virility" (5/16) beneath the feminine mask of the skirt and lace panties. A similar gender confusion is presented a page later when Juvenal (a masculine name) is referred to as the Perfidious Marquise (female) of the fable, drawing readers' attention to his feminine role.

Significantly, the predication of individual sentences frequently follows a similarly complicated and self-contradictory pattern. Indeed, the elaborate sentence structure mirrors the message, the labyrinthine rooms and halls of the house: "Lifting his skirts he raced down the corridors, cutting through bedrooms and halls, studies and drawing rooms, sewing and play rooms, twisting through passages and alcoves in the huge *empty house,* dodging past *wandering cousins*" (12/26; emphasis added). Note the contradiction, the lie, in the emphasized words. The empty house is not empty, contrary to the narrator's declaration; it is filled with wandering cousins. Or it might be the other way around: there are no wandering cousins. Nonetheless, both statements cannot be "true." The purpose of all this convolution seems to be to prove to us our capacity for accepting whatever absurdities and contradictions discourse might posit. For example, how many readers are immediately struck by the contradiction noted above (empty house, cousins) or by the absurdity when the text casually calls the picnic a "veritable dream" (172/246), or a few pages later when the text asserts that Casilda and Fabio had caught small game with the lance they did not know how to use?[25] Similarly, how likely are we to protest when the narrator assures that "this tone has become as *natural* to me *as a disguise*" (32/54; my translation and emphasis). We become accustomed to the convoluted prose and numb to its illogic.

Paradoxically, nonetheless, readers are likely to note the absurdity of the rhetoric and ostensibly meaningless discourse in the scenes from *La Marquise Est Sortie à Cinq Heures,* nonsense that ultimately does convey meaning to the extent that it connotes a specific ambience. For example, the speech with which chapter seven opens would appear to be meaningless drivel, yet it evokes (indirectly, to be sure) the violence, contradiction, destruction, triangular relations of betrayal, and even the unreliability of vision that are central to the novel. As was the case with the notion of truth, sometimes the discourse is tenable and sometimes not, in spite of appearances to the contrary, just as sometimes metaphors, adjectives, and similes are valid but more often not: the "impregnable railing of iron lances" (26/45) was not impregnable, and the plain "unchanged since the beginning of time" (34/57) was not unchanged.

Several readers have observed that *A House in the Country* is not just the (hi)story of the Venturas and Marulanda; it is also the (hi)story, the mise en scène, of writing. With an authority designed to mimic and make overt the covert authority and omnipotence with which any artist or historian approaches the creation, the narrator of the novel continually calls attention to his presence, power, and control over the fictitious world, making sure we recognize that it is he who chooses if and when to tell (17/32; for other examples see 239/339, 243/345, 261/371). Similarly, he allows events to take place (275–76/391–92) and chooses whether to reveal the destinies of the characters (347/490–91). Indeed he flagrantly asserts his narrative power and authority by noting that he has withheld the secret, and "the truth is that I have put it off until this point in the story on purpose so as to unveil now, in all its magnitude . . . " (68/104; note again the irony of the concept of truth as discussed above). Nevertheless, Donoso questions even this "absolute" power, suggesting that it, like that of the servants, is not as absolute as his narrator might like the reader to believe, for that narrator frequently abjures to an unnamed higher power or ethical force: for example, "I should confide to my reader" (239/339).

As in early Donoso works, the form of *A House in the Country* repeatedly mirrors the content and becomes indivisible from it. The narrator enters the story of the Venturas, just as Juan Pérez enters the trompe l'oeil as an eye that would register everything (227/323), and the characters of the trompe l'oeil eventually step out of it to interact with the characters of the novel. Similarly, the narrator's omnipotence and manipulation of the discourse (and by implication reality) are mirror reflections of the Venturas'. He too is given to drawing that dark curtain over taboo subjects: "Modesty counsels me, rather, to drop a dark curtain over these details" (243/346). And the theatrical curtain our narrator drops at the conclusion of the novel differs little from that of any writer (including writers of history) whose final curtain (blank page) is theatrically drawn at the moment the writer has answered all the questions she or he has chosen to pose and silenced those she or he has chosen not to answer. Although the statement "The curtain must now fall and the lights come up" (348/492) suggests that the lights have been off and we may not have seen well all along, that curtain in fact is twice dropped, and novel twice ends. It ends here with the announcement of its end and again on the final page as Celeste and Olegario disappear into the "impenetrable air" (if it is "impenetrable," how do they "penetrate" it?) while the figures of the optical illusion hover around the characters, ironically, to make sure they do not die.

Perhaps the originality of *A House in the Country* is that the narrator visibly manipulates both his characters and his readers, casting the latter as other characters in the mise en scène of writing. Not only does the narrator speak directly to the readers, but the authoritativeness of his discourse thrusts them into roles and postures as he tells them what to think, remember, or forget: "my reader will no doubt be wondering" (68/204); "my reader will not wonder" (263/373); "my startled reader must be wondering why" (337/477).[26] In one of the many narrative gestures in which style echoes content, the narrator concludes a paragraph on the question of power (of the servants over the children and vice versa) that seems absolute but is not by exercising his own power: "So nervous were they over every beating they gave that they turned them into dramatic spectacles—for instance, the drubbing the Majordomo handed Cipriano on that night which, as narrator of this tale, I saw fit to interrupt and which I will now use to return the reader to my story's present" (24/42). Surely our narrator mimics the servants and turns his own power play into a dramatic spectacle. Is that because the narrator too is insecure and nervous, knowing that his readers also have powers?

The narrator not only exercises his authority by manipulating the readers and projecting them into the roles he would have them play, remembering or forgetting, questioning or not questioning, at his direction and discretion, but he also exercises a divine right of possession—"*my* reader"—that echoes one of the themes of the novel made explicit in the early pages: "Wenceslao was [Melania's] toy . . . and Mauro . . . was hers too . . . and Juvenal too" (6/17). The original, however, does not speak of a toy; it merely says "Wenceslao was hers." The question of possession is carried a step further as our narrator declares that the material of the novel is "entirely" his own (31/53). Later he assures the readers that it is *his* monologue (247/349); all voices are his. The same chapter concludes with the eating of Amadeo, one of the least verisimilar (the dying Amadeo speaks eloquently and endlessly) and most self-contradictory scenes of the novel.[27] Readers cannot fail to note, however, the irony of the heroism portrayed in this chapter, both that of Amadeo, who gives his body to save "society," and that of the other small "heroes," who overcome social mores and taboos in the name of survival and the perpetuation of their ideals. Yet this heroism is for naught since their heroic action is immediately followed by the arrival of the adults, who bring food and means of physical survival (invalidating the heroic gesture), and Wenceslao's "Mama!" which signals his reversion to childhood and dependency as he abandons his ideals and joins the "enemy." So much for heroic gestures, Donoso proposes.

Thus the ultimate paradox of *A House in the Country* is that even the narrator is a trompe l'oeil, as unreliable and given to betrayal as the Venturas themselves. Distancing itself from other literary forms, particularly the conventions of the realistic novel, *A House in the Country* nowhere proffers a reliable voice, a trustworthy guide. As the narrator hides behind his dark curtain, he mirrors the children's game of the voice of the mirror, the ironic "Angel of Goodness" hidden behind a dark curtain, who exercises heartless authority as her discourse is unquestioningly obeyed by the others (239/339). But as I have posited, sometimes the narrative voice does what it says it will do and other times it does not, as for example when he says "Let us now hear Arabela's version, in her own words," but goes on, "But no. I have thought better of giving the text I promised in the last paragraph" (243/345). At other times the narrative voice contradicts itself ("But no, that wasn't true" [161/232]) or offers conflicting explanations of events (for example, the founding of the house). Think of the times we read statements like "I need not remind my reader" and "needless to say" (two expressions rendered by the same expression in Spanish: "it is in excess to say") or other qualifying statements that undermine the previous or following pronouncements—for example, "if my readers will permit me to call it thus" (calling the previous terminology into question) and "or rather" (deauthorizing the previous declarations). Numerous times he contradicts his assurances to readers that no other character knew of another's secret.[28] At still other moments the narrator seems caught up in his narrative and believes what his characters presumably believe. Thus Donoso dramatizes that there are no reliable voices; discourse is inherently as perfidious as the Marquise of the fable.

Figures of Speech and Literary Good Taste

Perhaps what marks the style of *A House in the Country* more than anything else is the manner in which it plays with the notion of good taste, literary and otherwise, a notion already foreshadowed in *Sacred Families*. The narrator directly addresses the issue of literary good taste at the beginning of chapter two and posits that "good taste" merely masks literary convention. In turn, the novel defies literary "good taste" with its hyperbolized artificiality of setting and language. Neither the children nor the adults speak like normal people. Much of the vocabulary is either archaic, erudite, or exaggeratedly grandiloquent; on the first page we find unusual terms (many of which are lost in the English translation) like laudanum, lackey, curfew (the Spanish term *toque de queda* has a more military connotation than its English translation), *bucles* (an old-fashioned word for curls, whose flavor is more accurately imparted by the word *ringlets*), *vaticinio* (a Latinized word for prophecy), none of which is incomprehensible but all of which are unconventional in modern usage.

Furthermore, the often forgotten or overlooked figurative nature of language is highlighted in the linguistic associations among eroticism, possession, fire, and cannibalism. These may seem strange bedfellows, but they are closely interrelated in *A House in the Country*, to some extent because of the rhetorical figures and tropes by which each is described. Eroticism is frequently presented in terms of fire, and, carried to its extreme, that fire might consume, devour, its object. Similarly, intercourse is often viewed as an act of possession or devouring. These idiomatic relations are, like all else, hyperbolized in the Donoso novel and carried to their (il)logical conclusions. Wenceslao threatens Melania with the arrival of the cannibals, who will rape her, then eat her. Melania will "give herself" to Mauro (note the metaphor: she means "have sexual relations with him," but it is imaged as a form of possession) like "a scrap of meat . . . for him to devour" (27/46). Mignon burns Aída's hair, repeating that all she desired was to see her burn to a crisp (be consumed by fire), a metaphor she makes reality when she roasts her head. In chapter four Olegario's desire for Celeste is figured as a voracious appetite that sorches her and had burned the image of his penis on her retina, thereby blinding her. Donoso's point is that all too often we forget the figurative nature of our language and come to accept figures as reality, or, like the Ventura family, see reality through the filter of those rhetorical figures.

Like any number of other metaphors, the notion of good taste is made literal on two levels in *A House in the Country.*[29] It is literalized in that the characters do taste one another, devour one another literally and figuratively as the word becomes reality. At the beginning, the children are described as "delicious," "exquisite," "sweet" (although it is lost in the English translation, Wenceslao is labeled a "sweet doll"), a tasty mouthful (translated *bonne bouche* in the English and rendered in Italian *bocato di cardinale* in the original). Similarly, on occasion, the parents would devour the children with kisses: " 'I could simply devour that luscious boy!' 'All children, thanks to their tender nature, are exquisite . . . you could just eat them alive with kisses' " (36/60; the ellipsis is Donoso's); it is pertinent that this conversation is part of a longer one that discusses Adriano's association with "cannibals." Elsewhere, Casilda's greed is imaged as hunger that might "devour him like a cannibal's" (136/199); note the double figure here—Casilda's greed is imaged as a hunger, then described with the simile of the cannibal. And, of course, the children do eat Amadeo.

The links among good taste, cannibalism, and figurative language are further apparent in the fact that literary "good taste" includes the use of appropriate and eloquent figures and tropes. But as noted above, these are capable of devouring the "original" referent, as they mask it and lead us to see only the figure, appearance. It may not be irrelevant that the Spanish word that marks the simile, one of Donoso's most frequent figures, is *como*, "like," which also means "I eat," a coincidence to which Donoso does not seem oblivious. Similarly, at the conclusion of the novel, even as he is blurring the division between literary characters and "real" people they are *like*, the narrator resorts to the figures of hunger and devouring. After insisting that the curtain must fall and the characters must die, he observes, "I must remember that if fantasies can come alive, they can also die, *to keep them from devouring the author like so many monsters*" (348/493; emphasis added). He continues, reminding his readers how *like* his characters the author/narrator is and how the text is a *mise en abîme* of self-reflecting (and devouring) mirrors, "the *tyrannical* momentum of this stage I keep mentioning carries me—carries us—yet a little further, so that I, for one, *who am hungry for them*, may witness at least one of the many final tableaux" (493/348–49; emphasis added). Yet the irony is that, although the metaphoric hunger functions in both directions, both the characters and the narrator (who is just one more character) die and the curtain (book) closes, devoured by rhetoric (the simile) and the metaphoric appetite of the readers who "consumed" the text, will go on to read (devour) yet another text, and will hold their own mirrors up to the paradoxical reality/trompe l'oeil of the text.

Notes

1. For the reader unfamiliar with political events in Chile, Marxist president Salvador Allende was elected in 1970 by a plurality but not a majority of votes. Candidate of the *Unidad Popular* (Popular Unity), a coalition of Communists and Socialists, he moved to nationalize first the copper industry (owned in a large degree by United States companies) and then many other industries (such as ITT and Ford), acts that aggravated tensions with the United States, which feared the spread of communism. On September 11, 1973, the military, led by General Augusto Pinochet, attacked the presidential palace, inside of which Allende died either by suicide or fire from the invading troops. Pinochet's government dissolved Congress, suspended the Constitution, and imposed a state of seige in its process of "national reconstruction." His military coup, which some believe was backed by the United States, has been considered one of the most violent and repressive of twentieth-century Latin America. Pinochet remained in power until March of 1990.

2. Mario Vargas Llosa is a well known contemporary Peruvian novelist. In 1990 he ran in (and lost) the presidential elections in Peru.

3. This is Donoso's version of the genesis of *A House in the Country* as reported to Z. Nelly Martínez in her "Entrevista con José Donoso," *Hispamérica* 7, 21 (1978):73.

4. *Preciosismo* and *modernismo* are explained in a later section of this chapter.

5. In Spain *casa de campo* generally refers to a summer house in the country, but as Iñigo Madrigal notes, such is not common usage in Latin America, especially in Chile. Nonetheless, since Donoso was living in Spain when he wrote *A House in the Country,* he may well have intended the phrase in the more traditional, peninsular Spanish usage. At the same time, the term *casa de campo* has a special referent in Spain: the *Casa de campo* in Madrid that once served as the hunting grounds for the royal family and later served as the final residence for Francisco Franco, dictator of Spain from 1939 until 1975. In addition, *campo* can refer to a rural area (the country or a field) and to a camp (the kind for children or the military kind) as well as to a faction or side. It is used in the terms "concentration camp," "labor camp," and "training camp."

6. There is an interesting play on words here, because *grandes* means not only adults but also great or eminent ones, as well as magnates or grandees.

7. See Martínez, p. 72.

8. This is my translation of Valente's assertions as quoted by Myrna Solotorevsky in *José Donoso: Incursiones en su producción novelesca* (Valparaiso: Universidad Católica, 1983), 43.

9. I have placed the words *childish* and *innocent* in quotation marks because it is doubtful that Mignon's acts are either. One of Donoso's points throughout the text is that children are far less innocent than they appear or than adults presume them to be. Furthermore, children's actions (games) are frequently a mimetic rendition of what they have seen adults do, in this case the unnecessary but ceremonial cruelty to the animal that is socially sanctioned.

10. A quick glance at the 1974 World Almanac reveals that the military dictatorship in Chile was not unique. Other countries that had military dictatorships or were involved in violent struggles for hegemony were South Vietnam, Cambodia, Israel, Egypt, the Philippines, Ethiopia, Syria, Cypress, and Greece.

11. Readers and critics will surely always disagree about whether one day or one year passes in the novel. In fact (and here we find some of the intentional and ironic "deceit" of

which the narrator is guilty and which I shall discuss later in this chapter), there is yet a third possibility that would invalidate both interpretations—that more than a year passes during the course of the novel. If one accepts the parents' view that only twelve hours have passed (177/254), it would be midnight when they arrive at the chapel (they left at noon) rather than sunset, as the narrator declares (171/245). On the other hand, if one accepts that a year passed while the parents were away, a year during which babies have been born and the children and natives have survived the inundation of the thistledown, then one must also recognize that several more months pass before the conclusion of the novel (from midsummer to the autumn arrival of the thistledown).

12. In one of our first views of Wenceslao, he is raising his skirts and "brandishing a respectable virility" (5/16).

13. Carlos Cerda, *José Donoso: Originales y metáforas* (Santiago: Planeta, 1988), 105–106.

14. On more than one occasion the text posits that what separates the adult Venturas from and makes them superior to other mortals, specifically the children, servants, and other less powerful beings, is not their possessions, their material wealth, but rather their immunity to doubt (see 189/279).

15. The English translation refers to a "pattern of life," but the original Spanish speaks of a "sector of life."

16. Such a system is clearly compatible with that of repressive governments throughout the world, particularly those of Latin America in recent decades. It is not the leaders themselves who actually torture people and make them disappear but rather their overly zealous lackeys.

17. By way of illustration of this general principle we might consider the major literary (and artistic) movements of Spain and Spanish America during the last century. Nineteenth-century romanticism, with its ornamentation and escape from verisimilitude or direct contact with quotidian reality, was replaced by realism and naturalism. In theory at least, the former depicted everyday life and social problems in a mimetic manner while the latter did the same but with a predilection for the ugliness and/or triteness of daily routine. Roughly contemporaneous with realism and naturalism in the prose genres (in the early twentieth century), *modernismo* dominated poetry in Spanish America and again proffered an escape into the exotic and the artificially beautiful. The swan was a symbol of *modernismo*, in part because of its beauty and exoticism and in part because of the question-mark shape of its neck.

More recently these movements seem to have been replaced by what might be labeled a neorealism or neonaturalism, which differs from the former schools in that the "reality" portrayed is now often that of the mind, that is, the internal rather than the external. This newer form of realism or naturalism stands at odds with a neobaroque movement that promotes beauty and ornamentation for their own sake as the primary goals of the work of art, thus once again rendering the sociopolitical goal secondary. Frequently this repeated oscillation between the two extremes is identified with a changing preoccupation with form (style) as opposed to content (sociopolitical theme).

Surely literary schools are never as neatly exclusionary as my generalities suggest, and in fact contradictory movements may well exist simultaneously or even respond to each other in the same work, as they do in *A House in the Country*.

18. *Preciosismo*, which translates "preciosity," is not frequently used in English. It is an affected, inflated, and mannered style.

19. Maxim Newmark, *Dictionary of Spanish Literature* (Towota, N.J.: Littlefield, Adams, 1970), 226.

20. Donoso is explicit that many things are not as antithetical as they might appear: "the border between present and past, good and evil, you and me, is often of patently weaker stuff" (222/316).

21. There is nonetheless an ironic note here. As utilitarian as it is, the garden of the new order retains a trace of the old, the *preciosismo* and frivolity of the Venturas' life-style, for in it grow not just practical lettuces and carrots, but also raspberries, a delicacy that surely is less essential (nutritionally at least) and surely more exotic than the other products.

22. Griselda Pollock, *Vision and Difference: Femininity, Feminism, and the Histories of Art* (New York: Routledge, 1988), 171.

23. Paul Valèry was a French Symbolist writer (1871–1945) who influenced the father of *modernismo*, Rubén Darío.

24. Significantly, too, the chapter entitled "The Marquise" is predominantly about erotic relationships and suggests that all our civilized trappings and finery may well be mere diversion from or covering for our baser, more animalistic sexual urges; for example, Celeste fears that the excursion will stimulate "a reversion to savagery . . . the brutal daily assault [intercourse, rape]" (98/145).

25. The translators' rendition of *verdadero sueño* as "veritable dream" is not incorrect, but it does elide the oxymoron implicit in the Spanish, which combines "true" and "dream."

26. The references to "reader" in the singular are a contribution of the translators; the original Spanish always alludes to "my readers."

27. This contradiction is foreshadowed by the narrator's easily overlooked self-contradiction and paradox at the beginning of the chapter. He aspires to set the scene so that his monologue can take on dimensions "of which not even my own intentions are ignorant" (349 in the Spanish; my translation). This double negative and the resulting complexity (and perfidy) of the sentence have been lost in the English translation.

28. For example, Hermógenes knew about Adriano's visits to the natives just as Malvina knew about Mauro's secret dislodging of the lances and Wenceslao's transmission of messages from his father to the natives in spite of all assurances to the contrary.

29. Solotorevsky has posited that literalization, a process by which a metaphor or a simile is eventually taken literally, understood as a nonfigurative truth, is a constant throughout Donoso's works. In regard to *A House in the Country*, she has discussed the literalization of the Spanish metaphor *comérselo* (eat him up) in the character of Amadeo. See Myrna Solotorevsky, "A Transmutation Device in Certain Texts of José Donoso" in *The Creative Process in the Works of José Donoso*, ed. Guillermo I. Castillo-Feliú (Rock Hill, SC: Winthrop College, 1982), 118–28.

It should be noted, however, that the question of devouring is not the only rhetoric figure that is literalized in the novel. For example, the Venturas also "kill time" in a literal sense by negating its passage. Similarly, in chapter eleven the narrator is explicit that the Venturas have literalized the metaphor "to be seated above the salt" by building the country house on top of a salt mine.

CHAPTER NINE

Curfew:
The Exile Goes Home

Surely the most important event in Donoso's life between the 1978 publication of *A House in the Country* and that of *La desesperanza (Curfew)* in 1986 was his 1981 return to Chile after his voluntary exile of so many years in Spain.[1] It is this experience that shapes *Curfew,* for the novel is Donoso's attempt to portray and understand Chile during the Pinochet dictatorship and his own relation (as an artist) to the political situation.[2] As Donoso has commented in the novel and elsewhere, once one returns to Chile one cannot write or speak about anything but the political situation there: "In love, art, business, even in death, . . . it was impossible to avoid politics" (245–46/259–60).[3] The title, which literally translates "Despair," expresses Donoso's response to the Chilean government and the impotence of art to alter the political horrors. Yet the experience of reading the novel is not as unilateral or despairing as the title suggests, for while readers do vicariously experience the oppression of the sociopolitical situation in Chile in the 1980s, they also glimpse Chile's mythical, lyrical past, its subtext of dreams and the supernatural (where any transformation is possible) as well as the magnificence of the country's natural wonders—the landscapes, sea, and mountains that remain impervious to the horrors perpetuated by human beings. And perhaps most of all, the text portrays the multiplicity of Chiles that exist and have always existed concurrently. The Chile of political oppression may have been the dominant one of the 1970s and 1980s, but other Chiles also endured, as evidenced by Judit's and Mañungo's disparate experiences of their past in spite of their common national background.[4] Curiously, however, although *Curfew* was translated and published in English within two years after it appeared in Spanish, the novel has been greeted with a critical silence (in both English and Spanish) unprecedented in response to Donoso's other works. To date there has been no study of the novel.

Story and Structure: Personal Politics

Set in January of 1985, *Curfew* takes place during a period of eighteen to twenty-four hours marked by two momentous events, one historical and one fictional: the funeral of Matilde Neruda, wife of Nobel Prize-winning Chilean poet Pablo Neruda, and Mañungo Vera's fictional return to Chile, which metaphorically signals his rebirth.[5] A thirty-four-year-old popular revolutionary singer, Mañungo comes back after a voluntary exile of thirteen years in Paris. Like so many Donoso texts, the novel is structured on the notion of the eternal return (ultimately acknowledged as fictional), the eternal search for the ideal(ized) paradise lost, which, as Donoso dramatizes, by definition is always somewhere else: as early as Mañungo's first hours back in Chile, he nostalgically evokes and yearns for other past moments in Paris. More specifically, *Curfew* revolves around a series of dualities, ostensible antitheses that are intricately intertwined and far less antithetical than might be immediately apparent: (1) the love story versus the political story; (2) Mañungo's story versus Judit's story; (3) the past versus the present and by implication life versus death; and (4) the qualities of human decency and compassion versus brutality and indifference (or oblivion) to human suffering.

First the novel narrates a political story as it simultaneously reveals a love story shaped and limited by the former. The political is not unconnected to the personal as much as we might like it to be, Donoso proposes here. The political story takes contemporary Chile as its overt referent, although, like the events of *A House in the Country,* those of *Curfew* might take (or have taken) place in any country under curfew or where human rights have been suspended. As was the case in *A House in the Country,* the political question in *Curfew* is both specific—the military dictatorship in Chile in the 1970s and 1980s—and generic—the use, abuse, and ubiquitous nature of power in all facets of life. Also like *A House in the Country,* *Curfew* reflects Donoso's ambivalence about the military regime in Chile and any possible solution to it. He portrays the horrors of the military dictatorship, demonstrating that even those who have not been directly and personally affected by it—that is, even those who have not suffered the abuses or tortures on their own bodies—have been touched by it indirectly, for perhaps the most deleterious by-product of an abusive dictatorship is psychological, the way it paralyzes the thoughts and actions of people who would be free or who would live another way. In addition, the dictatorship silences voices, particularly the voice of the artist, whether physically, by official censorship, or psychologically, by self-imposed censorship or the inability to express oneself (or perhaps even to think or perceive) in ways other than the "official."

Nevertheless, Donoso demonstrates that the alternatives to the military dictatorship (for example, socialism) are equally untenable. There is little reason to presume that someone like Lisboa, the leader of the Communist Youth, would behave much differently from the current government leaders if afforded their power. His dogmatism, envidiousness, and self-complacency attest to the fact that the power he would wield on the national level would vary only in degree and not in essence or form from the power he wields on the microcosmic level in his political group. Although he is presumably striving for a more just society, he echoes the government in his oppressive practices. For example, to benefit his political position, he would silence Matilde's dying wish for a mass at her funeral. Similarly, he exploits Ada Luz, using her for his own political and erotic ends in a relationship fraught with undertones of violence. His censorship technique differs little from that of the regime as he warns her not to talk to anyone about what she knows: "The threat in his eyes was more effective in silencing her than the hand he'd placed over hers"(29/35). At another moment he blackmails her erotically and threatens never to make love to her again if she is not silent (217/231). Furthermore, Lisboa's group insists on dogmatic certainties, but "their demands, their totalization, seemed just as noxious . . . as any system that promised heaven in exchange for servitude" (257/272).

In the midst of the political question, the novel's love stories are not to be overlooked, for not only is the text explicit about the love between Pablo Neruda and his wife Matilde, but Mañungo and Judit embark on what appears to be a rekindling of a love that will perhaps reflect that of the Nerudas. The suggestion, and one that is definitely not romanticized here, is that in spite of the despair perpetuated by the political tyranny, love survives, if indeed with difficulty and perhaps in an altered form.

During the eighteen to twenty-four hours that constitute the time frame of the text, these two thematic motifs converge. Mañungo returns to Chile to discover that his old friend Matilde has died. At her wake he encounters several of his former friends and acquaintances, many of whom dislike him for having "abandoned" their political position (Marxism) or envy his "artistic" success as a popular singer of "political" songs in Europe. Although Judit is also at the wake, he fails to recognize her until he encounters her later, when he is in the company of their mutual friend Lopito, a repugnant drunk, "filthy and abject and self-destructive and a failure" (93/99). Judit and Mañungo spend the night together in the streets of Santiago, avoiding the police as well as the restrictions of curfew. After Matilde's funeral the next day, Lopito insults the police for mocking his homely daughter and is taken into custody. His defense of his daughter is an aggressive overreaction, motivated at least in part by the excessive oppression under which they live. Donoso (through Mañungo's thoughts) is explicit about this at two moments: "one fine day it becomes impossible to stand things any longer and you shout a bit more than you should"(299/317); "Lopito's fury over a purely private, human, and individual thing . . . turned into a dangerous political row . . . all personal pain had to have at least a political subtext" (285/301–302).[6] Lopito's overreaction provokes a similar one on the part of the police, and a short time later he dies at the police station (while Judit and a friend watch from afar, impotent to do anything) when he is forced to do physical work beyond his capabilities. In this regard, the novel is also a story of parental love, for Lopito's death is prompted in part by his excessive love for his ugly daughter and his desire to protect her.

Although Donoso is indubitably criticizing police brutality here (and on a more universal note, indifference to human suffering and abuse of power on any level), the complexities of the issue are not to be underestimated. It is important to note that the police neither directly nor intentionally kill Lopito. Nonetheless, their lack of empathy and their indifference to human suffering (surely by-products of the oppression), as well as their exaggerated need to exercise power (perhaps a reflection of their sense of impotence), all occasion his death. At the same time, Lopito's death is due in part to his self-destructive nature, perhaps even suicidal inclinations. The police are unequivocally wrong to do what they do, but Lopito succumbs as rapidly as he does because of years of self-destructive behavior, a history of drunkenness and abuse of his body. Even his initial aggressive attitude toward the police is aggravated by his drunken state. That it should be Lopito who dies at the hands of the police is significant, for he is the least appealing character, the one for whom readers feel little empathy and the one with whom they are least likely to identify. Nonetheless, even though Lopito is a pathetic, unlikable character, readers are still outraged by his treatment at the hands of the police, a response that highlights even more acutely the ignoble nature of his mistreatment. Surely, Lopito's reaction when the police mock his daughter is poignant and posits a human core in all people, even the most repugnant or seemingly inhuman (including, paradoxically, the brutal police).

When he is apprised of Lopito's death, Mañungo rushes to the police station and is arrested himself. His fame and social position, coupled with help from Judit's powerful relative Freddy, lead to his release, however, as Donoso underlines the weight afforded to social status and the unequal treatment that status generates. The text ends as Mañungo decides first that he does not want to go on living "in a country capable of killing that idiot Lopito" (299/318), then changes his mind and announces his plans to stay in Chile forever and accepts an invitation to move in with Judit. In this way the "love" story and the political tale draw to a mutual conclusion. However, readers are not to perceive this ending in line with the traditional love story's "and they lived happily ever after." One of Donoso's points is that "happily ever after" occurs only in fiction; "real" stories do not end except in death. Lopito's story may be over, but Mañungo's and Judit's individual and joint stories are not. At the same time, the text is explicit about the lack of love between Mañungo and Judit. Although most readers will probably want to see a "love" relation between the two as a future possibility, Donoso instead posits an alternative to traditional "love," a new kind of interpersonal relationship (not unlike that of Matilde and Pablo or that of Fausta and Celedonio) based on mutual respect, need, and nurture, in contrast to the destructive, debilitating, exploitive "love" of Lisboa and Ada Luz, or perhaps that of Lopito and his wife, all of which may parallel what Freddy feels for Judit. Still, the ending does proffer a note of hope in the midst of so much despair, for the suggestion is that only by staying in Chile and trying to do something, trying to be heard in some small way, can the artist (Mañungo) and the activist (Judit) hope to improve (if only minimally) conditions in their homeland.

In addition to the political tale and the "love" story, *Curfew* is the narrative of Judit's and Mañungo's personal histories as it oscillates between their presents and their pasts in order to depict their private trajectories and make some sense of them (find a cause for the effects, as in *A House in the Country*). Mañungo's story is that of a singer raised on an island lost among the sea mists where "all reverberations dissolved in dreams or in the past" (265/280). Having left Chile a year before the 1973 military coup, he dedicated himself to singing political songs about Chile. In spite of his "role" as a revolutionary singer, Mañungo never directly suffered any of the persecution or oppression of the military regime about which he sings. With the passage of time, however, his role as a political singer became more and more of a mask, in part because of his distance from the referent of his songs, Chile, and in part because of his growing ambivalence about the political situation there and the possibility of any "right" solution (an ambivalence that echoes Donoso's). Both he and those envious of him perceive the revolutionary mask he has worn for so many years as just that, a mask, and specifically one created for mass (foreign) consumption: "A phony idol . . . made of plaster or papier-mâché, pure appearance, a commercial product created by the European mass media for an audience that was bored and wanted to consume revolution and protest" (55/61). Still, that mask afforded him a sense of potency (perhaps not unlike the policemen's uniform): "The guerrilla singer was possessed by the potency of his guitar-phallus-machine gun. . . . Using his voice and his gestures, he could still improvise the *perfect mask* for expressing *total potency*" (9/14; emphasis added). Nonetheless, and in keeping with a repeated Donoso theme, although Mañungo wants to "strip off the costume of his notorious cliché," he worries that beneath it there may be nothing "left of himself that hadn't been consumed by the mask" (9/15). Thus Donoso speculates again that human essence is lost as one becomes one's mask or role, while he underscores the sense of inadequacy or impotence that plagues all human beings and is alleviated only by donning a mask of potency (in whatever form it might take) as we all "cover up . . . weakness by exercising an authority only meant to frighten" (15/22).

Donoso's ironic characterization of Mañungo here is not to be missed, for in addition to the above-noted reasons, Mañungo returned to Chile because he is plagued by a physical ailment (the ringing in his ears) and because his popularity has waned: "Time passed, and Chile lost its allure because the TV generation needs action—bullets and blood—and if they don't get it, they get bored and try something else" (57/64). As the novel opens, he has returned to Chile, ostensibly "for no good reason" (5/11) but on some level, at least, to find himself and the "paradise lost," to transform himself into something else, or to assume some of the despair evoked in the title, despair that "has no music" (10/16). But at the same time, on a more optimistic note, he has also returned to be better able to hear the voice of art, although he recognizes that the ringing, the voices in his ears, "might be nothing more than the sinister musical scales of his own doubts" (16/23). These voices will be discussed in more detail below; let us note at this point the importance of this doubt. For Donoso the stance of the artist should be exactly that of doubt and not that of an ideologue who permits only limited emotions and fixed ideas. All political, philosophical stances should be (must be) permitted and encouraged, especially that of doubt, for the artist should question all and proffer multiple perspectives from which to view the world.[7]

Judit's tale is significantly different from and yet notably similar to Mañungo's. Hers is that of a political activist who has been more directly touched by the events and political abuses in Chile. Captured as a political prisoner, she was saved from further torture, disappearance, and death by her social position or "breeding" and the fact that she had friends and relatives in "high places" who secured her release from prison and helped her escape from the country.[8] That breeding or class apparently also deterred her torturer from raping her while she was in prison. Since her return to Chile, she has dedicated her life to seeking her "torturer" to punish (kill) him for having spared her. That is, on some level, she seeks to ease her own sense of guilt (one that perhaps parallels Mañungo's) for having been spared, for not having suffered as much as the women who were raped because they were not of her class. In this manner Donoso mixes the issues of violence and eroticism (rape as the ultimate form of violence) and relates them to the question of power and by implication potency, erotic or political; rape here is less an erotic act than a violent demonstration of power and dominance. Surely the reader is intended to perceive Judit's imprisonment and the violence against her as a microcosm of more general patterns of the abuse of power.

To undermine that power, to avenge the other women, and to ease her own guilt for having been born into a social class that has afforded her numerous privileges, Judit must find her torturer, the man with the moist hands and nasal voice (note again the importance of the voice), and kill him. Yet in spite of her continued efforts, she never "finds" him; or if she does, like Mañungo, she is plagued with doubts and cannot kill him.[9] Because her doubts paralyze her, she does not shoot Ricardo, the man who might be the one she seeks and who, even if he is not the right man, is still a government agent who perpetrates abuses like those inflicted on her. Instead, she shoots first the skylight (aiming over his head), then the white dog in heat being "raped" by the other dogs, an inverted revenge (perhaps all too human) taken not on those who "deserved to die, undifferentiated males sticking to her [the white bitch] and sullying her" (181/193), but rather on those with whom she identifies—the white bitch, symbolically herself.

Thus Donoso dramatizes here the complex interplay and continual shifting of identification and differentiation. That interplay is revealed by the fact that in spite of the ostensible disparity between Judit's and Mañungo's lives, they are unexpectedly similar. As a political activist, Judit has fought and risked her life for an egalitarian society that does not reward class and position. By sparing her, her torturer has acknowledged only that class and position: "People like them [Mañungo and Judit] . . . always manage to find tricks to escape from the definitive terror, and everything became a deal between equals who were experts in twisting the truth" (278/295). Perhaps Donoso's point is that not only are they comparable to each other, but paradoxically they are also similar to those they most hate. Donoso speculates that, horrible as the thought is, each of us is capable not only of being victimized but also of victimizing, inflicting abuse on the other. In his examination of the abuse of power (particularly by the police and other government agents), Donoso never simplifies the issue or presents it as a drama of "good guys" versus "bad guys." Not just the government officials are capable of acts of cruelty or insensitivity; we all are. For example, "good guy" Mañungo abandons his son overnight in a strange hotel room in a strange country; Lopito beats the daughter he loves so much; Celedonio is so wrapped up in his discussion about the eternal nature of poetry and its beauty that he is oblivious to any pain Freddy might feel about his mother's death (225/239).

Style

In many ways the style of *Curfew* duplicates the content and the twofold reading experience of the novel—the combination of politics and poetry. Indeed, moments of the text recall Neruda's poetry with its mixture of politics and poetry. The despair of his "Walking Around," a poem that conveys the poet's disillusionment with the human race and contemporary society ("It happens that I'm tired of being a man"), is echoed throughout the Donoso text, while the scene in chapter seven in which Ada Luz is described with a series of anaphoras highlighting what she does not want to do mimics the language of the poem. Thus, in spite of its political message and realistic style, *Curfew* is graced with a note of poetry, particularly in chapter twenty-three, a lyrical chapter that takes the reader to the mists and foggy transformations of Chiloé (Mañungo's homeland), where one can believe in witches and the supernatural and in the possibility of change.

Similarly, the text stylistically proffers assorted vantage points or perspectives from which to view this complex and multifaceted reality as it takes us into the minds and thoughts of several characters and alternates between their presents and their pasts on both the personal and the historical levels. This temporal oscillation in turn serves several ends. First, the repeated return to the past is an overt attempt to find the "beginning" of the story, to give it coherence and to understand the causes for the effects one lives in the present. But at the same time, that backward glance inevitably seeks a paradise lost, for surely the past remembered is always superior to the present lived. Furthermore, as the texts notes, one is probably not capable of evoking that past with any degree of precision, for "the past is . . . experience refracted through the memory of others" (107/115). Thus, like all history, even our personal histories are already fiction, transformed by the ship of art (a metaphor from the novel) as they are articulated in words.

The Voice of Art

As is typical of Donoso's other works, the political message of *Curfew* is interspersed with the theme of art and storytelling per se, often poetically imaged as a transformation on the ship of art. Specifically, Donoso deals here with the problems of telling a story, of finding a beginning, a past cause for the present effect, as well as with the sociopolitical responsibility of the artist whose voice has become ineffectual or silent. The impotence of the voice, both that of the artist and that of the people, is spotlighted in the opening paragraph in the related motifs of Carlitos the lion and Pablo Neruda, poet (voice) of the populace. By evoking Neruda, Donoso yearns for a poetic voice, an artistic vision and wisdom unburdened by doubts and capable of speaking for the populace, for it is precisely this freedom from doubt and willingness to assume the responsibility for representing a group that Mañungo (and by implication, Donoso) lacks but still wistfully craves. By juxtaposing the image of Neruda with that of Carlitos the lion, Donoso evokes the impotence that has silenced the voice of art. Neruda is dead, as is one of the last echoes of his voice, Matilde. Similarly, the lion Carlitos has "lost his voice" of potency and decisiveness, perhaps because he is alienated from his origins and his "people." He was born, not in the jungle, but in captivity, in a broken-down circus, many miles and generations from his fierce ancestors. Once a symbol of ferocity, potency, and dominance, epitomized by his resonant voice, Carlitos is now capable only of lamentations and "a cry more appropriate for a stuffed animal than for a real man-eater" (4/

9–10). Imprisoned in the zoo, he roars only at night or when he is afraid (3/9). Furthermore, he is old, has barely a tooth in his head and is thus incapable of attacking, suffers from melancholy, and is chronically indisposed. Lest there be any doubt about the thematic link between Neruda (the voice of the artist) and Carlitos, Mañungo's first thoughts connect the two as he wonders if the Nerudas had built their house where they did to be able to hear Carlitos. But Carlitos, already undermined as a symbol of the potent voice of the jungle, has been even further distanced from his "essence," from what he symbolizes, for he has been substituted by the toy lion (artistic reproduction) the Nerudas had with them in Paris. As a symbol, he has been replaced by yet another symbol, the placid toy lion who lets Matilde do with him as she would. Thus he is even more estranged from the potency of voice and dominance that he connotes. It is this replacement, this frivolous toy, that Mañungo remembers and yearns for as much as if not more than the "real" Carlitos. The confusion between the two incarnations, the "original" (which is already not original and certainly not potent) and its copy, the "useless and luxurious . . . apocryphal beast" (3/9), epitomizes the dangers in any artistic endeavor when the copy becomes more "real" or memorable than the "original."

Mañungo further connects the displacement of the lion's potency with himself and the sociopolitical situation in Chile as he realizes that once the illusion of change in his country has been lost, all that is left is the despair and the "whistle in his chest . . . like the voice of the poor plush lion in his final incarnation, that of today, that of defeat, that of death" (10/12). Donoso's suggestion is that the voices of art and the artist have been equally estranged from sociopolitical concerns. Mañungo sang political songs for thirteen years as the voice of art and the populace, but one who could add nothing to the discussion: all he could do was repeat what had already been said, what already belonged to the past and existed only as repetition of a repetition. Indeed, the "amusing story" Mañungo tells his son, Jean Paul, reflects his own predicament: the escaped parrot who had been taught to recite the rosary returns to the town with a flock of others, all of whom repeat the rosary, and the event is greeted as a miracle. The bittersweet irony not to be lost, however, is that not only are the parrots animals who have no conception of what they repeat, but they can recite only the second part of the rosary, only one perspective, not its entirety (16/22). Furthermore, Jean Paul, whom the story was meant to amuse, is neither amused nor impressed and misses the point. In his role of literary critic, he sees only the tale's departure from the realistic mode; he considers the tale untrue and foolish and misses its metaphoric dimension. In this regard, he epitomizes those who would restrict art to a narrow socio-political function: "For ideologues, there's no place in life for . . . art because for them artists shouldn't play or doubt or contradict themselves, or be themselves, but should simply accommodate themselves to a given 'truth' " (227/241).

In addition to its concern with artistic voices and responsibilities, *Curfew* also considers how fictions are created, both the political ones perpetuated by those in power and the personal ones we live. Donoso demonstrates that the mechanics of the two are not notably different, hence the bidirectional story line. In his exposure of the making of political fictions, Donoso joins the ranks of other contemporary Spanish-American writers who have taken this as their theme, either primary or secondary. He dramatizes how those in power use language and rhetoric to distort or reinvent reality, to lead others to perceive as they would have them perceive. This distortion of reality is overt at Mañungo's interview with the press when he is telling the "truth" of Lopito's story: "Freddy listened to him . . . explaining into Judit's ear that a telephone call would be sufficient to alter all those press articles, or eliminate them completely. After all, they didn't control the press for nothing: *reality could take the form they chose*" (303/322–23; emphasis added).

The artist's role in the representation and distortion of truth or reality, Donoso implies, is particularly dangerous, for artists (even if they are not on the side of those in power) specialize in changing the names of things, and it is through the name that we know: "when we know the names of things . . . we get to their essence, disarming them and making them manageable" (11/17; my translation from the original). Sometimes, however, the "naming" or re-creating is done innocently, that is, without malice of intent, but sometimes not, and it is difficult to know which is which. An interesting example is Chile in Miniature. The park simulates the country, but the country it duplicates is an ideal(ized) one, lacking the lurid and the tragic, unfortunately a substantial part of the "real" Chile. Exactly why it is painted in such paradisaic terms is unclear. Is that how the government would have people see the country? Is it how people would see themselves? Or is it just that "the reality of the entire country couldn't fit into the plot of land" (306/325)? As a result, fantasy is blended with sound judgment, "cutting or eliminating this or that . . . even erasing whole areas that were either totally uninteresting or monotonous or so poor or difficult to idealize that it was better to exclude them altogether. It had to be: after all, not everything can fit into a miniature, and unpleasant things should be left out" (306–07/325). Perhaps even more important is the fact that the work of art is distanced from its "consumers," fenced off from the visitors who would destroy it by trampling on it or stealing a piece of it for a souvenir "until there would be none left, or destroying for the simple human pleasure of doing evil" (306/325).[10] Again Donoso comments on the capacity of us all to create *and* destroy.

What is unique to this novel is the fact that Donoso carries the question of storytelling, and the reinvention of reality fundamental to any story, one step further and brings it back to the personal level. Judit has always resisted falling in love so she will not have to tell her story again from the beginning, for she no longer knows where that beginning is; her history (perhaps not unlike Chile's or Donoso's) is confused, intertwined with many others, and she cannot "establish a thread, and characters and realistic dates for her heart" (260/276). Indeed, the reader would be justified to ask if both Judit and Mañungo decide to remain in Chile at the end of the novel because the events associated with Lopito's death furnish a beginning, an originating point for their new (joint) stories. Earlier Judit needed to kill the man with the nasal voice (perhaps kill one voice to be able to hear another) so she could destroy the past and begin again at zero, have a starting point that perhaps can exist only in fiction. As she waits for the moment to kill Ricardo, she concurrently awaits "a revelation that would clarify the universe . . . [so] she would not hesitate to fire" (165/176), that is, not hesitate to act. But Donoso's point is that total certainty, like starting points and happy endings, occurs only in fiction (art). Those voices that Judit would have provide the revelation are either dead and relegated to the past (like Neruda's) or impotent (like Carlitos's).

Yet the role of art, like all else in *Curfew,* remains ambiguous. The ship of art, the Caleuche, is staffed by wizards (artists) who can transform everything and produce the eternal paradise; it thus functions as a symbol of seduction, revenge, and metamorphosis (105/113). Nonetheless, at times, as in Mañungo's dreams, the ship transforms itself into a cruel pirates' ship that carries people off to their deaths (114/122–23). As in *A House in the Country,* the same medium can serve contradictory ends. Fausta assures the children it is all a question of recognizing shades of difference, concentrating on the details, and seeing the differences (308/327), differences that art, perhaps all too often, blurs with its metaphors and similes. Perhaps for this reason Donoso has assumed such an uncharacteristically realistic style in *Curfew:* to highlight those obscure shades of difference that might be blurred or lost in the lyrical, where the re-creation or miniature (like the toy Carlitos) becomes more real than the original and where we are trapped by the lying miniatures. And, of course, everyone, the "naive ears that were perhaps not so naive" (309/328), listens to the artist as all listen to Fausta at the conclusion of the novel: because they want to participate in the fantasy and in turn create their own (as they do in their invention of Fausta's "family").

Donoso's ambivalence about the role of art in society and politics is perhaps most poignantly dramatized in the final two sentences of the text. Lopito has died, leaving his ugly daughter fatherless and perhaps never to be loved and protected in the same way, while the artists, Mañungo and Fausta, have been as impotent as the activist, Judit, to change that all-too-real fact. Yet the novel ends with the nonverbal communication between Fausta and Mañungo, the singer and the storyteller, two characters particularly given to verbal communication. Now silent, she recognizes (without words, without art) the difference within him, his transformation by a wicked wizard. Again the reader is left to wonder what good words are and whether all the "good" wizards are either dead like Neruda or impotent like Carlitos. Or was the existence of "good" artists or "voices of the people" another fantasy, a myth created by wishful thinking, not unlike Neruda's Chile?[11]

Constants

Reference has already been made to many of the constants found in *Curfew:* the question of power, witchcraft and the supernatural and their relation to art, the mask, the human being's capacity for cruelty and destruction. In *Curfew* this oblivion to human suffering is directly related to the constant of the dogs. This time the dogs unequivocally evoke human beings, at the service of their more powerful masters (usually men, not women), or launching their own instinctual acts of cruelty, violence, and eroticism. Like Alejo's dogs in *Hell Has No Limits,* the dogs in *Curfew* are at times afforded a position superior to that of some humans. For example, Judit notes that while she was in prison, the dogs were treated as the equals of the male guards and employed to help perpetuate violations against the women. Children too are important characters in *Curfew,* and, as in the other Donoso works (particularly *A House in the Country*), they are adults in miniature, capable of the same cruelty and domination as the adults. Women are again powerful figures (at times to be feared). It is not irrelevant that Ulda, the same woman who initiated Mañungo into the pleasures of the flesh, also taught him Marxism and to play the guitar. In addition, the text suggests that Ulda (in some sense the "good" witch/ mother who taught him and freed him, sent him away) and doña Petronila (the feared artist and "bad" witch/mother who would control him) have the power to call him back to the south. Fausta and Matilde also stand as powerful and influential figures, and while Lisboa mocks the women's group and perceives it as frivolous, the reader knows that it is dedicated to serious political activity. Finally, the underworld of the impoverished, ear- lier imaged as servants with structures and rituals that parallel those of the dominant class, reappears in *Curfew* in the underworld of beggars and thieves, led by the legless don César, all also intricately enmeshed in the political resistence.

None of Donoso's works can be said to end on a positive note, and *Cur- few* is no exception. Although the conclusion of the text offers little hope and certainly no answers, the despair of the Spanish title is alleviated somewhat by Mañungo's and Judit's decision to assume it. The text is ex- plicit that one has to lose the hope to which one stubbornly clings and as- sume the despair, begin over at point zero (247/261). Such is precisely what Mañungo and Judit do at the conclusion. Fraught with doubts as they are, they have nonetheless created a beginning for their (hi)story.

Notes

1. Between the 1978 publications of *A House in the Country* and that of *La desesperanza* (*Curfew*) in 1986, Donoso produced three other works: *La misteriosa desaparición de la Marquesita de Loria* (The Mysterious Disappearance of the Little Marquise of Loria) in 1980, *El jardín de al lado* (The Garden Next Door) in 1981, and *Cuatro para Delfina* (Four for Delfina) in 1982. Since these have not been translated into English, they will not be stud- ied in this work.

2. See note 1 of the previous chapter for a brief overview of the military dictatorship of Pinochet.

3. As Donoso stated categorically in an interview, "It is impossible to write about any- thing else. We are all condemned to this. I cannot stand writing about it, but nonetheless I cannot write about anything else. I find myself so completely obsessed by this problem, that I have no other option. May it be damned! But what other option is there?" Amalia Pereira, "An Interview with José Donoso," *Latin American Literary Review* 15, 30 (1987): 62. Sim- ilarly, in the novel Judit declares, "The dictatorship has imposed politics on us as the only respectable theme in conversation" (101/108).

4. For example, while in the cemetery Judit and Mañungo talk about their past and their childhood, as well as the cemeteries in which their families are buried. Her family's ceme- tery is one of permanence with marble mausoleums and stone grave markers. His family's is one of the "ephemeral wooden cemeteries" by the sea, where the "little houses for the dead were washed away" (265/280–81).

5. Donoso has stated that the action of the novel takes place during eighteen hours, but it may be closer to twenty-four. Mañungo arrives on the 6:00 P.M. plane from Paris; Matilde's funeral is at noon the next day; after that Lopito is arrested and dies, and the children spend the afternoon at Chile in Miniature.

Chilean poet Pablo Neruda was born in 1904 and died after Salvador Allende's overthrow in 1973. Politically active, he devoted his life and poetry to the socialist cause. His poetry is considered among the best from contemporary Latin America; he won the Nobel Prize for literature in 1971.

6. The Spanish text is more explicit than the English translation in this regard: "The fact that Lopito's fury over a totally private, human, and individual cause as was the offense against his poor, grotesque daughter should have developed into a dangerous political row, that his fury, that of the whole country, had no other outlet except violence and political protest, that love and music and laughter possessed nothing but that one tradition, and that all personal grief should proffer a political subtext was something that . . . Mañungo . . . had to accept as one accepts the definitive blow of a conqueror" (my translation from the Spanish, 301–02).

7. This is a charge Donoso has always taken seriously, if we are to judge by the repeated play of perspectives throughout this and other works.

8. "To disappear" is a euphemism frequently employed in contemporary Spanish America. One "disappears" after being captured by the police and accused of crimes against the regime. The "disappeared" are never heard from again; the specifics of their fate are uncertain, but in all likelihood they are tortured and eventually killed, their bodies dumped into unmarked communal graves.

9. Ada Luz indicates at one point that Judit cannot find the man because he exists only in her imagination. If this were the case, then it would be difficult to explain why Ada Luz and the other women continue to play this dangerous game with Judit.

10. This commentary on human nature and one's capacity to destroy what one loves best, albeit unintentionally, is also portrayed earlier as the crowd throngs around Mañungo at the cemetery, first wanting only to be near or to touch their idol but eventually turning violent, knocking him to the ground and trampling him.

11. As the text notes, "Neruda was a great inventor of geography" (18/25); the places he depicted in his poetry did not exist in the way he painted them: "Even this America to which Neruda's marvelous poetry has condemned us is more Nerudian than real—which, by the way, was what made it interesting" (19/25).

BIBLIOGRAPHY

Books by Donoso

Veraneo y otros cuentos. Santiago: Editorial Universitaria, 1955.

Dos cuentos. Santiago: Guardia Vieja, 1956.

Coronación. Santiago: Nascimento, 1957. [*Coronation.* Trans. Jocasta Goodwin. New York: Knopf, 1965.]

El charlestón. Santiago: Nascimento, 1960.

Los mejores cuentos de José Donoso. Santiago: Zig-Zag, 1965. Reprinted as *Cuentos.* Barcelona: Seix Barral, 1971. [*Charleston and Other Stories* (nine stories from *Los mejores cuentos de José Donoso*). Trans. Andrée Conrad. Boston: Godine, 1977.]

Este domingo. Santiago: Zig-Zag, 1966. [*This Sunday.* Trans. Lorraine O'Grady Freeman. New York: Knopf, 1967.]

El lugar sin límites. Mexico: Joaquín Mortiz, 1966. [*Hell Has No Limits.* Trans. Suzanne Jill Levine and Hallie Taylor. In *Triple Cross*, by Carlos Fuentes, José Donoso, and Severo Sarduy. New York: Dutton, 1972.]

El obsceno pájaro de la noche. Barcelona: Seix Barral, 1970. [*The Obscene Bird of Night.* Trans. Hardie St. Martin and Leonard Mades. Boston: Knopf, 1973.]

Historia personal del "boom". Barcelona: Anagrama, 1972. [*The Boom in Spanish American Literature: A Personal History.* Trans. Gregory Kolovakos, New York: Columbia University Press/Center for Inter-American Relations, 1977.]

Tres novelitas burguesas. Barcelona: Seix Barral, 1973. [*Sacred Families.* Trans. Andrée Conrad. New York: Knopf, 1977.]

Casa de campo. Barcelona: Seix Barral, 1978. [*A House in the Country.* Trans. David Pritchard with Suzanne Jill Levine. New York: Random House, 1984.]

La misteriosa desaparición de la Marquesita de Loria. Barcelona: Seix Barral, 1980.

El jardín de al lado. Barcelona: Seix Barral, 1981.

Poemas de un novelista. Santiago: Ganymedes, 1981.

Cuatro para Delfina. Barcelona: Seix Barral, 1982.

La desesperanza. Barcelona: Seix Barral, 1986. [*Curfew*. Trans. Alfred MacAdam. New York: Weidenfeld and Nicolson, 1988.]

With Carlos Cerda, *Este domingo* (play). Santiago: Andrés Bello, 1990.

Taratuta/Naturaleza muerta con cachimba. Madrid: Mondadori, 1990.

Books on Donoso

Achugar, Hugo. *Ideología y estructuras narrativas en José Donoso*. Caracas: Centro de Estudios Latinoamericanos, Rómulo Gallegos, 1979.

Adelstein, Miriam. *Studies on the Works of José Donoso: An Anthology of Critical Essays*. Lewiston, N.Y.: Edwin Mellen, 1990.

Castillo-Feliú, Guillermo I., ed. *The Creative Process in the Works of José Donoso*. Rock Hill, S.C.: Winthrop College, 1982.

Cerda, Carlos. *José Donoso: Originales y metáforas*. Santiago: Planeta, 1988.

Gutiérrez Mouat, Ricardo. *José Donoso: Impostura e impostación*. Gaithersburg, Md.: Hispamérica, 1983.

McMurray, George R. *José Donoso*. Boston: Twayne, 1979.

Morell, Hortensia R. *Composición expresionista en 'El lugar sin límites' de José Donoso*. Río Piedras: Universidad de Puerto Rico, 1986.

————. *José Donoso y el surrealismo: Tres novelitas burguesas*. Madrid: Pliegos, 1990.

Quinteros, Isis. *José Donoso: Una insurrección contra la realidad*. Miami: Hispanova, 1978.

Solotorevsky, Myrna. *José Donoso: Incursiones en su producción novelesca*. Valparaíso: Universidad Católica, 1983.

Vidal, Hernán. *José Donoso: Surrealismo y rebelión de los instintos*. San Antonio de Calonge, Spain: Aubi, 1972.

Articles on Donoso

Aguera, Victorio G. "Mito y realidad en *El lugar sin límites* de José Donoso." *Explicación de Textos Literarios* 4 (1975–76): 69–74.

Arana, Elsa. "Los pájaros de la noche de José Donoso" (an interview). *Plural* 3, 10 (1974): 65–69.

Bacarisse, Pamela. "Donoso and Social Commitment: *Casa de campo*." *Bulletin of Hispanic Studies* 60 (1983): 319–32.

————."*El obsceno pájaro de la noche:* The Novelist as Victim." *Modern Language Review* 81 (1986): 82–96.

————. "*El obsceno pájaro de la noche:* A Willed Process of Evasion." *Forum for Modern Language Studies* (Scotland) 15, 2 (1979): 114–29.

Baker, Rilda L. "Perfil del narrador desenmascarado en *Casa de campo*." *La Chispa '81*. Ed. Gilbert Paolini. New Orleans: Tulane University Press, 1981. 35–41.

Bockus Aponte, Barbara. "El niño como testigo: La visión infantil en el cuento hispanoaméricano contemporáneo." *Explicación de Textos Literarios* 11 (1982–83): 11–22.

Carnero, Guillermo. "*El obsceno pájaro de la noche.*" *Cuadernos Hispanoamericanos* 87 (1972): 169–75.

Castillo–Feliú, Guillermo I. "Aesthetic Impetus Versus Reality in Three Stories of José Donoso." *Studies in Short Fiction* 17 (1980): 133–39.

Cerezo, María del C. "La simetría en *Este domingo.*" *Explicación de Textos Literarios* 8 (1979–1980): 201–08.

Christ, Ronald. "An Interview with José Donoso." *Partisan Review* 49, 1 (1982): 23–44.

Coleman, Alexander. "Some Thoughts on José Donoso's Traditionalism." *Studies in Short Fiction* 8 (1971): 155–58.

Cornejo Polar, Antonio. "José Donoso y los problemas de la nueva narrativa hispanoamericana." *Acta Litteraria Academiae Scientiarum Hungaricae* 17 (1975): 215–26.

Feal, Rosemary Geisdorfer. " 'In my end is my beginning': José Donoso's Sense of an Ending." *Chasqui* 17, 2 (1988): 46–55.

Flori, Mónica. "Las ventanas en 'Paseo' de José Donoso." *Selecta* 2 (1981): 112–15.

Guerra Cunningham, Lucía. "Conformismo y liberación en 'Paseo' de José Donoso: Una dualidad no resuelta." *Texto e ideología en la narrativa chilena.* Minneapolis: Prisma Institute, 1987. 199–214.

Gutiérrez Mouat, Ricardo. "Carnavalización de la literatura en *Casa de campo* y *Cien años de soledad.*" *Sin Nombre* 13, 1 (1982): 50–64.

——— . "La figura infantil en *Este domingo* y 'Chatanooga Choochoo.' " *Revista de Estudios Hispánicos* 16 (1982): 223–39.

Iñigo Madrigal, Luis. "Alegoría, historia, novela: A propósito de *Casa de campo* de José Donoso." *Hispamérica* 9, 25–26 (1980): 5–31.

Kerr, Lucille. "Conventions of Authorial Design: José Donoso's *Casa de campo.*" *Symposium* 42 (1988): 133–52.

Lagos, Ramona. "Inconsciente y ritual en *Coronación.*" *Cuadernos Hispanoamericanos* 38, 335 (1979): 290–305.

Magnarelli, Sharon. "Amidst the Illusory Depths of the First-Person Pronoun and *El obsceno pájaro de la noche.*" *Modern Language Notes* 93 (1978): 267–84.

——— . "The Baroque, the Picaresque, and *El obsceno pájaro de la noche* by José Donoso." *Hispanic Journal* 2, 2 (1981): 81–93.

——— . "From *El obsceno pájaro de la noche* to *Tres novelitas burguesas:* Development of a Semiotic Theory in the Works of Donoso." *The Analysis of Literary Texts: Current Trends in Methodology.* Ed. Randolph Pope. Ypsilanti: Bilingual, 1980. 224–35.

―――― . "*El obsceno pájaro de la noche:* Fiction, Monsters, and Packages." *Hispanic Review* 45 (1977): 413–19.

Martínez, Z. Nelly. "El carnaval, el diálogo, y la novela polifónica." *Hispamérica* 6, 17 (1977): 3–21.

―――― . "*Casa de campo* de José Donoso: Afán de descentralización y nostalgia del centro." *Hispanic Review* 50 (1982): 439–48.

―――― . "Entrevista con José Donoso." *Hispamérica* 7, 21 (1978): 53–74.

―――― . "*El obsceno pájaro de la noche:* la productividad del texto." *Revista Iberoamericana* 46 (1980): 51–66.

McMurray, George R. "La temática en los cuentos de José Donoso." *Nueva Narrativa Hispanoamericana* 1, 2 (1971): 133–38.

Morell, Hortensia. "El doble en 'Gaspard de la nuit': José Donoso à la maniére de Ravel, en imitación de Bertrand." *Revista de Estudios Hispánicos* 15 (1981): 211–220.

Moreno Turner, Fernando. "La inversión como norma. A propósito de *El lugar sin límites.*" *Cuadernos Hispanoamericanos* 295 (1975): 19–42. Also published in the Cornejo Polar anthology of articles.

Nigro, Kirsten. "From *Criollismo* to the Grotesque: Approaches to José Donoso." *Tradition and Renewal: Essays in Twentieth–Century Latin–American Literature and Culture.* Ed. Merlin H. Forster. Urbana: University of Illinois Press, 1975. 208–32.

Pereira, Amalia. "An Interview with José Donoso." *Latin American Literary Review* 15, 30 (1987): 57–67.

Piña, Juan Andrés. "José Donoso: Los fantasmas del escritor" (an interview). *Mensaje* 246 (1976): 49–53.

Quain, Estelle. "Children and Their Games: Fiction and Reality in the Works of José Donoso." *Requiem for the "Boom"—Premature?* Eds. Rose S. Minc and Marilyn R. Frankenthaler. Upper Montclair, N.J.: Montclair State College, 1980. 74–81.

Rodríguez Monegal, Emir. "El mundo de José Donoso." *Mundo Nuevo* 12 (1967): 77–85.

Rowe, William. "José Donoso: *El obsceno pájaro de la noche* as Test Case for Psychoanalytic Interpretation." *Modern Language Review* 78 (1983): 588–96.

Sarduy, Severo. "Escritura/Transvestismo." *Mundo Nuevo* 20 (1968): 72–74.

Scott, Robert. "Heroic Illusion and Death Denial in Donoso's *El obsceno pájaro de la noche.*" *Symposium* 32 (1978): 133–46.

Swanson, Philip. "Donoso and the Post-Boom: Simplicity and Subversion." *Contemporary Literature* 28 (1987): 520–29.

―――― . "Una entrevista con José Donoso." *Revista Iberoamericana* 53 (1987): 995–98.

Tatum, Charles M. "The Child Point of View in Donoso's Fiction." *Journal of Spanish Studies Twentieth Century* 1 (1973): 187–96.

———— . "Enajenación, desintegración, y rebelión en *Tres novelitas burguesas*." *The American Hispanist* 2, 16 (1977): 12–15.

———— . "*El obsceno pájaro de la noche:* The Demise of a Feudal Society." *Latin American Literary Review* 1 (1973): 99–105.

Urbistondo, Vicente. "La metáfora don Alejo/Dios en *El lugar sin límites*." *Texto Crítico* 7, 22–23 (1981): 280–91.

Wyers Weber, Frances. "La dinámica de la alegoría: *El obsceno pájaro de la noche* de José Donoso." *Hispamérica* 4, 11–12 (1975): 23–31.